New Food of Life

*A Book of Ancient Persian and Modern Iranian
Cooking and Ceremonies*

By

NAJMIEH KHALILI BATMANGLIJ

MAGE PUBLISHERS
1994

To the memories of my mother
and father and my past in Iran
and to the future of my sons,
Zal and Rostam

CONTENTS

PREFACE

New Food of Life is the result of twelve years of testing recipes and creating new techniques for cooking Persian food in the West. It is also the culmination of my work on the three cookbooks I have written about Persian food and ceremonies in French, English, and Persian.

I am writing this book for those new to Persian food and culture, those who enjoy having creative fun in the kitchen, and for gourmet cooks, both Iranian and American.

I have revised and added many new recipes and incorporated 100 color photographs, since they complete the text and make it easier to grasp the way a recipe should look. I have also added more explanations where it has seemed necessary and included an up-to-date list of Persian stores and restaurants. I have also added to this book ancient ceremonies and rituals still maintained in various parts of Iran.

Persian food is a very important and integral part of our life and culture, so important that it is very frequently used as a metaphor for describing beauty. Farzaneh Milani tells us in her book, *Veil and Words*, for example: "Moon-faced beauties have almond-shaped eyes, peachy complexions, pistachio-like mouths, jujube colored lips, hazelnut-like noses, red apple cheeks, and lemon- or pomegranate-like breasts—a mobile green grocery, if you will."

I believe that the same qualities that govern the Persian arts, a sense of unity achieved by juxtaposing many elements—each a unit in itself—and what one might call a particular feeling for the "delicate touch," or as we say in Persian, *letafat*, govern the art of Persian cuisine. I have tried to demonstrate this by including not only photographs of the dishes but also textiles, copper ware and pottery, miniatures, poetry, calligraphy, and pieces from classical Persian literature all related to food. I have explored the rich garden of Persian literature and art through the ages and have picked some images: from the fourth-century Pahlavi language text, *King Khusrau and His Boy*, the story of a boy who, before being knighted, is tested by the King not on his prowess in archery, sword fighting or riding, but on his knowledge of food, to the sixteenth-century miniatures of Mir Mussavar; from the *Shahnameh* by the great tenth-century Persian poet Ferdowsi, who gives a detailed description of fillet of veal marinated in saffron, rose water, old wine, and pure musk, to the contemporary writer Simin Daneshvar, who begins her best-selling novel, *Savushun*, with a description of a loaf of flat *sangak* bread, the likes of which had never been seen before.

I hope that while you try the recipes in the book, you will also read and look at these images, all of which draw from the rich spring of Persian culture, where the first recipes were written four thousand years ago in a cuneiform script on clay tablets.

Najmieh Batmanglij

Georgetown, June 1992

Preface to the First Edition

When I am at home with the samovar steaming and the house fragrant with the smell of onions and garlic cooking, when the air is filled with the captivating aroma of mint and rare spices, what beautiful memories come back to me! I see the pantry behind the kitchen of my childhood home once again. The odors of savory, fenugreek, marjoram, and angelica burst through the white cloth sacks that hang from the ceiling. Perhaps this book was inspired most by those perfumed memories.

Above all, though, the cuisine of my country brings back to me the image of my parents and friends sitting cross-legged on a Persian carpet around the *sofreh*, a cotton table-cloth embroidered with poems and prayers.

Iranians wake up early, before the sun rises. In our family, my father and grandmother engaged in an amusing little contest every morning. The first one up was the proud winner. As soon as he awoke, my father would usually go out into the garden and head straight for the jasmine we had growing in red clay pots. He would pick all the flowers that had bloomed overnight and lay them at my mother's place on the *sofreh*. But sometimes Grandmother would get to the garden first. I can still hear father speaking in that mock-angry tone of his as he discovered that the jasmine bushes had been stripped of their flowers. "That grandmother has been here already!" he would say out loud. When our grandmother nonchalantly joined the rest of the family at breakfast, she casually plucked the concealed flowers from their hiding place under her shawl and dropped the fragrant bouquet near my father. He would pretend to ignore her as he waited to take his sweet revenge the next morning.

I have fond memories of those breakfasts, or *sobhaneh*. The meal itself usually consists of sweet tea, feta cheese, and *nan-e barbari*, a crusty, flat bread made fresh very early every morning. Breakfast sometimes includes other types of bread, jam and honey, fresh cream, butter, and hot milk. Fried or soft-boiled eggs, saffron cake or pudding (*halva* or *sholeh zard*) might also be served, or even, before a long mountain hike, a soup made of tripe (*sirab shir-dun*) and lamb head and feet (*kalleh pacheh*). *Sobhaneh* is a very important and pleasant moment in the life of an Iranian family, a time to be together before everyone leaves for work.

The cuisine of any country is a fundamental part of its heritage. The ingredients reflect its geography, while the savor and colors accent the aesthetic tastes of its inhabitants. And food is associated with so many major social events—births, weddings, funerals—that culinary traditions are intertwined with a country's history and religion. This is especially true of Iran (called "Persia" by Westerners in ancient times).

Thousands of years ago, Zoroaster elaborated the ancient myth of the Twins. One became good and the other evil, one the follower of truth and the other of falsehood. This concept of duality is typically Persian, and it extends beyond moral issues. We often balance light and darkness, sweet and sour, hot and cold.

For us, food is also classified as "hot" (*garmi*), which thickens the blood and speeds the metabolism, and "cold" (*sardi*), which dilutes the blood and slows the metabolism. Dates, figs, and grapes, for example, are hot fruits; plums, peaches, and oranges are cold.

It takes a certain skill to correctly select food for the family, since people too can have hot and cold natures. An extremely out-of-balance diet can lead to illness. For example, those with "hot" natures must eat cold foods to achieve a balance. My son, like many other five-year-olds, sometimes eats too many dates or chocolates. Because he has a hot nature—something I learned very early in his life!—too much of this hot food does not agree with him at all. Drinking watermelon or grapefruit juice, or the nectar from other cold fruits, quickly helps restore his balance—and his smile.

Increasingly, science is discovering links between food and health. And while the ancient Persian system of balance does not eliminate the need for doctors, experience has proven that it is an excellent nutritional adjunct to good health.

My objective in writing this book was not just to compile a collection of recipes, however delicious they might be. Instead I have tucked in among them other pearls of wisdom from my country—verses from our poets and old legends. I have described an Iranian wedding and some of our joyful holiday traditions. I have included photographs to show that our dishes are as colorful as our most beautiful carpets. For us, feasting our eyes is the first pleasure of a good meal.

I have always enjoyed cooking and have selected these recipes on the basis of my personal preferences and experience. I was aided in my research by my mother and other great cooks, who gave me valuable advice. As my knowledge grew, so did my curiosity and interest in my country's gastronomic heritage. This led me to research the origins of many of our ceremonies.

Among all the traditional recipes I have collected, only the simplest are included here. I have refined them over the years, first in France and then in the United States. In many instances, I have adapted old recipes to modern kitchen tools, like the food processor and the electric rice cooker. All the recipes were systematically tested using ingredients that are now, because of the increasing Iranian expatriate community, available almost everywhere in America.

When I think of a meal, I think of the family all together. I hope that my sons will have similar memories of the simple pleasures of life when they are grown. I dedicate this collection to them and to all Iranian children living far from the country of their heritage by the course of political events.

Najmieh Batmanglij
Georgetown, March 1986

APPETIZERS AND SIDE DISHES

A p p e t i z e r s   a n d   S i d e   D i s h e s

Traditionally, Iranian meals are served on the *sofreh*, a cotton cover embroidered with prayers and poems, which is spread over a Persian carpet or a table. The main dishes are surrounded with bread and a number of small bowls and relish dishes filled with appetizers and condiments. These are called *mokhalafat*. Among them might be:

—a plate of raw vegetables and fresh herbs (radishes, scallions, mint, basil, coriander or cilantro, tarragon, watercress) with feta cheese;

—all kinds of flat bread *(sangak, lavash,* and *barbari);*

—peeled, sliced cucumbers;

—sweetened melon slices;

—peeled steamed beets;

—a basket of grapes;

—shelled nuts and raisins;

—butter with a bowl of confectioners' sugar and a bowl of honey;

—yogurt;

—Persian pickles and relishes (*torshi*);

—yogurt with spinach or other vegetables;

—lentil dip, red kidney bean dip, yogurt and Persian shallots (*musir*);

—cucumber salad with mint and vinegar;

—cucumber, tomato, and onion salad;

—lemon juice, olive oil, and wine vinegar.

All those sitting around the *sofreh* are asked to help themselves according to their fancy.

Bread and Cheese with Fresh Vegetables and Herbs

No Persian table would be complete without *nan-o panir-o sabzi-khordan*, quite simply bread and fresh feta cheese with raw vegetables and herbs. The bread is spread with fresh cheese and garnished with raw vegetables and herbs.

Persian bread is called *nan*, and there are several kinds. *Nan-e-sangak*, or stone bread, is a large, flat, rectangular loaf, rounded on one end and about 3 feet long, 18 inches wide, and 1 inch thick. It is baked in the oven on hot stones and served warm. *Nan-e lavash* is a very thin, crisp bread in a round or oval shape. It keeps well for several days. *Nan-e barbari* is a flat, oval loaf, about 2 inches thick. It should be eaten very fresh and warm; it is usually served for breakfast.

Panir is a cheese similar to feta cheese. It can be made from either cow's or goat's milk.

Sabzi-khordan is an assortment of raw vegetables and fresh herbs. It usually includes radishes, scallions, cilantro or coriander, and watercress with tarragon, mint, and basil. The vegetables and herbs are arranged on a platter with a piece of feta cheese. *Nush-e Jan!*

نان و پنیر و سبزی خوردن

*Nan-o panir-o
sabzi-khordan*

Cheese and Egg Dip

½ pound white cheese
2 eggs, cooked 10 minutes until
    hard-boiled, then peeled and
    chopped
¼ cup mayonnaise
Juice of half a lime
1 tablespoon chopped basil
½ teaspoon salt
¼ teaspoon freshly ground
    black pepper

Makes 2 servings
Preparation time: 15 minutes

*Nan-o panir-o-
tokhm-e-morg*

1. In a food processor or in a bowl, blend together cheese and eggs. Add mayonnaise, lime juice, basil, salt, and pepper. Transfer to a bowl.

2. Cut bread in small 4-inch slices.

3. Place the bowl in the center of a platter and arrange *lavash* or pita brea around the bowl in the platter. *Nush-e Jan!*

Cheese and Walnut Dip

¼ pound white cheese, chopped
2 cups shelled walnuts, chopped
2 tablespoons chopped
   fresh scallions
2 tablespoons chopped fresh basil
2 tablespoons chopped fresh
   tarragon
2 tablespoons chopped fresh mint
1 clove garlic, peeled and crushed

½ teaspoon salt
¼ teaspoon freshly ground
   black pepper
Juice of one lime
¼ cup olive oil

Makes 2 servings
Preparation time: 15 minutes

Nan-o panir-o-gerdu

1. In a food processor or in a bowl, mix the cheese, chopped walnuts, scallions, fresh herbs, and garlic.

2. Add salt, pepper, lime juice, and olive oil; mix well.

3. Transfer the mixture to a serving bowl and place it on a round platter.

4. Cut *lavash* or pita bread into 4-inch pieces and arrange around the bowl on a platter. *Nush-e Jan!*

The Story of Yogurt

The word yogurt comes from the Turkish word *yoghurt*. In Arabic it is called *laban;* in India, *dahi;* in Armenia, *madzoon* or *matsun;* in Azerbaijan and Georgia, *matsuni;* and finally in Iran it is *mast.* Yogurt was introduced to Western Europe in the sixteenth century.

In 1931, the Armenian Colombosians family founded the first yogurt company in Massachusetts and called it Columbo. Although in America yogurt is considered a new product, it is one of the older foods known to mankind. Regional records of ancient civilizations from Egypt to Iran refer to the healthful properties of yogurt. Yogurt was probably discovered accidentally by a nomad long before people could write about it.

A well-known story goes like this: A desert nomad, possibly Persian, was carrying some milk in his goatskin canteen. During his journey, heat and the right bacteria (lactobacillus) transformed the milk into yogurt. The nomad took his chance and drank the mixture. Much to his astonishment he found a sour, creamy, and pleasant taste. When he did not get sick, he shared his discovery with others. In 500 B.C.E. India, the Yogis called the mixture of yogurt and honey "the food of Gods."

Throughout this century a number of healthful characteristics have been attributed to yogurt. They range from prolonging life, increasing sexual potency, remedying baldness, and calming the nervous system to curing skin diseases and gastrointestinal ailments.

Yogurt and Eggplant Dip

Makes 4 servings
Preparation time: 15 minutes
Cooking time: 1 hour

كلاش بادمجان

Borani-e bademjan

2 large or 3 small seedless eggplants
¼ cup olive oil
1 onion, peeled and thinly sliced
4 cloves garlic, peeled and crushed
1 teaspoon salt
¼ teaspoon freshly ground
    black pepper

1 cup yogurt, drained in cheesecloth
    for 3 hours
1 tablespoon chopped fresh mint, or
    1 teaspoon dried mint
¼ teaspoon saffron dissolved in
    1 tablespoon hot water
½ cup chopped walnuts (optional)

1. Preheat oven to 350°F.

2. Wash eggplant and prick in several places with a fork to prevent bursting. Place whole eggplants on oven rack and bake for 1 hour. Be sure to put a tray under the eggplant to catch drips.

3. Remove eggplant from oven, let cool, then peel and mash.

4. Heat the oil in a non-stick skillet and cook the onion and garlic until golden. Add the eggplant and mix well. Cover and cook for five minutes over low heat. Add salt and pepper. Remove from heat and let cool.

5. Transfer to a serving dish, mix with yogurt and garnish with mint, saffron water, and walnuts.

6. Place the eggplant dish on a platter. Cut up *lavash* bread and arrange around the dish on the platter. Serve as an appetizer. *Nush-e Jan!*

Whey and Eggplant Dip

Makes 4 servings
Preparation time: 50 minutes
Cooking time: 30 minutes

Kashk-o bademjan-e kubideh

Note: *Kashk*, or liquid whey, is available in food specialty shops and Iranian markets. Sour cream makes a good substitute.

3 medium eggplants
2 large onions, peeled and chopped
3 cloves garlic, peeled and crushed
¼ cup olive oil
½ cup liquid whey (*kashk*)
½ teaspoon salt,
¼ teaspoon freshly ground
    black pepper

Garnish
2 cloves garlic, crushed
1 tablespoon oil
1 tablespoon dried mint
2 tablespoons liquid whey (*kashk*)
¼ teaspoon ground saffron, dis-
    solved in 1 tablespoon hot water

1. Peel eggplants and cut into 4 slices lengthwise. Place in a colander and sprinkle with water and 2 teaspoons salt to remove bitterness. Let stand for 20 minutes, then rinse with cold water and pat dry.

2. Brown the eggplants, onions, and garlic in a non-stick skillet with ¼ cup of oil. Add 1 cup of water, cover, and cook over medium heat for 20 minutes. Mash in a food processor or with a masher, add ½ cup of whey, salt, and pepper, and mix well.

3. Just before serving, brown crushed garlic in 1 tablespoon oil. Remove skillet from heat, add dried mint, and mix well.

4. Place the eggplant in a serving bowl and garnish with 2 tablespoons whey, the garlic and mint mixture, and a few drops of saffron water. Serve with bread and fresh herbs. *Nush-e Jan!*

T h e   E g g p l a n t   S t o r y

They brought a yogurt-and-eggplant dish to Sultan Mahmud when he was very hungry. He liked it and said, "Eggplant makes a tasty dish." A court companion gave a lengthy lecture in praise of the eggplant. When the sultan was full, he declared, "Eggplant is a very harmful thing." Then the same courtier made an exaggerated speech on the harmfulness of the eggplant. The sultan said in amazement, "You wretch, you were just praising it." The man replied, "But sir, I am your courtier, not the eggplant's."

—Obeyd-e Zanaki

Yogurt and Spinach Dip

4 cups fresh spinach, washed and
    chopped, or 1 cup frozen spinach,
    chopped
2 onions, peeled and thinly sliced
2 cloves garlic, peeled and crushed
4 tablespoons olive oil
1½ cups drained yogurt

½ teaspoon salt
¼ teaspoon freshly ground
    black pepper
¼ teaspoon saffron dissolved
    in 1 tablespoon hot water

Makes 4 servings
Preparation time: 10 minutes
plus several hours' refrigeration
Cooking time: 10 minutes

Borani-e esfenaj

1. Steam the spinach in a steamer for 20 minutes or place the spinach in a pan, cover, and steam until wilted, about 5 minutes. Drain.

2. In a non-stick skillet, lightly brown the onions and garlic in oil over medium heat.

3. Stir in the spinach and cook for 2 minutes. Remove from heat and let cool.

4. In a serving bowl, mix yogurt and spinach and season to taste with salt and pepper. Refrigerate for several hours before serving.

5. Garnish with saffron water. Serve as an appetizer with Persian bread. *Nush-e Jan!*

Borani *recipes are attributed to their namesake, the Sasanian queen Pourandokht. Queen Pourandokht was fond of yogurt, and her chef made her many dishes with drained yogurt and vegetables. These dishes were called* Pourani *after her, and in time* Pourani *came to be known as* Borani.

Yogurt and Celery Dip

4 or 5 celery stalks (the inner, more
   tender stalks)
2 cups drained plain yogurt
½ teaspoon salt
¼ teaspoon freshly ground
   black pepper
2 tablespoons chopped fresh mint

Makes 2 servings
Preparation time: 10 minutes
plus 1 hours' refrigeration

Borani-e karafs

1. Chop the celery into one-inch pieces.

2. Place celery, yogurt, salt, pepper, and mint in a salad bowl. Toss well. Refrigerate for an hour.

3. Serve with bread as an appetizer. *Nush-e Jan!*

Yogurt and Cooked Beet Dip

Makes 4 servings
Preparation time: 5 minutes
Cooking time: 1 hour 30 minutes if fresh beets are used

بُلَنی لَبو

Borani-e labu

2 large uncooked beets or 1 can (16 ounces) cooked beets, drained
1 cup drained plain yogurt
2 tablespoons granulated sugar

1 tablespoon chopped fresh mint or 1 teaspoon dried mint

1. If using fresh beets, steam them with the skins on for about 1½ hours or longer until tender.

2. Peel and cut cooked or canned beets into ¾-inch cubes.

3. Place the beets in a serving bowl.

4. Immediately before serving add the yogurt and sugar to the beets and mix. Garnish with the mint. Present on a platter with Persian bread. *Nush-e Jan!*

Yogurt and Shallot Dip

Makes 4 servings
Preparation time: 10 minutes plus overnight soaking and chilling

ماست و موسیر

Mast-o musir

¼ pound dried Persian shallots (*musir*)
    or 1 pound fresh
2 cups yogurt
½ teaspoon salt
¼ teaspoon freshly ground
    black pepper

1. If using fresh shallots, peel and chop shallots and soak in cold water overnight. Change the water several times. Drain and pat dry. If using dried shallots, place in a saucepan, cover with water, bring to a boil over high heat, reduce heat, and simmer for 25 minutes until tender. Drain, rinse with cold water, and pat dry. Chop the shallots finely.

2. Combine the shallots with the yogurt, salt, and pepper. Chill in refrigerator for several hours before serving.

3. Serve as an appetizer with *lavash* or pita bread. *Nush-e Jan!*

Eggplant with Pomegranate Dip

2 medium eggplants
1 medium onion, peeled and grated
2 cloves garlic, peeled and crushed
3 tablespoons oil
2 medium tomatoes, peeled and
    thinly sliced
1 tablespoon pomegranate paste

½ teaspoon salt
¼ teaspoon freshly ground
    black pepper
1 teaspoon angelica powder
    (*gol-par*)
1 tablespoon chopped fresh mint
    or 1 teaspoon dried mint

Makes 4 servings
Preparation time: 5 minutes
Cooking time: 1 hour 45 minutes

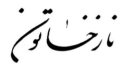

Nazkhatun

1. Preheat oven to 350°F. Prick eggplants with a fork to prevent bursting, and place on oven rack. Bake for 1 hour. Be sure to put a tray under eggplant to catch drips.

2. Place the eggplant on a cutting board and let stand until cool enough to handle. Peel and chop.

3. In a deep skillet, fry the onion and garlic in 3 tablespoons oil. Add tomatoes and pomegranate paste, cook for 10 minutes over medium heat, add the eggplant, and sprinkle with salt, pepper, angelica powder, and mint. Mix well, simmer over low heat for another 35 minutes, and adjust seasoning.

4. Transfer to a serving dish and serve hot or cold with *lavash* bread as an appetizer. *Nush-e Jan!*

Lentil Dip

Makes 6 servings
Cooking time: 2 hours 15 minutes

عدس

Adas pokhteh (Adasi)

2 cups lentils, cleaned and washed
2 large onions, peeled and thinly
  sliced
4 cloves garlic, peeled and crushed
3 tablespoons oil
1 teaspoon salt

½ teaspoon freshly ground
  black pepper
1 tablespoon angelica powder
  (*gol-par*)
½ cup Seville orange juice
  or vinegar

1. Place lentils in a saucepan and add 6 cups water and 1 teaspoon salt. Bring to a boil.

2. Cover and cook over medium heat for about 1½ hours, stirring occasionally; add more water if necessary.

3. In a skillet, fry the onion and garlic in 3 tablespoons oil until golden brown. Add it to the lentils, season with salt and pepper, and let simmer over low heat for another 45 minutes.

4. Add angelica powder and Seville orange juice or vinegar. Serve hot or cold with *lavash* bread as an appetizer. *Nush-e Jan!*

Lentil Salad

Makes 4 servings
Preparation time: 10 minutes
Cooking time: 30 minutes

سالاد عدس

Salad-e adas

1 cup lentils, cleaned and washed
1 cup chopped fresh scallions
2 cloves garlic, peeled and crushed
4 tablespoons olive oil
1 teaspoon salt
¼ teaspoon freshly ground
  black pepper

2 tablespoons angelica powder
  (*gol-par*)
Juice of 2 limes
2 tablespoons chopped fresh parsley

1. Place lentils in a heavy saucepan. Pour in 3 cups water and ¼ teaspoon salt and boil for 20 minutes, or until tender, over medium heat. Drain and set aside.

2. In a salad bowl, combine the scallions, garlic, oil, salt, pepper, angelica powder, and lime juice. Mix well.

3. Add lentils to the mixture, toss thoroughly, and serve with parsley sprinkled on top. *Nush-e Jan!*

Cucumber and Mint Salad

1 seedless cucumber
1 onion, peeled and thinly sliced
1 tablespoon chopped fresh mint, or
   1 teaspoon dried mint
2 tablespoons vinegar

½ teaspoon salt
¼ teaspoon freshly ground
   black pepper

Makes 4 servings
Preparation time: 15 minutes

1. Peel cucumber and chop into ¼-inch cubes.

2. Combine all ingredients in a bowl and mix thoroughly. Serve as an appetizer with Persian bread. *Nush-e Jan!*

Serkeh khiar

Tomato and Cucumber Salad

2 firm ripe tomatoes
1 seedless cucumber
3 tablespoons olive oil
Juice of one lime
1 clove garlic, peeled and crushed
½ teaspoon salt
¼ teaspoon freshly ground
   black pepper

2 scallions, chopped
3 radishes, sliced
1 cup chopped fresh parsley
¼ cup chopped fresh mint
¼ cup chopped fresh coriander

Makes 4 servings
Preparation time: 15 minutes

1. Drop tomatoes into scalding hot water. Remove immediately, drain under cold water, peel, and cut into quarters. Peel and cut cucumber into 1-inch cubes.

2. Whisk together the olive oil, lime juice, garlic, salt, and pepper. Add tomatoes, cucumber, remaining vegetables and herbs, and toss. Serve immediately. *Nush-e Jan!*

Salad-e gojeh khiar

Red Kidney Bean Dip

1 cup dried kidney beans or 1
   12-oz. can cooked beans*
2 large onions, peeled and
   thinly sliced
6 tablespoons olive oil
2 tablespoons tomato paste
½ teaspoon salt

¼ teaspoon freshly ground
   black pepper
Juice of 2 limes or juice of 2
   Seville oranges
2 teaspoons angelica powder
   (*gol-par*)

Makes 2 servings
Preparation time: 10 minutes
Cooking time: 1 hour 30 minutes

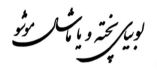

Lubia-Pokhteh
(Mashalah musho)

1. Place beans in a large saucepan; add 4 cups water and ¼ teaspoon salt; bring to a boil over high heat.

2. Reduce the heat, cover, and simmer for about 1 hour or more until tender. Add more water if needed.

3. Fry the onions in a skillet in 4 tablespoons oil over medium heat until golden brown. Add tomato paste, salt, and pepper, and mix well.

4. Combine with kidney beans.

5. Add 2 tablespoons oil, lime juice or Seville orange juice, and angelica powder, and mix well.

6. Adjust seasoning to taste; transfer to a salad bowl, and serve as an appetizer, warm or cold, with *lavash* bread. *Nush-e Jan!*

*Note: If using canned beans, fry the onions, mix them with the tomato paste and add the beans. Simmer for 15 minutes, and add the rest of the ingredients. If using dried beans, soak them overnight in 3 cups cold water and ½ teaspoon salt and drain.

Yogurt and Cucumber Dip

Makes 4 servings
Preparation time: 15 minutes
plus 1 hours' refrigeration

همس وخیار

Mast-o khiar

1 long seedless cucumber, peeled and diced
½ cup raisins, washed and drained
3 cups whole-milk yogurt
½ cup sour cream (optional)
¼ cup chopped scallions
1 tablespoon chopped fresh mint
2 tablespoons chopped fresh dill weed
2 cloves garlic, peeled and crushed

3 tablespoons chopped shelled walnuts
1 teaspoon salt
¼ teaspoon ground pepper

Garnish
½ teaspoon chopped fresh or dried mint
1 dried rosebud and 2 tablespoons petals

1. In a serving bowl, combine cucumber, raisins, yogurt, sour cream (if desired), scallions, mint, dill, garlic, and chopped walnuts. Mix thoroughly and season to taste with salt and pepper.

2. Refrigerate for at least 1 hour before serving.

3. Garnish with ½ teaspoon mint, rosebud, and petals. Serve with bread as an appetizer. *Nush-e Jan!*

Note: For fewer calories and less fat, you may use low-fat yogurt in place of whole-milk yogurt and eliminate the sour cream.

Variation: This may be transformed into a refreshing cold soup by adding 1 cup of cold water and 2 or 3 ice cubes to the mixture.

Persian Chicken Salad

Makes 6 servings
Preparation time: 1 hour 30 minutes plus 2 hours' chilling time in refrigerator

سلادالویه

Salad-e olivieh

1 frying chicken, about 2 or 3 pounds
1 onion, peeled and finely chopped
1 teaspoon salt
4 carrots, peeled and chopped
2 cups fresh shelled or frozen green peas
2 scallions, chopped
2 celery stalks, chopped
6 large potatoes, boiled, peeled, and chopped
3 hard-boiled eggs, peeled and chopped
3 medium cucumber pickles, finely chopped

½ cup chopped fresh parsley
⅔ cup green olives, pitted and chopped

Dressing
3 cups mayonnaise
2 tablespoons Dijon mustard
2 tablespoons sour cream (optional)
¼ cup olive oil
½ cup vinegar or lime juice
1½ teaspoons salt
½ teaspoon freshly ground black pepper

1. Place the chicken in a pot along with the onion and salt. Cover and cook for 1½ hours over low heat (no water is added because chicken makes its own juice). When done, allow to cool, debone the chicken, and chop finely.

2. Steam the carrots for 5 minutes and set aside.

3. Steam shelled peas for 5 minutes and set aside. (If using frozen peas, follow package directions.)

4. In a large bowl, whisk together mayonnaise, mustard, sour cream, olive oil, vinegar (or lime juice), salt, and pepper. Mix thoroughly with a fork.

5. Combine chicken and prepared vegetables with the rest of the ingredients. Pour the dressing over it and toss well. Adjust seasoning to taste.

6. Transfer salad to a flat plate and decorate with hearts of romaine lettuce. Chill for at least 2 hours. Serve with hot pita, *lavash*, or French bread. *Nush-e Jan!*

Caviar

4 ounces Caspian Sea caviar
Thin toast
Butter
2 fresh limes, cut in half

Makes 4 servings

خاویار

Khaviar

Caviar is the unfertilized, processed roe of the sturgeon fish. Its name probably comes from the Persian *mahi-e khayehdar,* literally meaning fish bearing eggs. The best caviar comes from the Caspian Sea. There are three main types of caviar, each from a different species of sturgeon. The largest eggs, known by the Russian name beluga, come from the *fil-mahi*, literally elephant fish. The average-sized roe, osetra, comes from *tas-mahi*, or the bald fish; and the smallest eggs, sevruga, are those from the *uzun-brun*, or the long-nosed fish. Besides the size, each type has its own particular flavor, and you have to try each one to see which you prefer.

The most important step in the production of caviar is the salting. The different brands available vary in quality. As long as it comes from the Caspian Sea it is the real thing, and then it is up to you to decide which type you prefer.

I have often been asked, "How does one know if the caviar is fresh or not?" The best answer I can give is that it should smell of the sea but never fishy.

Around the Caspian there are various recipes that include the roe of the sturgeon—one is with garlic chives in an omelet. The Russians also like to garnish theirs with onions and egg whites, but I believe good-quality caviar should be eaten simply. Place a good-sized dollop on a thin piece of lightly buttered toast and squeeze a little fresh lime over it. *Nush-e jan!*

The Masnavi, Jalaloddin Rumi, 1265
The Chick-pea Story

بنگر اندر نخودی در دیگ چون — می‌جهد بالا چو شد ز آتش زبون

هر زمان نخود برآید وقت جوش — بر سر دیگ و برآرد صد خروش

که چرا آتش به من در می‌زنی — چون خریدی چون نگونم می‌کنی

می‌زند کفلیز کابانو که نه — خوش بجوش و درمجه ز آتش تو زه

زآن نجوشانمت که مکروه منی — بلک تا گیری تو ذوق و چاشنی

یا غذایی گردی آمیزی به جان — بهر خواری نیست این رنج امتحان

آب می‌خوردی در بستان سبز و تر — بهر این آتش بدست آن آب خور

In a dialog between the chick pea in the noodle soup *ash-e reshteh* and the cook, the chick pea cries, "why are you setting the fire on me? Since you bought me and approved of me, why are you turning me upside down?"

The cook replies, "I am not boiling you because I hate you but rather to make you tastier and more savory, so that you may become nutriment and mingle with the vital spirit. You, when green and fresh, were drinking water in the garden: that water-drinking was for the sake of this fire."

Detail, making noodle soup (ash-e reshteh) *attributed to Mir Sayyid Ali, 1540*

Lettuce and Vinegar Syrup
Kahu va sekanjebin
Recipe page 370

34

Cooked Fava Beans with Angelica Petals
Baqala-pokhteh ba gol-par
Recipe page 357

35

Eggplant Dip
Kashk-e bademjan
Recipe page 20

Yogurt and Cucumber Dip
Mast-o khiar
Recipe page 29

37

Clockwise from center top: Cauliflower, fresh herb, potato, meat, yogurt, green bean and eggplant kuku in the center

38

Eggplant Kuku
Kuku-ye bademjan
Recipe page 96

39

Cauliflower Kuku
Kuku-ye gol-e kalam
Recipe page 94

Spinach Narcissus
Nargesi-ye esfenaj
Recipe page 104

41

Stuffed Cabbage Leaves
Dolmeh-ye kalam
Recipe page 80

Stuffed Apples
Dolmeh-ye sib
Recipe page 84

43

Stuffed Potatoes
Dolmeh-ye sibzamini
Recipe page 81

44

Stuffed Green Peppers, Eggplants, and Tomatoes
Dolmeh-ye felfel sabz-o bademjan-o gojehfarangi
Recipe page 82

Majnun brought in chains to Layla's tent, from the Khamsa of Nezami, *attributed to Mir Sayyid Ali, 1530*

Lamb Shank Soup with Yellow Split Peas and Meat Paste
Abgusht-e lapeh-o gusht-e kubideh
Recipe page 52

Noodle Soup
Ash-e reshteh
Recipe page 66

48

SOUPS AND ASHES

ملّا نصرالدین

D u c k   S o u p

A relative came to see Mulla Nasruddin from the country, and brought a duck. Mulla was grateful and had the bird cooked and shared it with his guest.

Presently another visitor arrived. He was a friend, as he said, "of the man who gave you the duck." Mulla fed him as well.

This happened several times. Mulla's home had become like a restaurant for out-of-town visitors. Everyone was a more and more distant friend removed from the original donor of the duck.

Finally Mulla was exasperated. One day there was a knock at the door and a stranger appeared. "I am the friend of the friend of the friend of the man who brought you the duck from the country," he said.

"Come in," said Nasruddin.

They seated themselves at the table, and Nasruddin asked his wife to bring the soup.

When the guest tasted it, it seemed to be nothing more than warm water. "What sort of soup is this?" he asked Mulla.

"That," said Mulla, "is the soup of the soup of the soup of the duck."

S o u p s   a n d   A s h e s

Soup plays a vital role in Iranian tradition. Many different kinds of soup are served to mark special occasions, and sharing a bowl of soup is believed to forge the bonds of friendship. Sometimes, in an act symbolizing great intimacy, friends or lovers sip from the same spoon to seal their devotion. Some soups are thin, but many are thick and substantial enough to serve as main course. An *ash* (rhymes with squash) is a wonderfully flavorful thick soup. In Persian, the cook is called *ash-paz*, or the soup preparer, and the kitchen is *ash-paz khaneh*, the place where the soup is prepared. For best results, make the *ash* a day in advance to give the flavors a chance to meld, and reheat it just before serving. Add the garnish at the last minute, after pouring the soup into the tureen. We Persians like to decorate our soups with various garnishes, creating patterns that are pleasing to the eye. Just before serving, stir in the garnish. Serve with warm crusty Persian bread like *sangak*, *lavash*, or pita.

Lamb Shank Soup with Yellow Split Peas and Meat Paste

Makes 6 servings
Preparation time: 10 minutes
Cooking time: 2 hours 15 minutes

آبگوشت لپه و گوشت کوبیده

Abgusht-e lapeh-o gusht-e kubideh

2 pounds lamb shanks and 1 pound breast of lamb
2 large onions, peeled and quartered
6–8 cups water
1 cup yellow split peas
1 teaspoon turmeric
2 teaspoons salt
½ teaspoon freshly ground black pepper
3 large potatoes, peeled and cut into halves
4 tomatoes, peeled and sliced
1 tablespoon tomato paste

2 teaspoons ground cinnamon
4 whole dried Persian limes (*limu-omani*), pierced, or ¼ cup lime juice
½ teaspoon ground saffron dissolved in 2 tablespoons hot water
1 teaspoon Persian allspice (*advieh*)

Garnish
1 large onion, peeled and sliced
1 teaspoon ground cinnamon

1. Place the meat, onion, and 6 cups of water in a large pot. Bring to a boil, skimming the froth as it forms. Add split peas, turmeric, salt, and pepper. Cover and let simmer for 1½ hours over low heat.

2. Add the potatoes, tomatoes, tomato paste, cinnamon, pierced Persian limes or lime juice, saffron water, *advieh*, and more water. Continue to simmer 45 minutes over low heat.

3. Test with a fork or knife tip to see if the meat and potatoes are tender. Adjust seasoning.

4. Using a slotted spoon, remove all of the stew ingredients. Debone the meat and reserve the bones. Mash the meat and vegetables together to make the paste called *gusht kubideh*. It should have the consistency of lumpy mashed potatoes. Iranian cooks would use a mortar and pestle to pound the *gusht kubideh* to just the right consistency. A food processor may be used instead, but take care not to let the paste get too smooth. Season to taste with salt and pepper and arrange on a serving platter. Pour 3 tablespoons hot soup over the paste. Sprinkle with cinnamon and garnish with fresh slices of raw onion.

5. Reheat the broth and scoop out the marrow from the bones. Mix the marrow with the broth, and serve in a bowl as soup. Serve the *gusht kubideh* separately with Persian pickles (*torshi*), a platter of spring onions, radishes, fresh tarragon, basil, and mint (*sabzi-khordan*) and *lavash* or pita bread. *Nush-e Jan!*

Variations: This soup may also be made with beef or veal. ½ cup chick-peas and ½ cup red kidney beans may be substituted for the split peas.

Note: Dried Persian limes (*limu-omani*) are available in Persian food specialty shops.

Lamb Shank Soup with Eggplant and Meat Paste

Makes 6 servings
Preparation time: 10 minutes
Cooking time: 2 hours 15 minutes

Abgusht-e bademjan

2 pounds lamb shanks and 1 pound breast of lamb
2 large onions, peeled and quartered
6–8 cups water
1 cup yellow split peas
1 teaspoon turmeric
2 teaspoons salt
½ teaspoon freshly ground black pepper
3 medium-sized eggplants, peeled and halved
⅓ cup oil
3 large potatoes, peeled and sliced

4 peeled tomatoes, cut in halves
1 tablespoon tomato paste
1 teaspoon Persian allspice (*advieh*)
1 cup sour grape juice (*ab-ghureh*) or ¼ cup lime juice

Garnish
1 large onion, peeled and sliced
1 teaspoon ground cinnamon

1. Place the meat, onion, and 6 cups of water in a large pot. Bring to a boil, skimming the froth as it forms. Add split peas, turmeric, salt, and pepper. Cover and let simmer for 1½ hours over low heat.

2. To remove the bitterness from the eggplant, soak the halves in water and 1 tablespoon of salt for 20 minutes. Drain and rinse with cold water. Pat dry with a paper towel and fry on both sides in ⅓ cup of oil. Set aside.

3. Add eggplant, potatoes, tomatoes, tomato paste, Persian allspice, and sour grape juice or lime juice to the large pot. Cover and simmer for 45 minutes over low heat.

4. Check to see if the meat and potatoes are tender. Add more water if necessary. Adjust seasoning.

5. Using a slotted spoon, remove all of the stew ingredients. Debone the meat and reserve the bones. Mash the meat and vegetables together to make the paste called *gusht kubideh*. It should have the consistency of lumpy mashed potatoes. Iranian cooks would use a mortar and pestle to pound the paste to just the right consistency. A food processor may be used instead, but take care not to let the paste get too smooth. Season to taste with salt and pepper and arrange on a serving platter. Garnish with fresh slices of raw onion and sprinkle with cinnamon.

6. Reheat the broth and scoop out the marrow from the bones. Mix the marrow with the broth, and serve in a bowl as soup. Serve the *gusht kubideh* with Persian pickles (*torshi*), a platter of scallions, radishes, fresh tarragon, basil, and mint (*sabzi-khordan*), and *lavash* or pita bread. *Nush-e Jan!*

Variation: Lamb Shank Soup with Quince and Meat Paste—2 peeled and sliced quinces and 2 cups sliced prunes may be substituted for the eggplant.

Unless we clap hands together in unison, we shall
*   Not stamp feet in joy upon the head of sorrow:*
Let us drink a morning cup before the hour of dawn,
*   For this dawn will often break when we no longer*
Breathe.

Omar Khayyam

تا دست با تّفاق در هم زنیم

پائی نشاط بر سر غـــم زنیم

پیش از که صبحدم صبوح بزنیم

کین صبح بسی دمد که بادم زنیم

خیّام

Lamb Shank Soup with Green Herbs

Makes 4 servings
Preparation time: 10 minutes
Cooking time: 2 hours 45 minutes

Abgusht-e bozbash

2 pounds lamb shanks and 1 pound lamb breast
2 onions, peeled and quartered
6–8 cups water
1 cup dried kidney beans
1 teaspoon turmeric
2 teaspoons salt
½ teaspoon freshly ground black pepper
3 cups chopped fresh parsley or ¾ cup dried
3 cups chopped scallions or ¾ cup dried

1 tablespoon dried or 4 tablespoons chopped fresh fenugreek leaves
3 tablespoons oil
4 whole dried Persian limes (*limu-omani*), pierced, or ¼ cup lime juice
5 large potatoes, peeled and cut in chunks
1 onion, peeled and sliced, for garnish

1. Place meat, onions, and 6 cups of water in a large pot or a large, heavy Dutch oven. Bring to boil, skimming the froth as it forms. Add beans, turmeric, salt, and pepper. Cover and simmer for 1½ hours over low heat.

2. Briefly saute parsley, scallions, and fenugreek in 3 tablespoons oil and add to the large pot.

3. Add Persian limes or lime juice. Simmer 30 minutes longer. Add 2 more cups water.

4. Add potatoes, cover, and simmer over low heat for another 45 minutes or until the meat and potatoes are tender. Add more warm water if necessary and simmer until the meat is done. Adjust seasoning.

5. Remove all of the stew ingredients, using a slotted spoon. Separate the meat from the bones, and mash the meat and the vegetables together to make the paste called *gusht kubideh*. Iranian cooks would use a mortar and pestle but a food processor may be used instead. Stop processing before the paste becomes smooth. Season to taste with salt and pepper and pile it up on a platter. Garnish with onion slices.

6. Reheat the broth and serve in a bowl as soup. Serve the *gusht kubideh* with Persian pickles (*torshi*), a platter of scallions, radishes, fresh tarragon, basil, mint (*sabzi-khordan*) and *lavash* or pita bread. *Nush-e Jan!*

Variation: This dish may also be made with veal or beef, either with the bone in or with a piece of bone added to the pot for flavor.

Note: Dried Persian limes (*limu-omani*) are available in Persian food specialty shops.

Note: If using dried herbs, place a sieve in a bowl of luke-warm water and soak the dried herbs for 20 minutes. Remove the sieve from the bowl and use the herbs.

Pomegranate Soup

Makes 6 servings
Preparation time: 20 minutes
Cooking time: 2 hours

آش انار

Ash-e anar

Note: If using dried herbs, place a sieve in a bowl of luke-warm water and soak the dried herbs for 20 minutes. Remove the sieve from the bowl and use the herbs.

Gol-par is angelica, which comes literally from the Persian compound word *gol* (flower) and *pari* (angel).

3 tablespoons olive oil
4 onions, 3 peeled and thinly sliced, 1 peeled and grated
3 cloves garlic, peeled and crushed
½ cup yellow split peas
10–12 cups water
1¼ teaspoons salt
½ teaspoon freshly ground black pepper
1 teaspoon turmeric
2 cups chopped fresh parsley or ½ cup dried
2 cups chopped fresh coriander leaves or ½ cup dried
1 cup chopped fresh mint or ¼ cup dried
1 beet, peeled and chopped

2 cups chopped fresh chives or scallions or ¼ cup dried
1 pound ground beef, veal or lamb
1 cup rice
⅔ cup pomegranate paste diluted in 2 cups water, or 4 cups pomegranate juice, or 4 cups fresh pomegranate seeds
⅓ cup sugar
2 tablespoons angelica seeds or powder (*gol-par*)

Garnish
2 tablespoons olive oil
5 cloves garlic, peeled and crushed
1 teaspoon dried mint flakes
½ teaspoon turmeric

1. Heat 3 tablespoons of oil in a large heavy pot and brown the 3 sliced onions and garlic. Add split peas, then 10 cups of water. Bring to boil, reduce heat, partially cover, and simmer over medium heat for 20 minutes.

2. Add 1 teaspoon salt, ¼ teaspoon pepper, turmeric, chopped parsley, coriander, mint, beet, and chives or scallions and continue cooking for 20 minutes longer, stirring occasionally to prevent sticking.

3. Combine the grated onion and the meat in a bowl. Season with ¼ teaspoon salt and ¼ teaspoon pepper. Mix ingredients thoroughly and shape into chestnut-size meatballs and add to the pot.

4. Add rice, half cover and cook for 30 minutes longer.

5. Stir in pomegranate paste, sugar, and angelica powder, and simmer over low heat for 35 minutes.

6. Check a meatball to see if it is cooked and taste soup for seasoning. It should be sweet and sour. Add warm water if the soup is too thick.

7. Just before serving, heat 2 tablespoons of oil in a skillet and brown the garlic. Remove from heat. Crumble the dried mint flakes in the palm of your hand and add to the garlic. Add ½ teaspoon turmeric; mix well.

8. Pour the warmed soup into a tureen and garnish with the mint-and-garlic mixture. *Nush-e Jan!*

Notes: For best results, make the ash a day in advance to give the flavors a chance to meld and reheat it just before serving. Add the garnish at the last minute, after pouring the soup into the tureen. If using pomegranate juice, reduce the water by 2 cups. Add more water or juice if the finished soup is too thick. Pomegranate paste and angelica powder (*gol-par*) are available in Persian food specialty stores.

Beggar's Soup

Makes 8 servings
Preparation time: 20 minutes
Cooking time: 3 hours

آش شله قلمكار

Ash-e sholeh qalamkar

3 onions, peeled and thinly sliced
5 cloves garlic, peeled and crushed
4 tablespoons olive oil
1 pound stewing beef, lamb, or veal (optional)
1 teaspoon turmeric
2 teaspoons salt
¼ teaspoon freshly ground black pepper
⅓ cup dried red kidney beans
½ cup dried lentils
¼ cup dried chick-peas
¼ cup dried mung beans
10–12 cups water
2 cups chopped fresh parsley or ½ cup dried
1 cup chopped fresh coriander or ¼ cup dried

¼ cup chopped fresh dill or 1 tablespoon dried
4 cups fresh spinach, washed and chopped, or 2 cups frozen spinach, chopped
1 cup chopped chives or scallions or ¼ cup dried
½ cup rice

Garnish
1 onion, peeled and thinly sliced
2 tablespoons oil
3 cloves garlic, peeled and crushed
2 tablespoons dried mint
¼ teaspoon turmeric

Long ago, people used to leave a kettle by the side of the road to make a wish come true. Passersby would throw in a few coins to be used to buy the ingredients for the soup. The more people pitched in, the better the chances of the wish coming true. Thus was born beggar's soup. Today, although kettles are no longer left at the roadside (perhaps for fear they would disappear!), the custom lives on in a new form. Friends are told in advance on what day a wish is going to be made. That morning, each one arrives bringing a few ingredients for the soup. They prepare it together and sit down to share it at the midday meal. This way everyone can join in making a loved one's wish come true.

Note: If using dried herbs, place a sieve in a bowl of luke-warm water and soak the dried herbs for 20 minutes. Remove the sieve from the bowl and use the herbs.

Suggestion: For best results, cook your *ash* a day in advance to give the flavors a chance to meld. Reheat the soup the next day just before serving. Fry and add the garnish at the last minute.

1. Saute the 3 onions and the garlic in 4 tablespoons oil in a large heavy pot. Push to one side and brown the meat. Add the turmeric, salt, pepper, kidney beans, lentils, chick-peas, and mung beans. Saute for a few minutes and pour in the water. Bring to a boil, partially cover, and simmer for 1 hour over medium heat.

2. Add parsley, coriander, dill, spinach, and chives or scallions. Cook 40 minutes longer, stirring occasionally to avoid sticking.

3. Add the rice. Cover and cook 55 minutes longer over low heat.

4. Check to be sure the meat is tender and beans are done. If you desire, use a slotted spoon to remove some of the ingredients and place in a food processor; blend thoroughly and return to the pot. Adjust seasoning and add warm water if the *ash* is too thick.

5. Just before serving, prepare the garnish. Fry the onion in a non-stick frying pan with 2 tablespoons oil until golden brown; add garlic and cook to a golden brown. Remove from heat; add mint and turmeric. Mix well. Reheat the soup and pour into a tureen, garnish, and serve. *Nush-e Jan!*

Barley Soup

Makes 6 servings
Preparation time: 20 minutes
Cooking time: 3 hours

Ash-e jow

2 onions, peeled and thinly sliced
½ pound stew meat (lamb, veal or
    beef) cut into ½-inch cubes
¼ cup oil
2 teaspoons salt
½ teaspoon freshly ground
    black pepper
1 teaspoon turmeric
¼ cup dried red kidney beans
    (optional)
¼ cup dried chick-peas (optional)
¼ cup lentils
12 cups water
1 cup barley
2 cups chopped fresh parsley
    or ½ cup dried

1 cup chopped fresh coriander
    or ¼ cup dried
½ cup chopped fresh dill
    or 2 tablespoons dried
4 cups fresh spinach, washed and
    chopped, or 1 cup frozen spinach,
    chopped
¼ cup rice
1 cup liquid whey (*kashk*) or sour
    cream or yogurt

Garnish
2 tablespoons oil
1 onion, peeled and thinly sliced
5 cloves garlic, peeled and crushed
¼ teaspoon turmeric
1 tablespoon dried mint leaves

1. Brown 2 onions and meat in ¼ cup of oil in a large pot. Sprinkle with salt, pepper, and turmeric. Add the kidney beans, chick-peas, and lentils and saute for a few minutes. Pour in the water, bring to a boil, reduce heat, and cover. Simmer for 50 minutes over medium heat, stirring occasionally.

2. Add barley. Cover and cook 50 minutes longer, stirring occasionally.

3. Add parsley, coriander, dill, spinach, and rice; cover and cook 50 minutes more.

4. Check to see that the meat is tender and beans are done. If you desire, use a slotted spoon to remove some of the ingredients and place in a food processor. Blend thoroughly, return to the pot, and adjust seasoning.

5. Stir in the liquid whey, and continue stirring constantly for 5 minutes with a wooden spoon to prevent curdling.

6. Just before serving, prepare the garnish. Pour 2 tablespoons oil into a small non-stick frying pan and brown the onion and garlic. Add turmeric and remove from heat. Crush dried mint in the palm of your hand and add to the pan. Mix well

7. Pour the simmering soup into a tureen. Garnish with mint-and-garlic mixture. *Nush-e Jan!*

Note: Liquid whey (*kashk*) is available in Persian specialty food shops.

For best results, cook your *ash* a day in advance so that the flavors meld. Reheat the soup the next day just before serving. Add *kashk* and the garnish at the last minute.

Note: If using dried herbs, place a sieve in a bowl of luke-warm water and soak the dried herbs for 20 minutes. Remove the sieve from the bowl and use the herbs.

Cream of Barley Soup

Makes 6 servings
Preparation time: 20 minutes
Cooking time: 3 hours

Soup-e jow

2 onions, peeled and thinly sliced
2 cloves garlic, peeled and crushed
3 tablespoons oil
½ cup barley
1 teaspoon salt
¼ teaspoon freshly ground
  black pepper
4 cups water
3 cups homemade beef or
  chicken broth)
1 carrot, grated
3 leeks, finely chopped
½ cup sour cream
Juice of one lime

Garnish
2 tablespoons chopped fresh parsley
Zest of ½ lime, minced (optional)

Beef or Chicken Broth
2 pounds beef or chicken bones
1 onion, peeled and chopped
1 teaspoon salt
¼ teaspoon freshly ground
  black pepper
4–6 cups water

1. To make the broth, combine the bones, onion, salt, and pepper in a pot. Cover with 4 cups of water. Bring to a boil, skimming the froth as it forms. Cover and let simmer for 2 hours over low heat.

2. In a large pot, brown onions and garlic in the oil, then add the barley, salt, and pepper and saute for a few minutes. Add the water and bring to a boil. Cover, reduce heat, and simmer for 1 hour or until barley is tender, stirring occasionally.

3. Add the beef broth, carrot, and leeks to the soup. Cover and simmer over low heat for 30 to 40 minutes longer. Using a slotted spoon, remove ingredients and place in a food processor; blend thoroughly and return to the pot. If the soup is too thick, add more warm water. Continue cooking for another five minutes.

4. Stir a few spoonfuls of soup into the sour cream. Mix well and then add the sour cream and lime juice to the soup. Correct seasoning to taste, adding more salt, pepper, or lime juice.

5. Just before serving, garnish the soup with parsley and the lime zest. *Nush-e Jan!*

Mung Bean Soup

Makes 6 servings
Preparation time: 20 minutes
Cooking time: 3 hours

Ash-e mash

3 large onions, peeled and thinly
  sliced
5 cloves garlic, peeled and crushed
⅓ cup oil
2 teaspoons salt
¼ teaspoon freshly ground
  black pepper
1 teaspoon turmeric
1 cup dried mung beans
10 cups water
½ cup rice
1 cup diced turnip
1 cup peeled and diced fresh pumpkin or other winter squash
1 cup chopped fresh coriander
  leaves or ¼ cup dried

2 cups chopped fresh parsley
  or ½ cup dried
½ cup chopped fresh dill
  or 2 tablespoons dried
1 cup chopped chives or scallions
  or ¼ cup dried
1 cup pearl onions, peeled
2 cups chicken broth
1 cup liquid whey or sour cream

Garnish
5 cloves garlic, peeled and crushed
2 tablespoons oil
1 teaspoon turmeric
1 tablespoon dried mint flakes

1. In a large Dutch oven, brown the onions and garlic in ⅓ cup oil. Add salt, pepper, and turmeric. Add the mung beans and saute for a few minutes. Pour in the water. Bring to a boil, skimming the froth as it forms. Reduce heat, cover, and simmer 50 minutes over medium heat, stirring from time to time.

2. Add the rice, turnip, pumpkin, coriander, parsley, dill, chives or scallions, pearl onions, and chicken broth. Cover partially and simmer gently for another 1½ hours, stirring occasionally.

3. Check to see if beans and vegetables are done. If desired, using a slotted spoon, remove some of the ingredients and place in a food processor; blend thoroughly and return to the dutch oven. Adjust seasoning and add whey; mix well.

4. Meanwhile, prepare the garnish: Brown the garlic in 2 tablespoons oil and remove from heat. Crumble the dried mint flakes in your hand and add to the garlic. Add the turmeric and mix well.

5. Pour soup into a tureen. Decorate the surface of the soup with the garnish. Stir the garnish in just before ladling soup into individual bowls. *Nush-e Jan!*

Note: Mung beans are tiny gray-green beans that are usually forced to germinate for bean sprouts. They are available in specialty stores.

Qeymeh (page 248) prepared without the potatoes may be used for garnish.

For best results, cook your *ash* a day in advance so that the flavors meld. Reheat the soup the next day just before serving. Add the garnish, warmed, at the last minute.

Note: If using dried herbs, place a sieve in a bowl of luke-warm water and soak the dried herbs for 20 minutes. Remove the sieve from the bowl and use the herbs.

Variation: 3 eggplants, peeled and sliced. Fry on both sides and add in step 3.

Women preparing bread and ash,
detail from the Tahmasb Shahnameh, *painted by Dust Mohammad, 1545*

Yogurt Soup

Makes 6 servings
Preparation time: 10 minutes
Cooking time: 2 hours 50 minutes

Ash-e mast

Note: If using dried herbs, place a sieve in a bowl of luke-warm water and soak the dried herbs for 20 minutes. Remove the sieve from the bowl and use the herbs.

3 large onions, 2 peeled and thinly sliced, 1 peeled and grated
¼ cup oil
2 teaspoons salt
½ teaspoon freshly ground black pepper
½ teaspoon turmeric
½ cup dried chick-peas or yellow split peas
½ cup lentils
8–10 cups water
½ pound lean ground beef
1 cup and 2 tablespoons chopped fresh parsley or ¼ cup dried
1 cup rice
2 cups chopped fresh coriander or ½ cup dried

½ cup chopped fresh chives or scallions or 2 tablespoons dried
3 sprigs fresh tarragon
1 cup chopped fresh dill or ¼ cup dried
4 cups fresh spinach, washed and chopped, or 1 cup frozen spinach, chopped
3 turnips, chopped
2–3 cups yogurt

Garnish
1 onion, peeled and thinly sliced
5 cloves garlic, peeled and crushed
2 tablespoons oil
½ teaspoon turmeric
3 teaspoons dried mint flakes

1. Brown the 2 sliced onions in ¼ cup oil in a large pot. Add 1½ teaspoons salt, ¼ teaspoon pepper, and turmeric. Add the chick-peas and lentils and saute for a few minutes. Pour in 8 cups of water. Bring to a boil, reduce heat, partially cover and simmer for 35 minutes over medium heat.

2. Combine the grated onion with the meat in a bowl. Season with ½ teaspoon salt, ¼ teaspoon pepper, and 2 tablespoons parsley. Mix and shape into chestnut-size meatballs and set aside.

3. Add rice and meatballs and simmer 25 minutes more.

4. Add chopped herbs, spinach, and turnips and cook another 1½ hours, stirring occasionally.

5. Check to see if peas are tender. If desired, remove ingredients with a slotted spoon and place in a food processor; blend thoroughly and return to the pot. Adjust seasoning; add more warm water if the *ash* is too thick and cook a bit longer.

6. Stir a few spoonfuls of hot soup into the yogurt, blend well and add to the pot, stirring constantly for 5 minutes to prevent curdling.

7. Just before serving, prepare the garnish by browning onion and garlic in 2 tablespoons oil in a non-stick frying pan and adding the turmeric. Remove from heat. Crush mint flakes in the palm of your hand and add to the pan. Mix well.

8. Pour hot soup into a tureen. Pour mint-and-garlic mixture on top. Serve with flat bread, *sangak, lavash,* or pita. *Nush-e Jan!*

Note: This soup is an excellent remedy for cold symptoms.

Variation: You may substitute the meat with ½ pound giblets. In this case, brown the sliced onions and giblets together in step 1.

Sweet and Sour Soup

Makes 6 servings
Preparation time: 30 minutes
Cooking time: 3 hours

Ash-e miveh

3 onions, 2 peeled and thinly sliced, 1 peeled and grated
1 pound ground meat or ground chicken
2½ teaspoons salt
½ teaspoon freshly ground black pepper
½ teaspoon ground cinnamon
1 cup chopped fresh parsley
¼ cup oil
½ teaspoon turmeric
½ cup yellow split peas or dried chick-peas
8–10 cups water
½ cup chopped fresh chives or scallions or 2 tablespoons dried
½ cup chopped fresh beet leaves
¼ cup fresh chopped mint

or 1 tablespoon dried
1 cup chopped fresh coriander leaves or ¼ cup dried
1 cup dried pitted prunes
1 cup dried apricots
½ cup rice
¼ cup chopped walnuts
¼ cup sugar
¼ cup red wine vinegar

Garnish
1 large onion, peeled and finely sliced
5 cloves garlic, peeled and crushed
2 tablespoons oil
1 teaspoon dried mint flakes, crushed
¼ teaspoon turmeric

1. In a bowl, combine grated onion with ground meat. Add ½ teaspoon salt, ¼ teaspoon pepper, ¼ teaspoon cinnamon, and 2 tablespoons parsley. Mix well and shape into meatballs the size of walnuts.

2. Brown the 2 sliced onions in ¼ cup oil in a large pot. Sprinkle with 2 teaspoons salt, ¼ teaspoon pepper, and turmeric. Add the split peas or chick-peas and saute for a few minutes. Pour in 8 cups water. Bring to a boil, reduce heat, cover, and simmer for 25 minutes over medium heat, stirring occasionally.

3. Add the remaining parsley, chives or scallions, beet leaves, fresh mint, and coriander and simmer, covered, 25 minutes longer.

4. Add prunes, apricots, and meatballs and cook, covered, 25 minutes more.

5. Add rice and walnuts. Cover and cook for 45 minutes longer.

6. Mix the sugar and vinegar together and stir into the soup. Cook for about 25 minutes longer. Add more warm water if *ash* is too thick. Taste for seasoning and add more sugar or vinegar if needed to balance the sweet and sour.

7. Shortly before serving, prepare the garnish by browning the onion and garlic in 2 tablespoons oil in a non-stick frying pan. Remove from heat; add crushed mint flakes and turmeric to the pan and mix well.

8. Pour warmed soup into a tureen. Pour the garlic-and-mint garnish on top and serve with Persian flat bread, *sangak* or *lavash. Nush-e Jan!*

Note: For richer, more developed flavors, make your soup the night before. Just before serving, warm up the soup and add the garnish mixture of browned onions, garlic, and mint.

Note: If using dried herbs, place a sieve in a bowl of luke-warm water and soak the dried herbs for 20 minutes. Remove the sieve from the bowl and use the herbs.

Onion Soup

4 onions, peeled and thinly sliced
½ cup oil
2 tablespoons flour
2 tablespoons dried fenugreek
   leaves
1 teaspoon turmeric
6 cups water
¼ cup lime juice, 1 cup dried pitted
   tart cherries, or 2 tablespoons
   pomegranate paste

3 potatoes, peeled and cut in halves
1 teaspoon salt
¼ teaspoon freshly ground
   black pepper
1 tablespoon sugar (optional)
3 eggs

Makes 6 servings
Preparation time: 20 minutes
Cooking time: 1 hour 30 minutes

Eshkeneh

1. In a large pot, brown the onions in the oil. This will take about 15 minutes. Add flour, fenugreek, and turmeric. Stir constantly for 1 minute with a wooden spoon. Add water, lime juice or an alternative, potatoes, salt, and pepper. Bring to a boil, reduce heat, cover, and cook for 55 minutes over medium heat. Taste and correct seasoning. If the soup is too sour, add the tablespoon of sugar. Check to see if the potatoes are tender.

2. Add eggs. Stir for 5 minutes with wooden spoon.

3. Pour soup into a tureen and serve with yogurt and bread. *Nush-e Jan!*

Eating Matter and Reading Matter

In one hand Mulla Nasruddin was carrying home some liver he had just bought. In the other hand he had a recipe for liver pie which a friend had given him.

Suddenly a crow swooped down and carried off the liver.

"You fool!" shouted Mulla. "The meat is all very well—but I still have the recipe."

Noodle Soup

Makes 6 servings
Preparation time: 20 minutes
Cooking time: 3 hours

Ash-e reshteh

3 large onions, peeled and thinly
   sliced
5 cloves garlic, peeled and crushed
3 tablespoons oil
2 teaspoons salt
½ teaspoon freshly ground
   black pepper
1 teaspoon turmeric
¼ cup dried red kidney beans,
   washed and soaked in cold water
   for 2 hours and drained
¼ cup dried navy beans
¼ cup dried chick-peas
10–12 cups water
½ cup lentils
2 cups homemade beef broth (recipe
   page 59)
½ cup coarsely chopped fresh chives
   or scallions or 2 tablespoons
   dried
½ cup chopped fresh dill or 2 tablespoons dried
1 cup coarsely chopped fresh
   parsley or ¼ cup dried

6 cups spinach, washed and
   chopped, or 3 cups frozen spinach, chopped
1 fresh beet, peeled and diced in ½-
   inch pieces
½ pound Persian noodles (*reshteh*)
   or linguine noodles, broken in
   half
1 tablespoon all-purpose flour
1 cup liquid whey (*kashk*), sour
   cream, or ¼ cup wine vinegar

Qeymeh (optional, page 248)

Mint Garnish
1 onion, peeled and finely sliced
6 cloves of garlic, peeled and
   crushed
2 tablespoons oil
1 teaspoon turmeric
3 teaspoons dried mint flakes,
   crushed
2 tablespoons liquid whey

In Iran it is customary to eat noodles before embarking on something new. For us they symbolize the choice of paths among the many that life spreads out before us. Eating those tangled strands is like unraveling the Gordian knot of life's infinite possibilities in order to pick out the best. Noodles, we believe, can bring good fortune and make new endeavors fruitful. That is why noodles are always served on Nowruz, the Iranian New Year's Day. Another traditional occasion is on the third day after friends and relatives have gone away on a trip. It is believed that by eating noodles we can send them luck as they follow the path of their journey.

1. Brown the 3 onions and garlic in 3 tablespoons oil in a large pot. Add 2 tea-spoons salt, ½ teaspoon pepper, and 1 teaspoon turmeric. Add kidney beans, navy beans, and chick-peas and saute for a few minutes. Pour in 10 cups water and bring to a boil, skimming the froth as it forms. Reduce heat, cover, and sim-mer for 45 minutes over medium heat.

2. Add lentils and beef broth. Cook 55 minutes longer.

3. Add chopped chives or scallions, dill, parsley, spinach, and the beet. Continue cooking, stirring from time to time for 1½ hours or until the beans are tender. Correct seasoning and add more water if the *ash* is too thick.

4. Add noodles and flour and cook about 10 minutes, stirring occasionally.

5. Stir in the liquid whey and mix well.

Note: If using dried herbs, place a sieve in a bowl of luke-warm water and soak the dried herbs for 20 minutes. Remove the sieve from the bowl and use the herbs.

6. Prepare the *qeymeh* without the potatoes by following the recipe on page 248.

7. Prepare the mint garnish. Brown the onion and garlic in oil in a non-stick frying pan. Remove from heat, add the turmeric and the crushed mint flakes and mix well.

8. Pour the soup into a tureen. Garnish with *qeymeh* and mint garnishes and the dollop of whey. *Nush-e Jan!*

Note: *Kashk* is Persian for liquid whey. Liquid whey is available in specialty stores. Persian noodles (*reshteh*) are also available at Middle Eastern food shops.

Whey Soup

Makes 6 servings
Preparation time: 20 minutes
Cooking time: 35 minutes

کله جوش

Kalleh jush

3 large onions, peeled and thinly
    sliced
2 cloves garlic, peeled and crushed
¼ cup oil
1½ tablespoons dried mint flakes,
    or ½ cup fresh mint, plus 2
    tablespoons for garnish
3 cups warm water
1 teaspoon turmeric or ½ teaspoon
    ground saffron

1 cup liquid whey (*kashk*)
½ teaspoon salt
½ teaspoon freshly ground
    black pepper
¼ cup ground walnuts or
    pistachios
1 tablespoon chopped walnuts for
    garnish

1. In a Dutch oven, brown the sliced onions and garlic in the oil. Sprinkle with 1 tablespoon mint flakes or ½ cup chopped fresh mint and cook for 2 minutes.

2. Add water and turmeric or saffron. Bring to a boil, reduce heat, cover, and simmer over medium heat for 20 minutes.

3. Slowly stir in liquid whey, stirring constantly. Taste and adjust seasoning with salt and pepper.

4. Add walnuts or pistachios and cook for 10 minutes longer over low heat.

5. Remove from heat and pour into a tureen. Garnish soup with the remaining mint flakes and chopped walnuts. *Nush-e Jan!*

Note: *Kashk* is Persian for whey. It is drained, salted, and sun-dried yogurt. It contains a lot of vitamins, and is fairly sour. It is available in both liquid and dried form in food specialty stores.

Lamb's Head and Feet Soup

1 mutton or lamb's head with
    the tongue
4 mutton or lamb's feet or 2 lamb
    shanks
6 cups water
2 large onions, peeled and quartered
4 cloves garlic, peeled and crushed
2 bay leaves

2 teaspoons salt
½ teaspoon freshly ground
    black pepper
1 teaspoon ground cinnamon
1 teaspoon turmeric
Croutons of sauteed *sangak* bread

Makes 4 servings
Preparation time: 30 minutes
*Cooking time: 4 hours 30
minutes*

Kalleh pacheh

1. Sear mutton head and feet over open flame to burn off hairs. Scrape and wash thoroughly. Remove the nose completely. Split the head in half vertically, with the tongue in one half, unless the butcher has already done so. Rinse with cold water.

2. Bring 6 cups of water to a boil and add the head, tongue, and feet or shanks as well as the onions, garlic, and bay leaves. Skim froth as it forms. When it stops forming, reduce the heat, cover, and simmer over low heat for 4 hours or until the meat separates easily from the bones. Skim broth occasionally while cooking. Add more warm water if necessary to keep the water level at a minimum of 3 cups. Do not add salt until soup is cooked to prevent ingredients from discoloring.

3. Remove the head from the soup and peel the tongue and the skin off the bones. Separate the meat and brains from the skull. Cut into bite-size pieces. Return meat to broth.

4. Remove bay leaves. Season to taste with salt, pepper, cinnamon, and turmeric.

5. Pour soup into a tureen. Place croutons in each soup bowl before ladling out the soup. Serve with lots of Persian pickles (*torshi*), fresh vegetables and herbs (*sabzi-khordan*), and *sangak* croutons. *Nush-e Jan!*

Note: Leftover *sangak* bread can be cut into pieces, or toast the bread to use as croutons.

Traditionally *kalleh pacheh* is made with the head (including the tongue) and the feet of a mutton or lamb. Shanks may be substituted for the feet, which are not available everywhere. The head can be ordered from butcher shops with Greek or Middle Eastern clientele. Lamb's head and feet soup has a surprisingly delicate flavor that is best set off with Persian pickles (*torshi*).

Tripe Soup

Makes 4 servings
Preparation time: 20 minutes
Cooking time: 4 hours

1 pound calf or lamb tripe, soaked,
   cleaned, rinsed, and cut into
   small pieces
2 large onions, peeled and quartered
2 cloves garlic, peeled and crushed
2 whole bay leaves
6 cups water
¼ teaspoon freshly ground
   black pepper
1 teaspoon salt

Sirab shir-dun

1. Place tripe, onions, garlic, and bay leaves in a large pot. Add the water and bring to a boil.

2. Cover and simmer over low heat for 3 to 4 hours or until tender. Skim broth occasionally while cooking. Add more warm water if necessary to keep level of water covering the tripe at a minimum of 3 cups.

3. Remove bay leaves. Season to taste with pepper and salt—do not add salt until cooking is finished, as it might discolor the tripe.

4. Pour into a tureen and serve with Persian eggplant pickles (*torshi*), a platter of raw vegetables, fresh herbs, and *sangak* bread. *Nush-e Jan!*

Note: Cleaned tripe is available at various ethnic butchers and some supermarkets. It is often necessary to order it in advance.

Golden Plum Soup

Makes 6 servings
Preparation time: 40 minutes
Cooking time: 2 hours

آش آلو

Ash-e alu

Note: If using dried herbs, place a sieve in a bowl of luke-warm water and soak the dried herbs for 20 minutes. Remove the sieve from the bowl and use the herbs.

3 onions, 1 peeled and grated, 2 peeled and thinly sliced
1 deboned chicken (1 pound) or ½ pound ground meat
2 teaspoons salt
¼ teaspoon freshly ground black pepper
½ teaspoon turmeric
6–8 cups water
½ cup dried yellow split peas or ¼ cup chick-peas
2 cups chopped fresh parsley leaves or ½ cup dried
1 cup chopped fresh chives or scallions or ¼ cup dried

1 cup chopped fresh mint or ¼ cup dried
2 cups chopped fresh coriander leaves or ½ cup dried
4 cups small fresh sour plums or 2 cups dried golden Persian plums (*alu*)
1 cup rice

Garnish
1 large onion, peeled and thinly sliced
5 cloves garlic, peeled and crushed
2 tablespoons oil
3 teaspoons dried mint flakes
¼ teaspoon turmeric

This soup is an excellent remedy for cold symptoms.

1. If using the chicken, place 2 sliced onions with the chicken in **a** large pot. Sprinkle with the salt, ¼ teaspoon pepper, and turmeric. Pour in the water and add the split peas or chick-peas. Bring to boil, cover, and simmer for 25 minutes over medium heat, stirring occasionally.

2. Add parsley, chives or scallions, mint, and coriander and simmer 25 minutes longer.

3. Add plums and cook 25 minutes more.

4. Add rice, cover and cook for 45 minutes longer.

5. Add more warm water if *ash* is too thick. Adjust seasoning to taste.

6. Shortly before serving, prepare garnish by browning one onion and garlic in 2 tablespoons oil in a non-stick frying pan. Remove from heat. Crush the mint flakes in the palm of your hand and add them to the frying pan, add turmeric, and mix well.

7. Pour soup into a tureen. Pour garlic-and-mint garnish on top and serve with Persian flat bread (*sangak* or *lavash*). *Nush-e Jan!*

Variation: If using meat instead of chicken, grate one onion and combine with ground meat. Add ½ teaspoon salt and ¼ teaspoon pepper. Mix well and shape into meatballs the size of a hazelnut. Add in step 4.

Note: The flavors will meld for a richer result if you make your soup the night before. Just before serving, warm up the soup and add the garnish mixture of browned onion, garlic, and mint to the soup.

Borscht

Makes 4 servings
Preparation time: 15 minutes
Cooking time: 2 hours 35 minutes

A Persian/Armenian Borscht

1 pound fresh corned beef brisket or beef bone
2 large onions, peeled and thinly sliced
6 cups water
2 bay leaves, chopped
1 teaspoon peppercorns
1 teaspoon salt
4 cups finely chopped white cabbage
1 carrot, peeled and chopped
1 stalk celery, chopped
1 parsnip, chopped
½ green pepper, chopped
2 cups tomato juice
½ cup chopped fresh parsley
1 cup sour cream or yogurt
1 teaspoon ground cumin (optional)

1. Place beef and onions in a large pot and add the water. Bring to a boil, skimming the froth as it forms.

2. Add bay leaves, peppercorns, and salt. Cover and simmer for 50 minutes over medium heat. Remove the bay leaves.

3. Add cabbage, carrot, celery, parsnip, green pepper, and tomato juice; cover and simmer for 1½ hours longer or until the meat is tender.

4. Adjust seasoning and add parsley.

5. Pour the soup into a tureen. Garnish with sour cream or yogurt and dust with ground cumin. *Nush-e Jan!*

Pistachio Soup

1 cup pistachios, shelled
2 tablespoons butter or oil
1 shallot, chopped
1 leek, chopped
1 clove garlic, peeled and chopped
1 tablespoon rice flour
6 cups homemade chicken broth
   (recipe page 59)

1 teaspoon salt
¼ teaspoon pepper
½ cup Seville orange juice or
   mixture of 2 tablespoons fresh
   lime juice and ¼ cup fresh orange
   juice
2 tablespoons slivered pistachios for
   garnish

Makes 4 servings
Preparation time: 10 minutes
Cooking time: 55 minutes

Soup-e pesteh

1. Grind pistachios in a food processor or grinder.

2. In a heavy pot, heat butter or oil over medium heat. Add shallot, leek, and garlic. Gently stew them. Cover until translucent. Add rice flour, stirring occasionally. Add chicken broth and bring to a boil.

3. Add pistachios, salt, and pepper and reduce heat. Simmer over low heat, stirring occasionally, for 20 minutes.

4. Add Seville orange juice. Adjust seasoning.

5. Pour the soup into a tureen, garnish with slivered pistachios, and serve hot or cold. *Nush-e Jan!*

Variation: Pistachios can be substituted with either almonds or hazelnuts.

Note: The name pistachio is from the Persian word *pesteh*.

Sumac Soup

Makes 6 servings
Preparation time: 10 minutes
plus 2 hours' soaking time
Cooking time: 2 hours

آش سماق

Ash-e somaq

3 cups and 1 tablespoon sumac
   powder
2 large onions, 1 peeled and thinly
   sliced, 1 peeled and grated
3 tablespoons oil
1¼ teaspoons salt
½ teaspoon freshly ground
   black pepper
½ cup lentils
½ cup split peas
8 cups water
2 cups and 2 tablespoons chopped
   fresh parsley or ¾ cup dried
2 cups chopped fresh coriander
   leaves or ½ cup dried

1 cup chopped fresh mint
   or ¼ cup dried
1 cup chopped fresh tarragon
   or ¼ cup dried
¼ pound ground meat
½ cup rice flour
1 tablespoon sugar (optional)

Garnish
2 tablespoons oil
5 cloves garlic, peeled and crushed
1 teaspoon dried mint
½ teaspoon turmeric

1. Cook 3 cups sumac in 6 cups of water for 35 minutes over medium heat. Drain through a strainer set over a bowl, reserving the sumac water.

2. In a heavy pot, brown the sliced onion in 3 tablespoons oil. Add 1 teaspoon salt, ¼ teaspoon pepper, and the lentils and split peas. Saute for a few minutes, then add 8 cups water.

3. Add herbs (except for 2 tablespoons of parsley) and the sumac water and simmer for 45 minutes longer.

4. Combine the grated onion, meat, rice flour, 2 tablespoons parsley, 1 tablespoon sumac powder, ¼ teaspoon salt, and ¼ teaspoon pepper. Mix ingredients thoroughly and shape into chestnut-size meatballs. Add to the pot and simmer for 1 hour 15 minutes.

5. Taste soup for seasoning—it should be both sweet and sour. Add sugar if the soup is too sour.

6. Just before serving, prepare the garnish. Heat 2 tablespoons oil in a skillet and brown the garlic. Remove from heat. Crumble the dried mint flakes in the palm of your hand and add to the garlic. Add the turmeric and mix well.

7. Pour the soup into a tureen and garnish with the mint, turmeric, and garlic mixture. *Nush-e Jan!*

Note: If using dried herbs, place a sieve in a bowl of lukewarm water and soak the dried herbs for 20 minutes. Remove the sieve from the bowl and use the herbs.

Note: For best results, make the *ash* a day in advance to give the flavors a chance to meld. Reheat it just before serving. Add the garnish after pouring the soup into the tureen.

Sumac, which is made from the ground berries of the sumac shrub, is available at Iranian specialty food stores.

VEGETABLES

مادرم ریحان می چیند .

نان و ریحان و پنیر ، آسمانی بی ابر ، اطلسی هایی تر .

رستگاری نزدیک : لای گل های حیاط .

نور در کاسه مس ، چه نوازش ها می ریزد !

My mother's picking basil.
Bread and basil and cheese, a cloudless sky, wet petunias.
Salvation is near, amidst the flowers in the courtyard.
What caresses the light pours into a copper goblet!

Sohrab Sepehri

سبزیجات

Vegetables

Persians rarely eat vegetables as separate side dishes. Instead, vegetables are usually combined with dried beans, grains, and fruits or stuffed with fruits, rice, and meats.

We are very partial to stuffed vegetables, called *dolmeh*. Some favorite *dolmehs* are grape and cabbage leaves, eggplant, zucchini, and tomatoes. Fruits such as quinces and apples are also excellent for stuffing. Generally speaking, *dolmehs* may be served cold as an appetizer or hot as a main dish accompanied with bread and yogurt.

The good cook always chooses vegetables in season, when they are at their height of flavor and nutritional value. Complementary herbs may vary in intensity even from season to season. For example, the perfume of dill in spring is strongest and therefore most desirable for cooking. Fresh fruits, vegetables, and herbs should be used in season whenever possible. They give superior results in every way.

Stuffed Grape Leaves

Makes 6 to 8 servings
Preparation time: 1 hour
Cooking time: 2 hours

دلمه برگ مو

Dolmeh-ye barg-e mo

Note: Canned grape leaves are available in specialty food shops and sometimes supermarkets. If grape leaves are too thin, use two, one on top of the other.

50 fresh grape leaves in season or canned leaves
⅔ cup rice
¼ cup yellow split peas
1 teaspoon salt
1 onion, peeled and thinly sliced
½ pound ground meat (lamb, veal, or beef)
3 tablespoons olive oil
1 cup chopped scallions
¼ cup summer savory
½ cup chopped fresh dill
¼ cup chopped fresh tarragon
¼ cup chopped fresh mint
2½ cups chopped fresh parsley
Juice of 1 lime
¼ teaspoon freshly ground black pepper
1 teaspoon ground cinnamon
1 cup homemade beef broth (recipe page 59)
¼ cup olive oil
⅔ cup sugar
⅓ cup vinegar
⅓ cup fresh lime juice

1. Preheat oven to 350°F.

2. If using fresh grape leaves, pick small and tender ones, blanch them in boiling water for 2 minutes, then drain in a colander and rinse with cold water. For canned grape leaves, drain in a colander and rinse under cold running water.

3. In a saucepan, cook rice and split peas for 20 minutes over medium heat in 3 cups of water and ½ teaspoon salt. Drain in a colander.

4. In a non-stick skillet, brown onion and meat in 3 tablespoons olive oil. Add the rice and split peas, scallions, summer savory, dill, tarragon, mint, parsley, and the juice of 1 lime. Season with ½ teaspoon salt, ¼ teaspoon pepper, and cinnamon. Mix this stuffing thoroughly, using hands or a wooden spoon.

5. Place three layers of grape leaves on the bottom of a well-oiled ovenproof dish.

6. Place a grape leaf on top of a wooden board with the vein side up and nip off the little stem. Top with 1 tablespoon stuffing. Roll up the leaf, folding in the ends to prevent the stuffing from leaking out while cooking. Place in the dish. Repeat, filling all the leaves.

7. Pour broth and the oil into the dish. Set a small ovenproof plate on top of the stuffed grape leaves. Cover and bake in the oven for 1 hour.

8. Mix the sugar, vinegar, and lime juice. Remove the baking dish from oven, uncover the grape leaves, and baste with this syrup. Cover and return to oven. Bake an additional hour.

9. When the grape leaves are tender, taste sauce and adjust seasoning. The sauce should be quite reduced. Serve in the same baking dish or on a platter, while hot or warm, with bread and yogurt, or use cool as an appetizer. *Nush-e Jan!*

Variation: Stuffed Grape Leaves with Pine Nuts (*Dolmeh-ye barg-e mo ba senobar*)—You may replace the meat with ⅓ cup pine nuts.

قومی متفکرند در مذہب و دین   جمعی متحیرند در شک و یقین

ناگاه برآورد منادی ز کمین   کای بیخبران راہ نه آنست و نه این

خیام

One group is in religious convictions devout
Another is full of uncertainty and doubt
Then appeared a messenger from without
"You've both got it wrong; you've both lost out."

Omar Khayyam

Stuffed Cabbage Leaves

Makes 6 servings
Preparation time: 1 hour
Cooking time: 2 hours

Dolmeh-ye kalam

2 large heads of green or savory cabbage
¼ cup rice
¼ cup yellow split peas
1 onion, peeled and thinly sliced
1 pound ground meat (lamb, veal or beef)
½ cup oil
2 tablespoons tomato paste
¼ cup chopped fresh parsley
2 tablespoon chopped fresh mint

2 tablespoons chopped fresh dill
1 tablespoon chopped fresh tarragon
1 teaspoon salt
¼ teaspoon freshly ground black pepper
1 teaspoon ground cumin
½ teaspoon ground cinnamon
1½ cups tomato juice
½ cup sugar
⅓ cup vinegar or fresh lime juice

1. Preheat the oven to 350°F.

2. Core cabbage and remove individual leaves. Plunge them into boiling salted water. Cover and boil for 5 minutes, drain in colander, and rinse under cold water.

3. Cook rice and split peas in 2½ cups water and ½ teaspoon salt for 30 minutes. Drain.

4. In a non-stick skillet, brown onion and meat in ¼ cup oil. Add tomato paste and mix thoroughly.

5. Combine meat, rice, split peas, and chopped herbs in a large bowl. Season with salt, pepper, cumin, and cinnamon. Mix well.

6. Place two layers of cabbage leaves in a well-greased ovenproof dish.

7. For each remaining leaf, place it on a plate. Top with 1 tablespoon of stuffing. Roll tightly, folding in the sides of the leaf to prevent the stuffing from leaking out while cooking. Arrange stuffed cabbage leaves side by side in the dish.

8. Pour the tomato juice and ¼ cup oil into the dish around the stuffed leaves. Cover and bake in the oven for 1½ hours.

9. Combine sugar and vinegar or lime juice. Pour this mixture into baking dish. Cover, return to oven, and bake 30 minutes more. Baste the stuffed cabbage leaves occasionally with pan juices.

10. When the stuffed cabbage leaves are done, taste sauce and adjust seasoning by adding more vinegar or sugar. Serve hot or warm in same baking dish with bread and yogurt on the side, or cool as an appetizer. *Nush-e Jan!*

Stuffed Potatoes

5 large potatoes of uniform size,
   peeled
⅔ cup oil
2 large onions, peeled and thinly
   sliced
½ pound ground meat
   (lamb, veal or beef)
2 tablespoons tomato paste

⅔ cup chopped fresh parsley
2 eggs, hard-boiled and chopped
1 teaspoon salt
¼ teaspoon freshly ground
   black pepper
½ cup beef broth (recipe page 59)
1 cup tomato juice

Makes 5 servings
Preparation time: 30 minutes
Cooking time: 1 hour

Dolmeh-ye sibzamini

1. Preheat the oven to 350°F.

2. Wash and peel potatoes. Cut off potato tops and set aside. Slice off the bottoms so potatoes can stand up straight. Hollow out potatoes with a potato peeler or a melon baller, leaving a shell about ½ inch thick. Discard potato pulp.

3. Brown potatoes in a non-stick skillet in ¼ cup oil.

4. Brown the onion and meat in the remaining oil. Stir in 2 tablespoons tomato paste, parsley, eggs, salt, and pepper. Mix thoroughly and continue cooking for several minutes.

5. Fill the potatoes with stuffing, replace tops, and arrange the potatoes in an ovenproof dish.

6. Mix tomato juice with the broth. Pour this mixture over and around potatoes. Cover and bake in the oven for 1 hour. Baste occasionally with pan juices.

7. Check to see if potatoes are tender; adjust seasoning. Serve in the same baking dish or arrange on a platter. Serve with bread, fresh herbs and Persian pickles (*torshi*). *Nush-e Jan!*

Stuffed Green Peppers, Eggplants, and Tomatoes

Makes 4 to 6 servings
Preparation time: 45 minutes
Cooking time: 2 hours 20 minutes

Dolmeh-ye felfel sabz-o bademjan-o gojeh farangi

2 eggplants or pattypan squash
1 tablespoon salt
2 green bell peppers
4 large tomatoes
¼ cup rice
¼ cup yellow split peas
1 tablespoon salt
½ cup oil
1 onion, peeled and thinly sliced
1 pound ground beef, lamb, or veal
2 tablespoons tomato paste
1 cup chopped fresh parsley
½ cup chopped chives or scallions

1 tablespoon chopped fresh mint
1 tablespoon chopped fresh tarragon
1½ teaspoons salt
¼ teaspoon freshly ground black pepper
1 cup tomato juice
1 cup beef broth (recipe page 59)
⅓ cup lime juice or vinegar
⅓ cup sugar
1 teaspoon ground cinnamon
½ teaspoon saffron dissolved in 2 tablespoons hot water

1. Preheat oven to 350°F.

2. Slice off the tops of the eggplants or pattypan squash and set aside. Slice off the bottoms so the eggplants or squash can stand on their own. Hollow them out, using the point of a knife or a melon baller, leaving a shell about ¾ inch thick, and discard the flesh. Sprinkle the shells with 1 tablespoon salt and place in a colander to drain for 20 minutes.

3. Cut off the tops of the green peppers ½ inch from the stem and set them aside. Blanch peppers for 5 minutes in boiling water. Rinse in cold water and drain.

4. Remove stems from tomatoes. Cut a slice off the tops and set aside. Scoop out tomato pulp using a melon baller and reserve.

5. Cook rice and split peas together for 30 minutes in 2 cups water and ¼ teaspoon salt. Drain.

6. Rinse eggplants or squash and pat dry. Brown on all sides in 3 or 4 tablespoons hot oil, adding more oil if necessary. Set aside.

7. In a non-stick skillet, brown onion and meat in 2 tablespoons oil. Stir in tomato paste.

8. In a large bowl, combine meat, rice and split peas, and the chopped herbs. Season with 1 teaspoon salt and pepper. Mix thoroughly.

9. Fill eggplants, tomatoes, and green peppers with stuffing. Replace their tops.

10. Place the stuffed eggplants and peppers side by side in an ovenproof dish, leaving room for the tomatoes, which do not need to cook as long. Mix the tomato juice in the broth and pour around the vegetables. Cover and bake in the oven for 1½ hours.

11. Combine the reserved tomato pulp, 2 tablespoons oil, lime juice or vinegar, sugar, cinnamon, remaining salt and saffron water. Mix well and bring to a boil.

12. Remove the dish from the oven, uncover, and add the stuffed tomatoes. Pour the tomato-pulp mixture around the stuffed vegetables, cover, and return to oven. Bake for 45 minutes longer or more until tender.

13. When the vegetables are done, taste the sauce and correct seasoning according to taste. Add more lime juice, sugar, or salt. Serve in baking dish or arrange on a platter. Serve with bread and yogurt. *Nush-e Jan!*

Variation: Whole peeled, cored onions are also excellent for stuffing. Core and use a melon baller to dig circular sections out of the onion to form a shell. Blanch in boiling water for 1 minute and drain before stuffing. Bake about 1½ hours at 375°F in a baking pan along with the sauce as directed for other stuffing.

Stuffed Quince

Makes 6 servings
Preparation time: 45 minutes
Cooking time: 2 hours

بُ مِه

Dolmeh-ye beh

1 onion, peeled and thinly sliced
½ pound ground meat (lamb, veal or beef)
4 tablespoons oil or butter
¼ cup rice, cleaned and washed
½ cup water
1 teaspoon salt
¼ teaspoon freshly ground black pepper
½ teaspoon Persian allspice (*advieh*), page 376

6 medium-size quince
1 cup beef broth or water
¼ cup fresh lime juice
½ cup brown sugar
¼ cup balsamic vinegar
¼ teaspoon saffron, dissolved in 1 tablespoon hot water

1. Brown onion and meat in a skillet in 4 tablespoons oil. Add rice, ½ cup water, 1 teaspoon salt, pepper, and *advieh*. Mix thoroughly. Cover and simmer for 15 minutes over low heat.

2. Wash and rub quince. Cut off tops and set aside. Hollow out quince, using the tip of a knife or a melon baller to scoop out the seeds and some of the pulp, leaving a shell about ½ inch thick.

3. Sprinkle each quince with 1 tablespoon sugar and then fill with stuffing. Replace tops and place in a deep-pan dish. Pour beef broth and the pulp around the fruit. Pour a drop of oil on top of each quince. Cover with 2 layers of paper towels, tightly place the lid on top of the towels, and simmer over low heat for 1 hour.

4. In a saucepan, combine lime juice, brown sugar, vinegar, and saffron water. Pour over the fruit in the pan. Cover and simmer 45 minutes to 1 hour longer, basting occasionally with pan juices.

5. Check to see if fruit is tender and adjust seasonings to taste with sugar or lime juice. Serve in same baking dish or on a platter. Serve with bread, yogurt, and fresh herbs. *Nush-e Jan!*

Variation: Stuffed Apples (*Dolmeh-ye sib*)—You may replace the quince with apples. Prepare apples as in steps 1 and 2 above, then in step 3, place the stuffed apples in a well-greased ovenproof dish. Pour broth around the fruit. Cover and bake for 30 minutes in a 350°F oven. Remove dish from oven and add the sauce from step 4. Return dish to oven and bake uncovered for another 10–20 minutes. *Nush-e Jan!*

Eggplant Puree

Makes 6 servings
Preparation time: 20 minutes
Cooking time: 3 hours

حلیم بادمجان

Halim-e bademjan

1 pound lamb, veal, or beef shank
2 onions, peeled and thinly sliced
6 tablespoons oil
4 cups water
2 cups lentils or 1 cup chick-peas
2 teaspoons salt
½ teaspoon freshly ground
   black pepper
2 medium eggplants
1 cup liquid whey (*kashk*), or 1 cup
   sour cream

Garnish
2 tablespoons oil
1 onion, peeled and thinly sliced
2 cloves garlic, peeled and crushed
2 tablespoons dried mint, crushed
3–4 walnut halves
2 tablespoons liquid whey (*kashk*)
   or 2 tablespoons sour cream
¼ teaspoon saffron dissolved in 1
   tablespoon hot water

1. Place meat in a large non-stick pot and brown with onions in 3 tablespoons oil. Add 4 cups water, lentils or chick-peas, salt, and pepper. Bring to a boil, skimming froth as it forms. Cover and simmer over medium heat for 1½ hours, or until very tender. Add more warm water if needed. Remove the bone—the meat will have fallen away during cooking.

2. Peel eggplants and cut into four lengthwise slices. Soak in a large container of water and 2 tablespoons salt to remove bitterness. Let stand for 20 minutes, then rinse and pat dry. Brown the slices on both sides in three tablespoons of oil. Add to the soup, cover, and simmer for 45 minutes longer.

3. Remove all the stew ingredients with a slotted spoon, reserving the cooking broth. Mash meat and eggplant with a mortar and pestle or roughly puree in a food processor.

4. Return the puree to the broth and cook 15 minutes over low heat, stirring constantly until an even puree is obtained. Add liquid whey or sour cream and stir thoroughly for about 5 minutes. Remove from heat. Taste and correct seasoning.

5. Place puree in a serving bowl. For the garnish, heat 2 tablespoons oil in a skillet and lightly brown the onion and garlic. Remove from heat and add mint. Decorate the puree with this mixture, pieces of walnut, and a dollop of liquid whey or sour cream and the saffron water. Serve with bread. *Nush-e Jan!*

Note: *Kashk*, or liquid whey, is available at Persian food specialty stores.

Eggplant with Traditional Whey

Makes 4 servings
Preparation time: 50 minutes
Cooking time: 1 hour 10 minutes

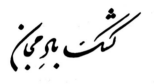

Kashk-e bademjan

3 medium eggplants
2 egg whites, beaten
¼ cup oil
3 large onions, peeled and thinly
   sliced
5 cloves garlic, peeled and crushed
½ cup water
2½ teaspoons salt
¼ teaspoon freshly ground
   black pepper

Garnish
5 cloves garlic, peeled and crushed
1 tablespoon oil
1 tablespoon dried mint, crumbled
½ cup liquid whey (*kashk*), diluted
   in ¼ cup water
¼ cup chopped walnuts (optional)
¼ teaspoon ground saffron dissolved in 1 tablespoon hot water

1. Peel eggplants and cut into four lengthwise slices. Place in a colander and soak in water and 2 tablespoons salt to remove bitterness. Let stand for 20 minutes. Rinse with cold water and pat dry.

2. Brush the eggplant with egg white on all sides to use less oil in the frying process.

3. Heat 2 tablespoons of the oil in a non-stick skillet and brown eggplant slices on all sides over medium heat. Drain over a paper towel.

4. Preheat the oven to 350°F.

5. Brown the onions and garlic in 2 tablespoons oil and set aside.

6. Alternate layers of eggplant with layers of onion and garlic in a long oven-proof dish. Pour ½ cup water over the layers, sprinkle with salt and pepper, cover, and bake in the oven for about 20 minutes or until tender.

7. For the garnish, just before serving, lightly brown the garlic in oil. Remove skillet from heat and add mint, whey, walnuts, and saffron water. Pour over the eggplant, cover, and bake for another 15 minutes in a 300°F oven.

8. When the eggplant is done, adjust seasoning with salt and pepper and keep it warm until serving. Serve from the baking dish with bread and chopped herbs. *Nush-e Jan!*

Note: Liquid whey (*kashk*) is available in food specialty shops. I recommend Gol-naz kashk.

Wheat Puree

Makes 6 servings
Preparation time: 15 minutes
plus 1 hour soaking time
Cooking time: 2 hours 45
minutes

حلیم گندم

Halim-e gandom

1 pound boned shoulder of lamb,
   veal, or beef, cut up, or 1 pound
   boned turkey
2 onions, peeled and thinly sliced
1 cup dried chick-peas (optional)
8 cups water
1½ teaspoons salt
1 pound whole wheat grain, soaked
   for 1 hour in 2 cups water

Garnish
¼ cup butter, melted
1 teaspoon cinnamon
2 teaspoons confectioners' sugar

This is a rich and hearty meal for winter.

1. Place the meat in a large pot. Add onions, chick-peas, 8 cups water and 1½ teaspoons salt. Bring to boil, skimming the froth as it forms. Cover and simmer over low heat for 1½ hours, adding warm water if needed. Stir occasionally to prevent sticking to the bottom.

2. Add soaked wheat grain with its water to the pot and cook for 55 minutes over low heat. Remove the ingredients from the pot, puree in a food processor, and then return to pot. Cook for another 35 minutes over low heat, stirring constantly until the mixture reaches the consistency of smooth porridge.

3. Spoon puree into a serving bowl. Garnish by pouring the butter over the wheat puree. Sprinkle cinnamon and confectioners' sugar on the top. *Nush-e Jan!*

Variation: This dish may also be prepared by replacing whole wheat with 2 cups wheat germ dissolved in 2 cups milk.

گر تو افتم نظر چهره به چهره رو به رو   شرح دهم عنم ترا نکته به نکته مو به مو

از پی دیدن رُخت همچو صبا نا فغانم   کو چه به کوچه، در به در، خانه به خانه، کو به کو

دور دهان تنگ تو عارض عنبرین خطت   غنچه غنچه، گل به گل، لاله به لاله، بو به بو

می رود از فراق تو خون دل از دو دیدم   دجله به دجله، یم به یم، چشمه چشمه، جو به جو

مهرِ ترا دل خزین بافته بر قماش جان   رشته به رشته، نخ به نخ، تار به تار، پو به پو

If I see you, face to face, eye to eye
I will tell you of my sadness, point by point, item by item.

For you I search like the east wind
In the streets, door to door, house to house.

For your sweet lips, your gentle features
Your fragrance, blossom to blossom, flower to flower.

Separated from you my heart bleeds through both eyes
To the sea, spring to spring, river to river.

Love for you has woven this afflicted heart
To the stuff of life, strand to strand, thread to thread.

Ghoratalaine

EGG DISHES

ملا نصرالدین

The Smell of a Thought

Mulla Nasruddin was penniless and sat huddled in a blanket while the wind howled outside. At least, he thought, the people next door will not smell cooking from my kitchen, so they can't send round to cadge some food.

At that, the thought of hot, aromatic soup came to his mind, and he savored it mentally for several minutes. Then there came a knocking on the door.

"Mother sent me," said the little girl, "to ask whether you had any soup to spare, hot seasoned soup."

"Heaven help us," said Mulla, "the neighbors even smell my thoughts."

E g g   D i s h e s

Eggs and egg dishes are popular throughout the Middle East. Iranians are specially fond of *kuku*, a type of omelet similar to the Italian frittata and the Arab *eggah*. It is filled with vegetables and herbs. A good *kuku* is thick and rather fluffy.

Although nowadays this dish is usually prepared in the oven, traditionally it was cooked in a large covered skillet that was set on hot coals. Coals were placed on the cover as well.

Kukus are served as appetizers or side dishes or as main dishes with yogurt or salad and bread. They may be eaten hot or cold and they keep well in the refrigerator for two to three days.

Most Iranian households keep *kukus* on hand for snacks or to serve unexpected guests. They are ideal for picnics as well.

Plain Egg Omelet

Makes 2 servings
Preparation time: 10 minutes
Cooking time: 15 minutes

Khagineh

5 eggs
1 onion, peeled and grated
    (optional)
¼ teaspoon saffron dissolved in 1
    tablespoon hot water
½ teaspoon salt
½ teaspoon baking powder
1 tablespoon flour
½ cup oil or melted butter
2 tablespoons confectioners' sugar
    (optional)
Rose water syrup (optional),
    page 369

1. Break the eggs in a bowl and whisk with onion, saffron water, salt, baking powder, and flour.

2. In a large non-stick skillet, heat the oil or butter over high heat.

3. Pour the egg mixture into the middle of the skillet and reduce the heat.

4. Cover and cook for 2 to 5 minutes over medium heat, until the edge sets and the eggs are golden brown on the bottom.

5. With a spatula, turn over the omelet and let the second side cook for another 5 minutes or until it is done, or cut into wedges and turn them over one by one to finish cooking.

6. Transfer into a serving dish and sprinkle with confectioners' sugar or rose water syrup. Serve hot with bread. *Nush-e Jan!*

Fresh Herb Kuku

Makes 4 servings
Preparation time: 25 minutes
Cooking time: 1 hour

گوگوی سبزی

Kuku-ye sabzi

5 to 6 eggs
1 teaspoon baking powder
1 teaspoon Persian allspice (*advieh*), page 376
1 teaspoon salt
¼ teaspoon freshly ground black pepper
2 cloves garlic, peeled and crushed
1 cup finely chopped fresh garlic chives or scallions
1 cup finely chopped fresh parsley leaves
1 cup finely chopped fresh coriander leaves
1 cup chopped fresh dill
1 tablespoon all-purpose flour
1 tablespoon dried fenugreek (optional)
2 tablespoons dried barberries (optional)
½ cup oil or clarified butter

Herb kuku is a traditional New Year's dish in Iran. The green of the herbs symbolizes rebirth. Eggs represent fertility and happiness for the year to come.

1. Preheat oven to 350°F.

2. Break eggs into a large bowl. Add baking powder, *advieh*, salt and pepper. Beat with a fork. Add garlic, chopped herbs, fenugreek or barberries, and flour. Mix thoroughly. Adjust seasoning to your taste.

3. Pour ¼ cup of the oil or butter into an 8-inch ovenproof baking dish and place it in the oven for 10 to 15 minutes. Pour in the egg mixture and bake uncovered for 30 minutes. Remove the dish from the oven and gently pour the remaining oil or butter over the *kuku*. Put the dish back in the oven and bake for 20 to 30 minutes longer, until golden brown.

4. Serve *kuku* in the baking dish or unmold it by loosening the edge with a knife and inverting it onto a serving platter. Cut the *kuku* into small pieces and serve hot or cold with *lavash* bread and yogurt. *Nush-e Jan!*

Note: If using dried herbs, reduce the amount to ¼ of the fresh herb amount. Place a sieve in a bowl of lukewarm water and soak the dried herbs for 20 minutes. Remove the sieve from the bowl and use the herbs.

Variation: *Kuku* can also be cooked on top of the stove. Heat the oil or butter in a non-stick skillet, pour in the egg mixture, then cook, covered, over low heat until it has set, about 25 to 30 minutes. Cook the second side by cutting into wedges and turning them over one by one, adding more oil or butter if needed. Cover and cook for 20 to 30 minutes longer, or until golden brown.

Cauliflower Kuku

1 small head cauliflower, half a large
 head, or 1 pound frozen florets
1 onion, peeled and thinly sliced
2 cloves garlic, peeled and crushed
½ cup oil or butter
4 eggs
1½ teaspoons salt
¼ teaspoon freshly ground
 black pepper
½ teaspoon baking powder

Makes 4 servings
Preparation time: 25 minutes
Cooking time: 1 hour

Kuku-ye gol-e kalam

1. Wash cauliflower and break into florets; steam cauliflower in a steamer for 20 minutes, or cook in saucepan for 15 minutes over medium heat in 2 cups water and ¼ teaspoon salt. If using frozen cauliflower, follow package instructions. Drain and mash. Allow to cool.

2. In a skillet, brown onion and garlic in 3 tablespoons of the oil or butter and set aside.

3. Preheat oven to 350°F.

4. Break eggs into a bowl. Add salt, pepper, and baking powder. Beat thoroughly with a fork.

5. Mix the mashed cauliflower, onion, and garlic into beaten eggs. Taste and adjust seasoning.

6. Pour ¼ cup of the oil or butter into an 8-inch ovenproof baking dish and place it in the oven. Heat the oil; pour in the egg mixture and bake uncovered for 30 minutes. Remove the dish and gently pour the remaining oil or butter over the *kuku*. Put the dish back in the oven and bake for 20 to 30 minutes longer, until golden brown.

7. Serve the *kuku* in the baking dish or unmold it by loosening the edge with a knife and inverting it onto a serving platter. Serve hot or cold with yogurt and bread. *Nush-e Jan!*

Note: *Kuku* can also be cooked on top of the stove. Heat the oil or butter in a skillet, pour in the egg mixture, then cook, covered, over low heat until it has set, about 15 minutes. Turn the *kuku* over by cutting it into wedges and turning them over one by one; cover and cook for 15 to 20 minutes longer, or until golden brown.

Chicken Kuku

1 small chicken, about 2½ pounds,
  cut up (leftover cooked chicken
  or turkey may be used)
2 onions, peeled and thinly sliced
½ cup oil or butter
4 eggs
¼ teaspoon saffron dissolved in 1
  tablespoon hot water

½ teaspoon baking powder
1 tablespoon lime juice
1 teaspoon salt
¼ teaspoon freshly ground
  black pepper

Makes 4 servings
Preparation time: 1 hour
Cooking time: 1 hour

Kuku-ye jujeh

1. Place the chicken in a saucepan with one of the onions, cover, and simmer for 45 minutes over low heat. It is not necessary to add water; the chicken and onion will produce enough juice. Remove chicken, debone it, finely chop and set aside to cool.

2. In a skillet, brown the other onion in 3 tablespoons of the oil.

3. Preheat oven to 350°F.

4. Break eggs into a bowl. Add the browned onion, saffron water, baking powder, lime juice, salt, and pepper. Beat the mixture thoroughly with a fork.

5. Add the chicken pieces to the beaten eggs. Mix, taste and adjust seasoning.

6. Pour ¼ cup of the oil or butter into an 8-inch ovenproof baking dish and place it in the oven. Heat the oil or butter for 10 to 15 minutes; pour in the egg mixture and bake uncovered for 30 minutes. Remove the dish and gently pour the remaining oil or butter over the *kuku*. Put back in the oven and bake for 20 to 30 minutes longer, until golden brown.

7. Serve *kuku* in the baking dish, or unmold it by loosening the edge with knife and inverting onto a serving platter.

8. Serve hot or cold with fresh herbs, yogurt, and bread. *Nush-e Jan!*

Note: *Kuku* can also be cooked on top of the stove. Heat the oil or butter in a skillet, pour in the egg mixture, then cook, covered, over low heat until it has set, about 15 minutes. Turn the *kuku* over by cutting it into wedges and turning them over one by one. Add more oil if needed, cover, and cook for 15 to 20 minutes longer, or until golden brown.

Eggplant Kuku

Makes 4 servings
Preparation time: 35 minutes
Cooking time: 1 hour

کوکو بادمجان

Kuku-ye bademjan

2 large eggplants, about 2 pounds
¾ cup olive oil or butter
2 large onions, peeled and thinly
   sliced
2 cloves garlic, peeled and crushed
4 eggs
1 tablespoon chopped parsley
   (optional)
¼ teaspoon ground saffron, dissolved in 1 tablespoon hot water
Juice of 1 lime

1 teaspoon baking powder
1 tablespoon all-purpose flour
1 teaspoon salt
¼ teaspoon freshly ground
   black pepper

1. To remove bitterness from the eggplant, peel them and cut each into 5 length-wise slices. Soak in a large bowl of water with 2 tablespoons salt. Let stand for 20 minutes, then drain. Rinse with cold water and pat dry.

2. In a skillet, brown eggplant on both sides in ¼ cup oil. Remove from skillet, cool, and mash with a fork. (You may also broil eggplant in the oven. Broil for 10 minutes on each side, or until golden brown, brushing oil on both sides.)

3. In the same skillet, lightly brown onion and garlic in 3 tablespoons oil and add to mashed eggplant.

4. Preheat oven to 350°F.

5. Break eggs into a bowl. Add parsley, saffron water, lime juice, baking powder, flour, salt, and pepper. Beat thoroughly with a fork. Add the eggplant mixture to beaten eggs. Mix thoroughly and mash. Adjust seasoning to taste.

6. Pour ¼ cup of the oil into an 8-inch ovenproof baking dish and place it in the oven. Heat the oil; pour in the egg mixture and bake uncovered for 30 minutes. Remove the dish and gently pour the remaining oil over the egg mixture. Put the dish back in the oven and bake for 20 to 30 minutes longer, until golden brown.

7. Serve *kuku* in the baking dish or unmold it by loosening the edge with knife and inverting it onto a serving platter. *Nush-e Jan!*

Note: *Kuku* can also be cooked on top of the stove. Heat ¼ cup of oil or butter in a skillet, pour in the egg mixture, then cook, covered, over low heat until it has set, about 25–30 minutes. Cook the second side by cutting into wedges and turning them over one by one; add the rest of the oil, cover, and cook for 15 to 20 minutes longer, or until golden brown.

Eggplant Omelet

2 small eggplants
½ cup olive oil or butter
3 cloves garlic, peeled and crushed
1 large onion, peeied and finely
   sliced
2 large tomatoes, peeled and
   chopped
¼ teaspoon turmeric
2 eggs
½ teaspoons salt
¼ teaspoon freshly ground
   black pepper

Makes 4 servings
Preparation time: 1 hour
Cooking time: 30 minutes

Mirza qasemi

1. Preheat oven to 350°F.

2. Prick eggplants with a fork to prevent bursting and place on oven rack. Bake for 60 minutes. Be sure to put a tray under the eggplants to catch drips.

3. Remove eggplants from oven, peel, and chop.

4. Heat the oil in a non-stick skillet and saute the garlic, onion, eggplant, and tomatoes. Add the turmeric. Cook over medium heat for 10 minutes.

5. Break eggs into a bowl; add salt and pepper. Beat well with a fork.

6. Add eggs to the eggplant mixture in the skillet and cook over low heat until eggs are firm, stirring occasionally with a wooden spoon.

7. Transfer to a serving platter. Serve with bread, fresh herbs, and yogurt. *Nush-e Jan!*

Fava Bean or Lima Bean Kuku

1 pound fava beans, shelled and peeled, or lima beans, fresh or frozen
2 medium onions, peeled and thinly sliced
2 cloves garlic, peeled and crushed
½ cup olive oil or butter
4 eggs

1 teaspoon salt
¼ teaspoon freshly ground black pepper
½ teaspoon baking powder
1 cup chopped fresh or ½ cup dried dill

Makes 4 servings
Preparation time: 35 minutes
Cooking time: 1 hour

Kuku-ye shevid-obaqala

1. Preheat oven to 350°F.

2. Steam the beans in a steamer for 20 minutes, or place the beans in a saucepan with 3 cups water and ½ teaspoon salt and boil for 10 minutes over medium heat. If using frozen beans, follow package instructions. Drain and allow to cool.

3. In a skillet, brown onions and garlic in 3 tablespoons oil or butter. Add beans and stir. Remove from heat and set aside.

4. Break eggs into a bowl. Add the salt, pepper, and baking powder.. Beat thoroughly with a fork. Add chopped dill.

5. Add bean mixture to beaten eggs. Mix and season to taste.

6. Pour ¼ cup of the oil or butter into an 8-inch ovenproof baking dish and place it in the oven. Heat the oil; gently pour in the egg mixture and bake uncovered for 30 minutes. Remove the dish and gently pour the remaining oil or butter over the egg mixture. Put the dish back in the oven and bake for 20 to 30 minutes longer, until golden brown.

7. Serve *kuku* in the baking dish or unmold it by loosening the edge with knife and inverting onto a serving platter. Serve with bread and yogurt. *Nush-e Jan!*

Note: *Kuku* can also be cooked on top of the stove. Heat the oil or butter in a skillet, pour in the egg mixture, then cook, covered, over low heat until it has set, about 15 minutes. Cook the second side by cutting into wedges and turning them over one by one; add the rest of the oil or butter, cover, and cook for 15 to 20 minutes longer, or until golden brown.

Garlic Kuku

**3 cups finely chopped fresh chives
  or scallions**
**1 pound garlic, peeled and crushed,
  or 1 pound whole green garlic,
  chopped**
½ cup olive oil or butter
2 teaspoons turmeric
4 eggs
1 teaspoon salt
**¼ teaspoon freshly ground
  black pepper**
1 teaspoon baking powder

*Makes 4 servings
Preparation time: 25 minutes
Cooking time: 1 hour*

Kuku-ye sir bij

1. In a skillet, lightly brown chives or scallions and garlic in 3 tablespoons oil for 10 minutes over medium heat. Add turmeric and mix well. Remove from heat and allow to cool.

2. Preheat oven to 350°F.

3. Break eggs into a bowl. Add the chive-and-garlic mixture, salt, pepper, and baking powder. Beat thoroughly with a fork.

4. Pour ¼ cup of the oil into an 8-inch ovenproof baking dish and place it in the oven. Heat the oil; pour in the egg mixture and bake uncovered for 30 minutes. Remove the dish and pour the remaining oil over the egg mixture. Put it back in the oven and bake for 20 to 30 minutes longer until golden brown.

5. Serve *kuku* in the baking dish or unmold it by loosening the edge with a knife and inverting it onto a serving platter. Serve with yogurt and hot bread. *Nush-e Jan!*

Note: *Kuku* can also be cooked on top of the stove. Heat the oil in a skillet, pour in the egg mixture; then cook, covered, over low heat until it has set, about 15 minutes. Cook the second side by cutting into wedges and turning them over one by one; add the rest of the oil, cover, and cook for 15 to 20 minutes longer, or until golden brown.

Green Bean Kuku

1 pound fresh or frozen green beans, finely chopped
2 medium onions, peeled and thinly sliced
2 cloves garlic, peeled and crushed
½ cup oil or butter
4 eggs

1 tablespoon flour
1 teaspoon baking powder
1 tablespoon lime juice
1 teaspoon salt
¼ teaspoon freshly ground black pepper

Makes 6 servings
Preparation time: 20 minutes
Cooking time: 1 hour

Kuku-ye lubia sabz

1. Steam the green beans in a steamer for 20 minutes, or place them in a saucepan with 3 cups of water and ½ teaspoon salt and boil for 10 minutes over medium heat. If using frozen beans, follow package instructions. Drain, cool, and chop.

2. In a skillet, brown the onions and garlic in 3 tablespoons oil or butter. Add green beans and mix. Remove from heat and set aside.

3. Preheat oven to 350°F.

4. Break eggs in a bowl. Add flour, baking powder, lime juice, salt, and pepper. Beat thoroughly with a fork.

5. Add the green-bean mixture to beaten eggs. Mix and season to taste.

6. Pour ¼ cup of the oil or butter into an 8-inch ovenproof baking dish and place it in the oven. Heat the oil; pour in the egg mixture and bake uncovered for 30 minutes. Remove the dish and pour the remaining oil or butter over the egg mixture. Put the dish back in the oven and bake for 20 to 30 minutes longer, until golden brown.

7. Serve *kuku* in the baking dish or unmold it by loosening the edge with a knife and inverting it onto a serving platter. Serve with yogurt and bread. *Nush-e Jan!*

Note: *Kuku* can also be cooked on top of the stove. Heat the oil or butter in a skillet, pour in the mixture, then cook, covered, over low heat until it has set, about 15 minutes. Cook the second side by cutting into wedges and turning them over one by one; add the remaining oil or butter, cover, and cook for 15 to 20 minutes longer, or until golden brown.

Green Pea Kuku

1 pound shelled green peas, fresh or frozen
1 onion, peeled and thinly sliced
2 cloves garlic, peeled and crushed
½ cup oil or butter
4 eggs
1 cup chopped fresh dill or ½ cup dried dill

1 teaspoon salt
¼ teaspoon freshly ground black pepper
½ teaspoon baking powder

Makes 4 servings
Preparation time: 10 minutes
Cooking time: 1 hour

Kuku-ye nokhod sabz

1. Steam the peas in a steamer for 10 minutes or boil the peas in 2 cups water and ½ teaspoon salt for about 5 minutes. If using frozen peas, follow package instructions. Drain and allow to cool.

2. In a skillet, lightly brown onion and garlic in 3 tablespoons oil.

3. Preheat oven to 350°F.

4. Break eggs into a bowl. Add onion and garlic mixture, green peas, dill, salt, pepper, and baking powder. Beat thoroughly with a fork.

5. Pour ¼ cup of the oil or butter into an 8-inch ovenproof baking dish and place it in the oven. Heat the oil or butter; pour in the egg mixture and bake uncovered for 30 minutes. Remove the dish and pour the remaining oil or butter over the egg mixture. Put the dish back in the oven and bake for 20 to 30 minutes longer, until golden brown.

6. Serve *kuku* in the baking dish or unmold it by loosening the edge with a knife and inverting it onto a serving platter. Serve with yogurt and bread. *Nush-e Jan!*

Note: *Kuku* can also be cooked on top of the stove. Heat the oil or butter in a skillet, pour in the egg mixture, then cook, covered, over low heat until it has set, about 15 minutes. Cook the second side by cutting into wedges and turning them over one by one; add the rest of the oil or butter, cover and cook for 15 to 20 minutes longer, or until golden brown.

Meat Kuku

1 pound ground beef
2 onions, peeled and thinly sliced
½ cup olive oil or butter
1 cup chopped fresh parsley
½ cup chopped fresh chives
    or scallions
1¼ teaspoons salt

¼ teaspoon freshly ground
    black pepper
5 eggs
¼ teaspoon ground cinnamon
1 teaspoon curry powder

Makes 4 servings
Preparation time: 20 minutes
Cooking time: 1 hour

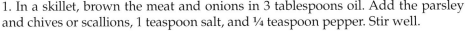

Kuku-ye gusht

1. In a skillet, brown the meat and onions in 3 tablespoons oil. Add the parsley and chives or scallions, 1 teaspoon salt, and ¼ teaspoon pepper. Stir well.

2. Preheat the oven to 350°F.

3. Break eggs into a bowl. Add cinnamon, curry powder, and ¼ teaspoon salt. Beat the mixture thoroughly with a fork.

4. Add meat to beaten eggs. Mix, taste, and adjust seasoning.

5. Pour ¼ cup of the oil into an 8-inch ovenproof baking dish and place it in the oven. Heat the oil; pour in the egg mixture and bake uncovered for 30 minutes. Remove the dish and pour the remaining oil over the egg mixture. Put it back in the oven and bake for 20 to 30 minutes longer, until golden brown.

6. Serve *kuku* in the baking dish or unmold it by loosening the edge with a knife and inverting it onto a serving platter. Serve with yogurt and bread. *Nush-e Jan!*

Note: *Kuku* can also be cooked on top of the stove. Heat the oil in a skillet, pour in the egg mixture, then cook, covered, over low heat until it has set, about 15 minutes. Cook the second side by cutting into wedges and turning them over one by one; add more oil if needed; cover and cook for 15 to 20 minutes longer, or until golden brown.

Potato Kuku

2 large potatoes (1 pound)
5 eggs
1 teaspoon salt
¼ teaspoon freshly ground
  black pepper
1 teaspoon baking powder
2 medium-size onions, grated
½ cup olive oil or butter
3 tablespoons confectioners' sugar
  for garnish (optional)

Makes 4 servings
Preparation time: 35 minutes
Cooking time: 1 hour 20 minutes

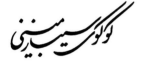

Kuku-ye sibzamini

1. Boil potatoes in 4 cups water and ½ teaspoon salt for 30 minutes. Peel, mash, and allow to cool.

2. Preheat oven to 350°F.

3. Break eggs into a bowl. Add salt, pepper, and baking powder. Beat thoroughly with a fork.

4. Add mashed potatoes and grated onions to beaten eggs. Mix, taste, and adjust seasoning.

5. Pour ¼ cup of the oil into an 8-inch ovenproof baking dish and place it in the oven. Heat the oil; pour in the egg mixture and bake uncovered for 30 minutes. Remove the dish and pour the remaining oil over the egg mixture. Put it back in the oven and bake for 20 to 30 minutes longer, until golden brown.

6. Serve *kuku* in the dish or unmold it by loosening the edges with the tip of a knife and inverting it onto a serving platter. Serve with bread, yogurt, and fresh herbs, or sprinkle with confectioners' sugar. *Nush-e Jan!*

Note: The egg-and-potato mixture can also be cooked into patties 3 inches in diameter by scooping ladlesful of the batter and pouring them onto a skillet. Cover and fry in hot oil on both sides until golden brown.

Spinach Narcissus

3 pounds fresh spinach, washed and chopped, or 1 pound frozen spinach, chopped
2 large onions, peeled and finely chopped
6 tablespoons olive oil or butter
1 clove garlic, peeled and crushed

¼ teaspoon salt
¼ teaspoon freshly ground black pepper
4 eggs

Makes 4 servings
Preparation time: 20 minutes
Cooking time: 25 minutes

Nargesi-ye esfenaj

1. Steam spinach in a steamer for 10 minutes. If using frozen spinach, follow package instructions. Set aside.

2. Brown onions in a non-stick skillet in the oil until golden; add garlic and cook briefly. Stir in spinach and season with salt and pepper. Mix well and cook over medium heat for 3 minutes. Spread out the mixture evenly in the skillet.

3. Reduce the heat. Break open an egg into a bowl, then pour onto the layer of spinach. Continue until all eggs are used. Do not mix the eggs. Cover and cook over very low heat for 3 to 5 minutes, or until the eggs have set.

4. Transfer to serving platter and serve immediately. *Nush-e Jan!*

Note: *Nargesi* is the Persian word for narcissus, a flower with white petals and a bright yellow center. To the imaginative, the colors of a dish of eggs poached on a bed of green suggest this early springtime flower.

Variation: One pound steamed zucchini or green beans may be substituted for the spinach.

Yogurt Kuku

4 eggs
1 teaspoon flour
¼ teaspoon saffron dissolved in 1 tablespoon hot water
½ teaspoon salt
¼ teaspoon freshly ground black pepper

½ cup chopped fresh chives or scallions
1 large carrot, grated
½ cup drained yogurt (page 372)
1 teaspoon slivered almonds
4 tablespoons olive oil or butter

Makes 4 servings
Preparation time: 35 minutes
Cooking time: 35 minutes

کوکوی ماست

Kuku-ye mast

1. Preheat oven to 350°F.

2 Break eggs into a bowl. Add flour, saffron water, salt and pepper, chives or scallions, and carrot. Beat thoroughly with a fork.

3. Add yogurt and slivered almonds to the egg mixture. Mix, taste, and adjust seasoning.

4. Pour oil into an 8-inch ovenproof baking dish or mold and place it in the oven. When the oil is hot, pour in egg mixture and return to oven. Bake for 20 to 35 minutes until golden brown.

5. Serve the *kuku* in the dish or unmold it by loosening the edges with the tip of a knife and inverting it onto a serving platter. Serve with bread and yogurt. *Nush-e Jan!*

Note: *Kuku* can also be cooked on top of the stove. Heat the oil in a skillet, pour in the egg mixture, then cook, covered, over low heat until it has set, about 15 minutes. Cook the second side by cutting into wedges and turning them over one by one; add more oil if necessary, cover, and cook for 15 to 20 minutes longer, or until golden brown.

Zucchini Kuku

Makes 4 servings
Preparation time: 15 minutes
Cooking time: 1 hour

کوکوی کدو

Kuku-ye kadu

1 pound (4 medium) zucchini, sliced
3 large onions, peeled and thinly
    sliced
2 cloves garlic, peeled and crushed
¾ cup olive oil or butter
4 eggs
1½ teaspoons salt
¼ teaspoon freshly ground
    black pepper
1 tablespoon flour
1 teaspoon baking powder

1. In a skillet, brown zucchini, onions, and garlic in 5 tablespoons oil or butter. Mash and set aside.

2. Preheat the oven to 350°F.

3. Break eggs into a bowl. Add the salt, pepper, flour, and baking powder. Beat thoroughly with a fork.

4. Add the mashed zucchini mixture to beaten eggs. Mix, taste, and adjust seasoning.

5. Pour ¼ cup of the oil or butter into an 8-inch ovenproof baking dish and place it in the oven. Heat the oil; pour in the egg mixture and bake uncovered for 30 minutes. Remove the dish and pour the remaining oil or butter over the egg mixture. Put it back in the oven and bake for 20 to 30 minutes longer, until golden brown.

6. Serve *kuku* in the baking dish or unmold it by loosening the edges with knife and inverting it onto a serving platter. Serve with yogurt, bread, and fresh herbs. *Nush-e Jan!*

Note: *Kuku* can also be cooked on top of the stove. Heat the oil or butter in a skillet, pour in the egg mixture, then cover and cook over low heat until it has set, about 15 minutes. Cook the second side by cutting into wedges and turning them over one by one, adding more oil or butter if necessary. Cover and cook for 15 to 20 minutes longer, or until golden brown.

Pistachio Kuku

¼ cup sugar cubes
½ cup finely ground shelled
   pistachios
4 eggs
2 tablespoons milk
1 teaspoon flour
½ teaspoon baking powder
¼ teaspoon ground saffron, dissolved in 1 tablespoon hot water

½ teaspoon salt
¼ teaspoon freshly ground
   black pepper
4 tablespoons oil or butter
1 teaspoon slivered pistachios
1 tablespoon confectioners' sugar

Makes 4 servings
Preparation time: 10 minutes
Cooking time: 20 minutes

کوکوی پسته

Kuku-ye pesteh

1. Preheat oven to 350°F.

2. In a food processor, finely grind sugar cubes and pistachios.

3. Break eggs into a bowl. Add milk, flour, baking powder, saffron water, salt, and pepper. Beat thoroughly with a fork.

4. Add the pistachio and sugar mixture to the egg mixture. Mix well and taste for seasoning.

5. Pour oil into an ovenproof dish or mold and place in oven. When the oil is hot, pour in egg mixture, sprinkle slivered pistachios on top and return to the oven. Bake uncovered for 15 to 20 minutes, until golden brown.

6. Serve the *kuku* in the dish or unmold it by loosening the edges with the tip of a knife and inverting it onto a serving platter. Dust the top with confectioners' sugar. *Nush-e Jan!*

Note: Pistachio kuku can also be cooked on top of the stove. Heat the oil in a skillet, pour in the egg mixture, sprinkle slivered pistachios on top, and then cover and cook over low heat until it has set, about 15 minutes. Cook the second side by cutting into wedges and turning them over one by one; add more oil if necessary, cover, and cook for 15 to 20 minutes longer, or until golden brown.

Variation: Almonds or hazelnuts can be substituted for pistachios.

Journeys in Persia and Kurdistan
Isabella Bird, 1891

. . . the Khan's wives called, and pressed me very hospitably to leave my tent and live with them, and when I refused they sent me a dinner of Persian dishes with sweetmeats made by their own hands. The *kababs* were quite appetizing. They are a favorite Persian dish, made of pieces of seasoned meat roasted on skewers, and served very hot, between flaps of very hot bread. Each bit of meat is rubbed with an onion before being put on the skewer, and a thin slice of tail fat is put between every two pieces. The cooks show great art in the rapidity with which they rotate a skewer full of *kababs* over a fierce charcoal fire.

"Rostam barbecues while his horse, Rakhsh, looks on," from Shahnameh, *circa 1540*

MEAT, CHICKEN, AND FISH

گر دست دهد ز مغز گندم نانی

و ز می دو منی ز گوسفند رانی

با لاله رخی نشسته در بستانی

عیشی بود این نه حد هر سلطانی

If one may have a loaf of the flower of wheat, a two-
   Maund jar of wine, a thigh of mutton, seated with
A heart's darling in a ruined place—that is a pleasure
That is not the attainment of any sultan.

Omar Khayyam

Meat, Chicken, and Fish

Lamb or mutton is the meat used most in Persian cuisine. All the parts of the sheep are used, not only the prime cuts or the leg, shoulder, and loin, but also the feet and the head, as well as all the organs, such as lamb fries, known in America as Rocky Mountain oysters (the testicles).

Lamb kababs, convenient and virtually foolproof, are very popular. The meat is marinated in herbs, onion, garlic, and vinegar or lime juice or yogurt. Then, when it is nearly time to eat, the meat is threaded onto skewers (a small piece of lamb tailfat is put between every two pieces of meat) and cooked over glowing charcoals for a subtly perfumed, flame-rich flavor. We like to use the very tender meat from the loin, but leg of lamb can also be used as long as it is marinated for at least 24 hours before grilling.

Kababs are also easy to make and bound to please. The meat is mixed with onions and spices, and molded onto flat swordlike skewers. Then it is cooked just long enough to be seared on the outside, pink and juicy within.

Such dishes can be broiled indoors in the broiler, but the flavor will not be as haunting as when the meat is imbued with the odor of a charcoal flame.

Whole Stuffed Baby Lamb with Pistachios

Makes 12 servings
Preparation time: 1 hour 30 minutes
Cooking time: 5 to 6 hours

برّهٔ درستهٔ تو پر

Bareh-ye doroste ye tu por ba pesteh

The name pistachio is from the Persian word Pesteh.

1 baby lamb, 14 to 18 pounds
Juice of 2 onions
1 teaspoon salt
10 cloves garlic, peeled
2 teaspoons ground saffron dissolved in ¼ cup hot water
½ cup butter or margarine, melted

Stuffing
3 cups long-grain basmati rice
9 cups water
2 tablespoons salt
4 large onions, peeled and thinly sliced
10 cloves garlic, peeled and crushed
½ cup butter or margarine, melted
1 cup chopped fresh scallions
1 cup chopped fresh parsley
¼ cup chopped fresh tarragon
1 cup chopped fresh coriander

1 cup chopped almonds
2 cups chopped pistachios
2 cups raisins
2 cups slivered walnuts
2 cups slivered apricots
2 cups dried barberries, cleaned, soaked for 20 minutes in water, and drained
2 cups chopped, pitted dates
4 apples, peeled, cored, and chopped
2 teaspoons turmeric
2 teaspoons salt
1 teaspoon freshly ground black pepper
2 tablespoons Persian allspice (*advieh*), page 376

1. Order your lamb ahead of time. Ask your butcher to prepare the lamb for stuffing and to bone the legs.

2. Rinse the lamb inside and out, and wipe dry with a towel.

3. Rub inside and out with mixture of onion juice and 1 teaspoon salt.

4. Using the point of a small knife, make 10 slits in the lamb and insert a clove of garlic in each. Set aside while preparing the stuffing.

5. In a saucepan, cook rice for 20 minutes in 9 cups water and 2 tablespoons salt. Drain and set aside.

6. In a large skillet, saute the onions and garlic in the butter. Add the scallions, parsley, tarragon, coriander, almonds, pistachios, raisins, walnuts, apricots, barberries, dates, apples, turmeric, 2 teaspoons salt, pepper, and Persian allspice. Cook for 5 minutes.

7. In a large bowl, combine all the stuffing ingredients with the rice and mix well. Preheat the oven to 350°F.

8. Stuff the lamb tightly with the mixture and sew up the belly. Use a large trussing needle and strong kitchen thread.

9. Place the lamb in a roasting pan in the oven and cook for about 4 to 5 hours, or until meat separates easily from the bone. Using a pastry brush, baste the lamb occasionally with a mixture of the saffron water and melted butter, and the pan juices.

10. Lay the lamb on an oval platter in the center of a huge mound of saffron-flavored rice (*chelow*, page 146).

11. Serve with Persian pickles (*torshi*) and fresh herbs and vegetables (*sabzi-khordan*). *Nush-e Jan!*

Note: More simply, you may wrap the lamb in foil and roast it in a preheated 375°F oven for 3 or 4 hours. Uncover it for the last ½ hour of cooking. Roast until well done because well-done lamb is tender.

As an alternative, you may use a leg of lamb. Place it in an ovenproof baking dish, stuff it, using half the ingredients, and bake for 3 or 4 hours.

This spectacular dish is served on festive occasions. It is often the centerpiece of a lavish wedding feast. Several lambs would be prepared to serve all the guests.

If using dried barberries, they must first be soaked in a colander and placed in a container of cold water for 20 minutes. Lift them out carefully and rinse well. Dried barberries are available at Iranian specialty stores.

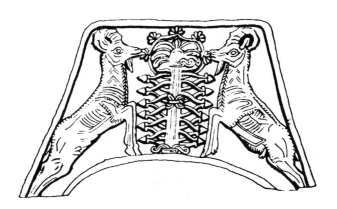

Meat Casserole

Makes 6 servings
Preparation time: 15 minutes
Cooking time: 2 hours 30 minutes

Tas kabab

4 tablespoons oil
4 large onions, peeled and sliced
2 pounds lean filet or shoulder of lamb, veal, or beef, boned and thinly sliced
2 cloves garlic, peeled and crushed
2 quinces or, if not available, 2 apples, cored and sliced
1 small eggplant, peeled and sliced
2 carrots, peeled and sliced
3 tomatoes, peeled and sliced
2 large potatoes, peeled and sliced
1 cup pitted prunes
2 cups dried apricots

1 teaspoon Persian allspice (*advieh*), page 376
¼ teaspoon turmeric
2 teaspoons salt
¼ teaspoon freshly ground black pepper
1 cup tomato juice
½ teaspoon ground saffron dissolved in 1 tablespoon hot water
1 tablespoon unripe grape powder (*gard-e-ghureh*)
1 tablespoon dried Persian limes (powdered *limu-omani*), page 377

1. Preheat oven to 350°F.

2. Pour 2 tablespoons oil into a large ovenproof casserole. Layer the ingredients in the following order: onion, meat, garlic, quince or apple, eggplant, carrots, tomatoes, and potatoes. Top with a layer of prunes and apricots. Pour in the remaining oil. Sprinkle allspice, turmeric, salt, and pepper on top. Mix together the tomato juice, saffron water, grape powder, and dried Persian limes and pour over the meat and vegetables. Cover and cook in the oven for 2 to 2½ hours or until it is done. Season to taste.

3. Serve in the same dish with bread, yogurt, salad, and fresh herbs. *Nush-e Jan!*

Variation: This casserole may also be cooked in a heavy Dutch oven on the stove over low heat for 2 hours, or until done.

Note: Dried Persian limes (*limu-omani*), Persian allspice (*advieh*), and unripe grape powder (*gard-e-ghureh*) are available at Iranian specialty stores.

Lamb Kabab

Makes 4 servings
Preparation time: 20 minutes
plus 24 hours' marinating
Cooking time: 10 minutes

Kabab-e barg

2 pounds boned tenderloin lamb, beef, or veal
¼ pound tailfat of lamb (optional)
3 large onions, peeled and grated
4 cloves garlic, peeled and crushed
1 cup fresh lime juice
1 teaspoon salt
1 tablespoon rose water (optional)
¼ teaspoon ground saffron dissolved in 1 tablespoon hot water
1 cup yogurt

8 cherry tomatoes or 4 large tomatoes, cut in quarters
Baste
2 tablespoons butter or margarine
1 teaspoon salt
1 12-ounce package of *lavash* bread
2 tablespoons sumac powder (optional)
1 lime, cut in half

6 flat, swordlike skewers

1. Have your butcher remove back bones from the lamb loins, then the fillets from the loins, and then trim all fat and gristle from the main muscles.

2. Cut meat into 2-inch cubes and pound each piece of meat with a small mallet. Cut tailfat into 1-inch cubes. Place meat and tailfat in a large bowl.

3. Add onions, garlic, lime juice, salt, saffron water and the yogurt. Mix well. Cover the meat and marinate for at least 24 hours in the refrigerator.

4. Start a bed of charcoal at least 30 minutes before you want to cook and let it burn until the coals glow. (You may use a hair dryer to speed up the process.)

5. During this time, thread 5 or 6 pieces of meat onto each flat and swordlike skewer and thread 1 piece of tailfat between every two pieces of meat, leaving a few inches free on both ends. Spear tomatoes onto separate skewers.

6. In a small saucepan, melt butter. Add the salt. Set aside and keep warm.

7. When the coals are glowing, first place tomatoes on grill; after 1 minute, place the skewered meat on the grill. Paint the kabab on all sides with the melted butter. Cook for 3 or 4 minutes on each side, turning frequently. The meat should be seared on the outside, pink and juicy on the inside.

8. Spread *lavash* bread on a serving platter. When the meat is cooked, place the skewers of meat on the bread and brush them with the melted butter mixture. Garnish with grilled tomatoes. Sprinkle the kababs with sumac powder to taste and squeeze half of a fresh lime over them. Try a piece to taste (cook's privilege). Cover with *lavash* bread to keep warm.

9. Serve immediately with *chelow, lavash* bread, or Persian pickles (*torshi*) and a dish of fresh herbs, especially scallions and basil. Remove the meat from each skewer by taking a piece of *lavash* bread, placing it over several pieces of meat, and using it to slide the meat off the skewer. *Nush-e Jan!*

Variation: Lamb Rib Chops Kabab (*Shish lik*) may be substituted for tenderloin. In this case there is no need for the tailfat.

Note: Traditional *Kabab-e barg* Cut meat into strips 3 inches wide, 4 inches long, and ¼ inch thick. Split each fillet without cutting entirely through the meat, and open out. Pound each piece with a heavy-bladed knife to make shallow incisions along the meat. Marinate meat and, before grilling, brush all sides with a mixture of butter and salt.

Shish Kabab

2 pounds lamb, veal, or beef, from the boned loin or leg, or boneless chicken breast, cut into 2-inch cubes
10 cloves garlic, peeled
1 large onion, peeled and grated
⅔ cup vinegar
½ cup olive oil
1 teaspoon dried oregano
4 green peppers
6 large tomatoes, quartered

10 pearl or 3 large onions, peeled and cut into 2-inch cubes
10 mushrooms

Baste
2 tablespoons melted butter or olive oil
Juice of 1 lime
½ teaspoon salt

1 12-ounce package of *lavash* bread

Makes 4 servings
Preparation time: 30 minutes plus 24 hours' marinating
Cooking time: 10 minutes

Shish kabab

1. Pound each piece of meat with a small mallet and place meat and garlic cloves in a large bowl. Add grated onion, vinegar, olive oil, and oregano. Mix well. Cover and marinate for at least 24 hours in a refrigerator.

2. Start charcoal at least 30 minutes before you want to cook and let it burn until the coals are glowing. (You may use a hair dryer to speed up the process.)

3. Remove the seeds and ribs from peppers and cut them into 2-inch squares.

4. Spear meat cubes onto skewers, alternating them with pieces of pepper, tomato, garlic, onions, and mushrooms.

5. In a saucepan, combine the melted butter, lime juice, and ½ teaspoon salt and brush this mixture over the skewered meat and vegetables.

6. When coals are evenly lit with white ash around each coal and the grill is hot, place meat on grill rack. Grill for 3 to 5 minutes on each side. Baste frequently with the baste mixture, and turn often.

7. Spread whole *lavash* bread on a serving platter. Arrange the skewers of meat on the bread and brush with melted butter. Remove the meat and vegetables from each skewer by taking a piece of *lavash* bread, placing it over several pieces, and using it to slide the food off the skewer.

8. Cover the meat and vegetables with another piece of *lavash* to keep it warm and serve immediately with scallions, basil, and yogurt. *Nush-e Jan!*

Variation: As an alternative, you may use 1 cup of yogurt, 1 grated onion, 2 tablespoons fresh lime juice, ½ teaspoon ground saffron dissolved in 2 tablespoons hot water, and ⅓ teaspoon freshly ground black pepper for marinating.

Liver, Heart, and Kidney Kabab

1 lamb's liver or ½ pound piece
   calf's liver
4 lamb kidneys or 1 veal kidney
4 lamb hearts or ¼ of a calf's heart
½ teaspoon salt
¼ teaspoon freshly ground
   black pepper
Juice of 3 limes

Makes 4 servings
Preparation time: 20 minutes
Cooking time: 6 minutes

Kabab-e jigar-o
del-o qolveh

1. Clean liver and cut into strips 1 inch thick. Cut kidneys into 1-inch cubes and slice hearts lengthwise into strips 1½ inches thick.

2. Light a bed of charcoal and let it burn until the coals glow evenly, or preheat the broiler in your oven.

3. Skewer strips of liver, cubes of kidney, and slices of heart onto separate skewers (cooking times are different for each).

4. Grill over hot coals for approximately 6 minutes for heart, 5 minutes for kidney, and 4 minutes for the liver. Turn them frequently.

5. After cooking, sprinkle with salt, pepper, and lime juice.

6. Serve immediately with bread, scallions, and Persian pickles (*torshi*) or serve as an appetizer with drinks. *Nush-e Jan!*

Note: A marvelous way to cook these meats is to grill them while you are sitting around the fireplace. Devise an ingenious cooking grill for inside your fireplace.

Lamb Fries Kabab

4 lamb fries
2 tablespoons melted butter
Salt
Freshly ground black pepper

Makes 4 servings
Preparation time: 10 minutes
Cooking time: 6 minutes

Kabab-e donbalan

1. Place the lamb fries in a large bowl of cool water; wash and drain them and cut each one in half.

2. Remove the thin outer membrane from the fries.

3. Light a bed of charcoal and let it burn until the coals glow evenly, or preheat the broiler in your oven.

4. Thread the fries onto the skewers. Paint them with melted butter and grill them over hot coals for about 4 to 6 minutes, turning them over often and quickly.

5. Serve very hot and season to taste with salt and pepper. *Nush-e Jan!*

Note: Wherever lamb is raised for meat, the fries, or testicles, are considered a great delicacy. They are usually referred to by terms such as Rocky Mountain or prairie oysters, or swinging steak in the United States, or *caprices de femme* (lady's whims) in France. Whatever you call them, they are excellent as an appetizer served with drinks.

Chicken Kabab

Makes 4 servings
Preparation time: 20 minutes
plus 6 hours' marinating
Cooking time: 15 minutes

Jujeh kabab

1 teaspoon ground saffron dissolved in 2 tablespoons hot water
1 cup fresh lime juice
2 tablespoons olive oil
2 large onions, peeled and thinly sliced
2 teaspoons salt
2 broiling chickens, about 4 pounds, each cut into 10 pieces, or 4 pounds of chicken drumettes
10 cherry tomatoes or 5 large tomatoes, cut in quarters

Baste
Juice of 1 lime
¼ cup butter, melted
½ teaspoon salt
½ teaspoon freshly ground black pepper
Garnish
Limes
Parsley sprigs

2 12-ounce packages of *lavash* bread

Chicken drumettes are tastier and cheaper.

1. In a large bowl, combine half the saffron water and the lime juice, 2 tablespoons olive oil, onions, and salt. Beat well with a fork. Add the pieces of chicken and toss well with marinade. Cover and marinate for at least 6 hours and up to 2 days in the refrigerator.

2. Start a bed of charcoal at least 30 minutes before you want to cook and let it burn until the coals glow evenly. (You may use a hair dryer to speed up the process.) Otherwise, preheat the oven broiler.

3. Skewer the tomatoes onto the skewers.

4. Spear wings, breasts, and legs onto different skewers (they require different cooking times).

5. Add the juice of 1 lime and the remaining saffron water to the melted butter. Add ½ teaspoon salt and ½ teaspoon pepper. Mix well and set aside.

6. Paint the tomato and chicken with the basting mixture. Grill the chicken and tomatoes 8 to 15 minutes (drumettes need less time to cook), putting the legs on first, then the breasts and wings. Turn and baste occasionally. The chicken is done when the juice that runs out is yellow rather than pink.

7. Spread a whole *lavash* bread on a serving platter. Paint the chicken with the butter mixture. Remove the grilled chicken from skewers and arrange the pieces on the bread. Garnish with limes cut in half and sprigs of parsley. Cover the platter with more bread.

8. Serve immediately with fresh herbs, Persian pickles (*torshi*), and french fries. *Nush-e Jan!*

Note: You may broil the chicken pieces in a pan in a broiler for 10 minutes on each side. During the cooking the door of the broiler should be shut. In this way the broiled chicken will be tender. There is no need to spear chicken pieces onto skewers.

Chicken Stuffed with Rice

Makes 4 servings
Preparation time: 35 minutes
Cooking time: 2 hours 25 minutes

Morgh-e tu por ba berenj

2 small frying chickens, about 6 to 7 pounds, or 2 Cornish game hens
2 teaspoons salt
2 large onions, peeled and thinly sliced
2 cloves garlic, peeled and crushed
¼ cup butter or oil
½ cup rice, cleaned and washed
½ tablespoon Persian allspice (*advieh*), page 376
1 teaspoon dried rose petals
¼ teaspoon freshly ground black pepper

1 cup chicken stock
¼ cup dried barberries, cleaned, soaked for 20 minutes, and drained, or ¼ cup dried tart cherries
2 tablespoons slivered almonds
2 tablespoons raisins
2 tablespoons fresh lime juice
¼ teaspoon ground saffron dissolved in 1 tablespoon hot water
¼ cup butter or olive oil
Lime slices for garnish

This is an excellent stuffing for turkey as well.

1. Clean and wash chickens or hens and rub with 1 teaspoon salt.

2. Brown onions and garlic in a skillet in ¼ cup butter or oil. Add rice, Persian allspice, rose petals, 1 teaspoon salt, and pepper. Cook for 5 minutes, stirring occasionally.

3. Add chicken stock; cover and simmer over low heat for 20 minutes.

4. Add barberries, almonds, raisins, and lime juice.

5. Preheat the oven to 350°F. Stuff chicken with the rice mixture and pin or sew the cavities shut.

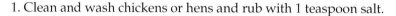

6. Place chicken in a greased ovenproof dish or roasting pan, paint with melted butter and cover with aluminum foil.

7. Place pan in the oven and roast for 1 hour. Remove chicken from the oven and paint it with a mixture of saffron water and butter. Cook uncovered for another hour, or until the meat separates easily from the bone. Baste occasionally with the pan juices.

8. Serve the chicken in the baking dish or on a serving platter. Garnish with lime slices and accompany with bread, raw vegetables, fresh herbs, and salad. *Nush-e Jan!*

Note: You may use wild rice in place of white rice. Follow directions on the package.

Rose petals are as much part of Persian cooking as they are part of Persian literature.

Barberries are available from Iranian specialty food stores. Clean sand from barberries (*zereshk*) by removing their stems and placing barberries in a colander. Place colander in a large container full of cold water and allow barberries to soak for 20 minutes. The sand will settle to the bottom of the container. Take the colander out of the container and run cold water over the barberries; drain and set aside.

Sweet and Sour Stuffed Chicken

Makes 4 servings
Preparation time: 30 minutes
Cooking time: 2 hours

Morgh-e tu por-e torsh-o-shirin

2 Cornish game hens or 2 small
  frying chickens
2½ teaspoons salt
3 tablespoons oil
1 large onion, peeled and thinly
  sliced
2 cloves garlic, peeled and crushed
1 cup pitted and finely chopped
  prunes
1 apple, cored and chopped

1 cup finely chopped dried apricots
½ cup raisins
¼ teaspoon freshly ground
  black pepper
1 teaspoon ground cinnamon
¼ teaspoon ground saffron dissolved in 2 tablespoons hot water
1 teaspoon sugar
½ cup melted butter or olive oil

This is an excellent stuffing for turkey as well.

1. Clean and rinse the hens or chickens in cold water, then pat dry and rub with ½ teaspoon salt.

2. Heat 3 tablespoons oil in a skillet and brown onion and garlic. Add prunes, apple, apricots, raisins, 2 teaspoons salt, pepper, cinnamon, saffron water, and sugar. Mix well.

3. Preheat oven to 350°F. Stuff the hens or chickens with the fruit mixture and pin or sew the cavities shut.

4. Place the hens or chickens in a greased ovenproof dish or roasting pan and paint with butter. Cover and place in the oven and bake for 1 hour, basting with pan juices, and bake uncovered for another hour, or until the meat separates easily from bone.

5. Serve game hens or chicken in the ovenproof dish or arrange them on a serving platter. Serve with plain rice (*chelow*) or bread and salad and fresh herbs. *Nush-e Jan!*

Variation: Sweet and Sour Stuffed Duck (*Ordak-e tu por-e torsh-o shirin*)—Stuff a whole duckling, about 5 pounds, with 1 large onion, 4 cloves garlic, ½ teaspoon cinnamon, ½ teaspoon cumin, ½ teaspoon cardamom, 1 teaspoon dried rose petals, 1 teaspoon salt, ¼ teaspoon pepper, ½ cup chopped fresh coriander, ½ cup pomegranate paste, and 3 tablespoons sugar. Proceed as above, basting the duck with the pan juices and ¼ cup orange juice.

Sweet and Sour Stuffed Turkey

Makes 4 servings
Preparation time: 30 minutes
Cooking time: 3 hours (20 minutes per pound of turkey)

بقلمون تو پرتش وشیرین

Buqalamu-ye tu por-e torsh-o shirin

Variation: Sweet and Sour Lamb Stuffing (*Buqalamu-ye tu por-e torsh-o shirin ba bareh*)—Cook ½ cup rice in 2 cups water with ½ teaspoon salt and drain. In a large skillet, fry ¼ pound ground lamb and two large peeled and chopped onions. Add salt, pepper, 1 teaspoon turmeric, ½ cup ground walnuts, ½ cup dried chopped apricots, ½ cup dried barberries, ½ cup raisins, and the rice.

Barberries are available from Iranian specialty food stores.

1 turkey, about 8 to 9 pounds
2½ tablespoons salt
1 cup butter
Juice of 1 lime
1 cup oil
2 large onions, peeled and thinly sliced
5 cloves garlic, peeled and crushed
½ cup rice
1 cup peeled and slivered carrot
1 cup dried barberries, cleaned, soaked for 20 minutes in water and drained, or ¼ cup dried tart cherries
½ cup dried apricot, chopped
2 tablespoons slivered, candied orange peel with bitterness removed (page 380)

½ cup raisins
1 cup ground walnuts
¼ teaspoon freshly ground black pepper
1 teaspoon ground cinnamon
1 teaspoon ground saffron dissolved in 2 tablespoons hot water
½ cup sugar
3 cups chicken broth

Sauce
2 tablespoons flour
salt
pepper
1 cup turkey broth

1. Clean and rinse the turkey in cold water, then pat dry and, with 2 tablespoons salt, ½ cup butter and the lime juice, rub thoroughly inside and out, lifting up the skin and placing 2 tablespoons of the butter under the skin.

2. Heat ½ cup of the oil in a saucepan and brown onion and garlic. Add rice, sauté for a few minutes and then add carrot, barberries, apricot, orange peel, raisins, walnuts, 2 teaspoons salt, pepper, cinnamon, saffron water, and sugar. Add chicken broth, cover, and simmer for 20 minutes over low heat.

3. Preheat the oven to 350°F. Stuff the turkey with this mixture and pin or sew the cavity shut.

4. Set the rack in a roasting pan, and place the turkey breast side down on the rack. Roast for 1 hour at 350°, then remove the pan from the oven, turn the turkey on one side, and rub with the remaining butter. Return the turkey to the oven and roast for another hour. Repeat for all sides of the turkey, and continue cooking until the meat separates easily from the bone (about 2½–3 hours). For good results use a meat thermometer.

5. Transfer the turkey to a serving platter. Let it cool for 20 minutes at room temperature. For the sauce, transfer all the pan drippings to a saucepan. Add 2 tablespoons flour, salt, pepper, and 1 cup turkey broth, stirring constantly over medium heat until the mixture thickens. Serve with Rice with Sour Cherries, page 190, salad, and fresh herbs. *Nush-e jan!*

Note: You may use wild rice in place of white rice. Follow directions on the package.

Sweet and Sour Stuffed Quail with Rose Petal

Makes 4 servings
Preparation time: 45 minutes
Cooking time: 25 minutes

بلدرچین تو پُر

Belderchin-e tu por

8 quails, with all small bones removed from the cavity
3 teaspoons salt
¾ teaspoon freshly ground black pepper
1 large onion, peeled and thinly sliced
4 cloves garlic, peeled and crushed
⅓ cup olive oil or butter
1 large tomato, peeled and chopped
½ cup ground walnuts
¼ cup barberries, cleaned and washed (page 379)

1 cup dried tart pitted cherries
¼ cup dried apricot or peaches
2 tablespoons sugar
2 tablespoons dried rose petals
¼ cup fresh lime juice
½ cup fresh orange juice
¼ teaspoon ground saffron, dissolved in 2 tablespoons hot water
Rose petals for garnish

1. Remove all the visible bones from the quail cavities; wash and pat dry.

2. Place the quail in a greased baking dish. Rub each bird inside and out with 1 teaspoon salt and ¼ teaspoon pepper.

3. In a non-stick skillet, brown the onion and garlic in 3 tablespoons of the butter or oil. Add the tomato and continue cooking for five minutes.

4. Add walnuts, barberries, cherries, apricot, sugar, 1 teaspoon salt, ¼ teaspoon pepper, and 2 tablespoons rose petals. Mix well.

5. Preheat oven to 425°F.

6. Divide the stuffing into 8 portions. Stuff each quail and pin or sew the cavity shut.

7. Mix lime juice, orange juice, saffron water, and remaining butter or olive oil and pour over the quail. Bake for 20–25 minutes, basting occasionally.

8. When done, the quail should be golden. Arrange quail on a serving dish, garnish with rose petals, and serve with rice. *Nush-e jan!*

Rose petals are as much part of Persian cooking as they are part of Persian literature.

Sauteed Brains

4 lambs' brains
2 tablespoons vinegar
1½ teaspoons salt
1 onion, peeled
2 eggs
1 teaspoon freshly ground
   black pepper
2 cloves of garlic, peeled and
   crushed

3 tablespoons milk
¼ cup flour
1 cup dry bread crumbs
1 cup oil
2 tablespoons balsamic vinegar or
   fresh squeezed lime juice

Makes 4 servings
Preparation time: 15 minutes
Cooking time: 10 minutes

Kotlet-e maghz

1. Place brains in a pot of boiling water with vinegar, ½ teaspoon salt, and peeled onion for 10 minutes. Drain. Remove membrane with a sharp knife and cut each brain in half. If the membrane is already removed, skip this step.

2. Break eggs into a bowl. Add remaining salt, pepper, garlic, and milk. Beat well with a fork.

3. Sprinkle brains with flour. Dip into egg mixture and let excess drip off. Coat the brains with a mixture of 1 cup bread crumbs and 2 tablespoons flour.

4. Deep fry brains in a skillet in hot oil over medium heat until golden brown.

5. Place the fried brains on a serving dish, sprinkle them with balsamic vinegar or lime juice and serve immediately with bread, fresh herbs, salad or steamed vegetables, and french fries. *Nush-e Jan!*

Meat Patties

Makes 4 servings
Preparation time: 45 minutes
Cooking time: 45 minutes

Kotlet-e gusht

2 large potatoes
1 pound ground lamb, veal, or beef
1 medium onion, peeled and grated
2 eggs
1 teaspoon salt
½ teaspoon freshly ground
    black pepper
¼ teaspoon ground cinnamon
¼ teaspoon Persian allspice (*advieh*)
    (optional), page 376

¼ teaspoon ground saffron dis-
    solved in 1 tablespoon hot water
½ teaspoon turmeric
¾ cup dry bread crumbs
¾ cup oil
4 ripe tomatoes, peeled and sliced
Parsley for garnish

1. Boil the potatoes until cooked. Peel, mash, and set aside.

2. In a bowl, combine meat, onion, eggs, mashed potato, salt, pepper, cinnamon, Persian allspice, saffron water, and turmeric. Knead for 10 minutes to form a smooth paste.

3. Using damp hands, shape the meat mixture into lumps the size of eggs. Flatten them into oval patties and roll them in bread crumbs. Brown the patties on both sides in a skillet in ½ cup hot oil over medium heat. Add more oil if necessary.

4. If you desire to make a tomato sauce, saute the tomatoes in 2 tablespoons oil in a skillet. Cover and cook over low heat for 10 minutes. Season with salt and pepper.

5. Arrange the patties on a serving platter. Pour the tomato sauce on top, if desired, and garnish with parsley. Serve with french fries, bread, salad and fresh herbs, and Persian pickles (*torshi*). *Nush-e Jan!*

Split-Pea Patties

Makes 15 to 18 patties
Preparation time: 10 minutes
Cooking time: 20 minutes plus 30 minutes for sweet and sour sauce

شامی آکه نخوچی

Shami-e-lapeh

3½ cups split peas
1 pound ground lamb, beef, or veal
1 large or 2 medium onions, peeled and finely grated
2 eggs
½ teaspoon ground saffron dissolved in 1 tablepoon hot water
2 teaspoons Persian allspice (*advieh*), page 376
1½ teaspoons salt
¼ teaspoon freshly ground black pepper
2 cups oil or more, for frying

Garnish
Parsley, basil, and mint sprigs

Sweet and Sour Sauce
1 onion, peeled and thinly chopped
3 tablespoons oil
½ teaspoon turmeric
1 teaspoon dried mint
½ cup water
½ cup vinegar
½ cup sugar

1. Cook split peas in 8 cups water over high heat for 30 minutes. Remove from heat, drain, and set aside to cool.

2. In a large bowl or a food processor, grind the split peas to a powder.

3. Combine the meat, onion, split peas and eggs. Add saffron water, Persian allspice, salt, and pepper. In a mixing bowl, knead well for about 15 minutes to create a soft paste. Cover and place in the refrigerator for at least 1 hour.

4. Place a bowl of warm water next to your cooking pan. With damp hands, separate the meat mixture into lumps the size of walnuts. Flatten each lump between your palms into a flat, thin shape and press a hole in the center with your finger (thin, even patties may also be made by spreading the walnut-size lump over an inverted saucer or cup). Fry on both sides in 2 cups hot oil in a skillet over medium heat for about 5 minutes on each side, or until golden brown. Add more oil if necessary. (These patties must fry in very hot oil.)

5. Arrange the patties on a platter, garnish with parsley, basil, and mint sprigs and serve very hot, warm, or even cold with warm, flat bread, pickled fruits and fresh herbs and vegetables (*sabzi khordan*). *Nush-e Jan!*

6. Split-pea patties may also be served with a sweet and sour sauce. In a pan, fry 1 chopped onion in oil. Add turmeric, mint, water, vinegar, and sugar. Bring to a boil. Before serving, place the patties in the sauce and let simmer for 3 minutes. Serve hot.

Variation: Chick-Pea Patties (*Shami-e ard-e nokhodchi*). Follow the above recipe, except replace the eggs and split peas with 3½ cups roasted chick-pea flour, 1 teaspoon baking powder, and ¾ cup of warm water. Chick-pea flour or powder is available in Iranian specialty stores.

Tabriz-Style Meatballs

Makes 4 servings
Preparation time: 40 minutes
Cooking time: 1 hour 20 minutes

Kufteh tabrizi

Note: If dried barberries are used, they must first be soaked in a colander and placed in a container of cold water for 20 minutes. Lift them out carefully and rinse well.

Dried barberries and Persian allspice (*advieh*) are available in Iranian specialty stores.

6 eggs, 4 hard boiled and 2 slightly beaten
½ cup yellow split peas
2 teaspoons salt
4 large onions, 1 peeled and grated and 3 peeled and thinly sliced
¼ teaspoon freshly ground black pepper
1 teaspoon ground saffron dissolved in 2 tablespoons hot water
1 teaspoon Persian allspice (*advieh*), page 376
½ cup rice flour
1 pound ground meat (lamb, beef, or veal shank)
¼ cup chopped fresh summer savory, or 2 tablespoons dried

2 cloves garlic, peeled and crushed
3 tablespoons oil or butter
2 cups beef broth
2 cups water
1 cup tomato juice
1 teaspoon turmeric
1 tablespoon tomato paste
2 tablespoons fresh lime juice
¼ cup dried barberries, cleaned, soaked for 20 minutes in water and drained
8 pitted prunes
4 walnut pieces
4 apricot halves

1. Hard boil 4 of the eggs. Shell and set aside.

2. Cook split peas for 20 minutes in 2 cups water and ½ teaspoon salt. Drain and set aside.

3. Beat 2 eggs in a large bowl or in a food processor. Add 1 grated onion, 1½ teaspoons salt, ¼ teaspoon pepper, ½ teaspoon saffron water, Persian allspice, rice flour, split peas, ground meat, and summer savory. Knead well for about 10 minutes until the mixture has reached the consistency of a smooth paste.

4. In a large pot, brown the 3 sliced onions and garlic in oil or butter. Add the beef broth, water, tomato juice, turmeric, ½ teaspoon salt, tomato paste, the remaining saffron water and lime juice. Bring to a boil.

5. Preheat the oven to 350°F. Shape the meat paste into 4 large balls the size of oranges. Stuff the center of each with 1 hard-boiled egg, 1 teaspoon barberries, 2 pieces of prune, 1 piece of walnut and 1 apricot half. Reshape the meatballs. Place them in an ovenproof glass baking dish. Pour the boiling broth around the meatballs. Cover and bake for 1 hour or more in the oven, turning the meatballs twice. Baste occasionally with pan juices to prevent them from drying out.

6. Check to see if the juices have reduced. Taste sauce and adjust seasoning to taste.

7. Serve the meatballs in the baking dish with bread and yogurt. *Nush-e Jan!*

Variation: In a large pot, make your sauce (step 4) and bring it to boil. Gently place the meatballs in the sauce and cook half-covered over medium heat for 1½ to 2 hours, adding more hot water if necessary.

pictured pg 200

Rice Meatballs

Makes 6 meatballs
Preparation time: 35 minutes
Cooking time: 1 hour 20 minutes

كوفته برنجی

Kufteh berenji

Note: If using dried herbs, place a sieve in a bowl of lukewarm water and soak the dried herbs for 20 minutes. Remove the sieve from the bowl and use the herbs.

½ cup yellow split peas
1 cup rice, cleaned and washed
2 teaspoons salt
2 eggs
2 teaspoons Persian allspice (*advieh*), page 376 (optional)
¼ teaspoon freshly ground black pepper
3 large onions, 1 peeled and grated and 2 peeled and thinly sliced
1 pound ground meat (lamb, veal, or beef)
2 cups chopped fresh or ½ cup dried parsley
1 cup chopped fresh dill or ¼ cup dried

½ cup chopped fresh or 2 tablespoons dried summer savory
¼ cup chopped fresh tarragon or 1 tablespoon dried
2 cups chopped fresh chives or scallions or ½ cup dried
2 cloves garlic, peeled and crushed
½ cup oil
1 cup tomato juice
2 cups water
2 cups beef broth
1 cup unripe plums (*gojeh sabz*) or ¼ cup fresh lime juice
1 teaspoon turmeric
¼ teaspoon ground saffron dissolved in 1 tablespoon hot water

1. Cook split peas and rice in a saucepan in 4 cups water with ½ teaspoon salt for 30 minutes over medium heat. Drain, reserving the liquid, and set aside to cool.

2. Break eggs into a mixing bowl; add ½ teaspoon salt, *advieh*, and the pepper and beat well. Add the grated onion, ground meat, parsley, dill, summer savory, tarragon, chives or scallions, split peas, and rice. Knead the mixture thoroughly for about 10 minutes until it reaches the consistency of a smooth paste.

3. In a heavy pot, brown the 2 sliced onions and garlic in the oil. Add tomato juice, water, beef broth, the rice and split pea liquid, unripe plums or lime juice, turmeric, 1 teaspoon salt, and saffron water. Bring to a boil.

4. Shape meat paste into balls the size of oranges. Gently place the meatballs into the boiling pot of broth. Cover partially and simmer gently for 45 minutes over low heat, basting the meatballs occasionally with the broth to prevent them from drying out.

5. Cover and cook for 15 minutes longer.

6. Check to see if pan liquids have thickened, and adjust salt to your taste. Place the meatballs in a bowl and gently pour the pan sauce on top. Serve hot with yogurt and bread. *Nush-e Jan!*

Note: Unripe plums (*gojeh sabz*) are available fresh in season at Iranian specialty stores.

Variations:

Sumac Meatballs (*Kufteh somaq*)—Sumac meatballs can be made by replacing the lime juice or unripe plums in step 2 with 2 tablespoons powdered sumac.

Curried Meatballs (*Kufteh curry*)—Curried meatballs can be made by adding 2 tablespoons curry powder and 1 teaspoon red pepper in step 2. Roll the meatballs in bread crumbs and fry them in ¼ cup oil; then add to the sauce. During the last 10 minutes of cooking, add ½ cup *kashk* or yogurt. Serve hot with bread.

Fava Bean or Lima Bean Meatballs (*Kufteh baqali*)—Fava bean meatballs can be made by replacing all the herbs such as savory, tarragon, and scallions with 4 cups chopped fresh dill and 1 pound shelled fava or lima beans. The beans should be washed, shelled, and have their outer skins removed before using. Cook the fava beans with the rice and split peas for 20 minutes and drain. Add dill. All the cooking times and proportions of spices are the same.

Ground Meat or Ground Chicken Kabab

Makes 6 servings
Preparation time: 40 minutes
Cooking time: 10 minutes

Kabab-e kubideh

1 pound ground lamb (it should contain fat)
1 pound ground beef or veal
1 medium onion, peeled and grated
1 egg (optional)
1 tablespoon yogurt
2 teaspoons salt
¼ teaspoon freshly ground black pepper
4 tablespoons butter
¼ teaspoon ground saffron dissolved in 1 tablespoon hot water (optional)
2 teaspoons powdered sumac or juice of 1 lime
1 12-ounce package of *lavash* bread

Chicken Kabab
2 pounds ground boneless chicken breast
1 large onion, peeled and grated
5 cloves garlic, peeled and grated
1 teaspoon salt
¼ cup butter or *ghee*, page 147
¼ teaspoon ground saffron, dissolved in 1 tablespoon hot water (optional)
½ cup sumac powder
2 limes, cut in half
1 12-ounce package of *lavash* bread

12 flat, swordlike skewers

1. In a large bowl, combine meat or chicken and the rest of the ingredients (except the butter, saffron water, sumac, limes, and *lavash* bread). Knead this mixture with your hands or with the aid of a mixer for 15 minutes to form a paste that will adhere well to cooking skewers. Cover the paste and let stand for 15 minutes at room temperature.

2. Start charcoal at least 30 minutes before you want to cook and let it burn until the coals are glowing evenly. (You may use a hair dryer to speed up the process.)

3. Melt the butter in a small saucepan and if desired add the saffron water and a pinch of salt.

4. Using damp hands, divide the meat paste into 12 equal lumps about the size of oranges. Roll each into a 5-inch sausage shape and mold it firmly on a flat, swordlike skewer.

5. Arrange the skewered meat on the grill 3 inches away from the coals; after a few seconds, turn the meat gently to prevent it from falling off.

6. Grill the meat 3 to 5 minutes on each side, brushing occasionally with the melted butter. Avoid overcooking it. The meat should be seared on the outside, juicy and tender on the inside. After cooking, remove the meat from the grill and baste with the melted saffron butter.

7. Spread *lavash* bread on a serving platter. Slide the meat off the skewer with another piece of bread. Arrange the meat on the bread, sprinkle with sumac or lime juice, and cover meat with more *lavash* bread to keep it warm. Serve immediately with *chelow* or bread, fresh herbs, scallions, salad, yogurt and cucumbers (*mast-o khiar*), and Persian pickles (*torshi*). *Nush-e Jan!*

Note: Sumac is sold powdered or whole in Iranian specialty stores.

Tongue with Tomato Sauce

Makes 4 servings
Preparation time: 20 minutes
Cooking time: 4 hours

خوراک زبان

Khorak-e zaban

1 large beef tongue or
    2 calf or lamb tongues
2 large onions, peeled and
    thinly sliced
4 cloves garlic, peeled and crushed
2 bay leaves
4 whole cloves
½ teaspoon freshly ground
    black pepper
3 tablespoons tomato paste

3 tablespoons butter or olive oil
2 tomatoes, peeled and sliced
½ pound mushrooms, sliced
1 tablespoon flour
2 tablespoons sour cream (optional)
    or 1 cup plain yogurt
Juice of 1 lime
1 teaspoon salt
2 tablespoons chopped fresh parsley
    for garnish

I have particularly fond memories of tongue-and-tomato-sauce sandwiches during my school years in Iran.

1. Wash and rinse the tongue and place in a large pot. Cover with water and add 1 onion, 3 cloves of garlic, bay leaves, cloves, and ¼ teaspoon pepper (do not add salt because it changes the color of the tongue). Bring to a boil, skimming off the foam. Add 2 tablespoons tomato paste, cover, and simmer over low heat for 2½ hours for calf and 3½ hours for beef, until cooked.

2. Remove the bay leaves and tongue from the broth and allow the tongue to cool. Reserve the broth. Remove the skin and excess fat from the tongue and cut it into thin slices.

3. In a saucepan, melt the butter or margarine over low heat. Saute the remaining onion, garlic, 1 tablespoon tomato paste, fresh tomatoes, and mushrooms and sprinkle in 1 tablespoon flour.

4. Add 1½ cups of the tongue broth, sour cream or yogurt, lime juice, and 1 teaspoon salt and ¼ teaspoon pepper to the saucepan. Mix well and simmer 10 minutes over low heat. Adjust seasoning to your taste.

5. Arrange sliced tongue on a serving platter and pour the sauce over the slices. Sprinkle with chopped parsley. Serve hot with plenty of Persian pickles (*torshi*), fresh herbs, and vegetables (*sabzi khordan*) and warm bread. *Nush-e Jan!*

Variation: You may prepare this dish without mushrooms and tomato, but add to the sauce the yogurt, 2 teaspoons *advieh,* and 2 teaspoons turmeric.

Sauteed Shrimp with Herbs and Tamarind

Makes 4 servings
Preparation time: 25 minutes
Cooking time: 45 minutes

میگو با تمر هندی

Maygoo ba tamr-e hindi

1 large onion, peeled and thinly sliced
4 cloves garlic, peeled and crushed
½ cup olive oil or butter
1 large tomato, peeled and crushed
1 cup fresh chopped coriander leaves
3 tablespoons dried fenugreek
¼ cup fresh basil, chopped
¼ cup coarsely chopped walnuts
2 teaspoons curry powder
¼ teaspoon freshly ground black pepper
½ teaspoon cinammon
¼ teaspoon ground cumin
½ teaspoon ground cardamom
1 teaspoon dried rose petals
⅔ cup tamarind liquid, page 375
1 pound raw peeled shrimp
2 tablespoons butter

1. In a non-stick skillet, brown the onion and garlic in 3 tablespoons olive oil over medium heat. Add tomato and continue cooking for 5 minutes.

2. Add coriander, fenugreek, basil, walnuts, curry powder, pepper, cinnamon, cumin, cardamom, rose petals, and ⅔ cup taramind liquid. Mix well and simmer over low heat for 20 minutes.

3. Cut the shrimp in half; wash and pat dry.

4. In a non-stick skillet, heat the rest of the olive oil and the butter and saute the shrimp for 5 minutes. Add to the sauce, and simmer for 10 minutes.

5. Add salt to your taste and adjust seasoning. Serve with *chelow* (plain rice, page 146). *Nush-e Jan!*

Platonic Fish

Makes 4 servings
Preparation time: 20 minutes
Cooking time: 5 to 10 minutes

1 cup washed and chopped scallions
2 cloves garlic, peeled and crushed
½ cup oil or butter
1 cup pomegranate juice or 1 tablespoon pomegranate paste dissolved in ½ cup water
½ cup unripe grape juice (*ab ghureh*)
  or 1 teaspoon powdered unripe
  grape (*qard-e ghureh*)
1 cup Seville orange juice

1 cup tomato juice
1 teaspoon salt
2 teaspoons Persian allspice (*advieh*)
1 tablespoon sugar or honey
  (optional)
4 thick fish fillets, sea bass, trout,
  orange roughy, or rockfish
1 tablespoon flour
Pomegranate seeds for garnish

Mahi-e aflatuni

1. In a saucepan, fry the scallions and garlic in 3 tablespoons oil or butter. Add pomegranate juice, unripe grape juice, Seville orange juice, tomato juice, ½ teaspoon salt, and Persian allspice. Bring to a boil and taste the sauce: it should be sweet and sour. If necessary, add 1 tablespoon sugar or honey.

2. Preheat the oven to 450°F.

3. Wash the fish and pat dry. Sprinkle the fish with ½ teaspoon salt and flour.

4. In a frying pan, fry the fish on both sides in the remaining oil or butter.

5. Place the fried fish in an ovenproof baking dish. Pour the sauce over the fish, cover, and bake it in the oven for 5–10 minutes. Remove it from the oven, garnish it with a few pomegranate seeds, and serve with rice. *Nush-e Jan!*

Stuffed Fish with Pomegranate Sauce

Makes 4 servings
Preparation time: 15 minutes
Cooking time: 50 minutes

Mahi-ye tu por ba anar

1 large or 2 pounds firm-fleshed white fish, about ½ inch thick: sea bass, halibut, cod, rockfish, or orange roughy
1 teaspoon salt
⅓ cup olive oil or butter
1 onion, peeled and thinly sliced
3 cloves garlic, peeled and crushed
¼ teaspoon freshly ground black pepper
¼ cup chopped walnuts
1 cup pomegranate juice or 3 tablespoons pomegranate paste

1 tablespoon slivered candied orange peel
2 tablespoons fresh lime juice
¼ teaspoon ground saffron dissolved in 2 tablespoons hot water

Garnish
1 tablespoon angelica petals or powder (*gol-par*)
2 tablespoons chopped walnuts
2 tablespoons pomegranate seeds

1. Rinse fish in cold water. Pat dry with paper towel and rub both sides with 1 teaspoon salt.

2. Heat ¼ cup oil in a large frying pan and brown onion and garlic. Add all the ingredients except the saffron water and lime juice and cook for 3 minutes. Mix well and remove from heat.

3. Preheat oven to 400°F. Place the fish in a baking dish. Stuff it with the mixture from step 2 and pin or sew the cavity shut. Pour the saffron water, the rest of the oil, and lime juice over the fish.

4. Place the fish in the oven and bake for 10–15 minutes (until the fish flakes easily with a fork), basting from time to time.

5. Arrange the fish on a serving platter. Pour the sauce from the baking dish over the fish. Garnish with angelica petals, walnuts, and pomegranate seeds.

6. Serve with saffron-steamed plain rice (page 146). *Nush-e Jan!*

Variation: You may substitute pomegranate juice or paste with 1 cup liquid tamarind.

Grilled Fish with Sumac

Makes 4 servings
Preparation time: 10 minutes
plus 3 hours' marinating time
Cooking time: 5 to 7 minutes

ماهی باسماق

Kabab-e mahi ba somaq

4 thick firm-fleshed white fish fillets of red snapper, sea bass, salmon, rockfish, swordfish, or orange roughy
1 teaspoon salt
¼ teaspoon freshly ground black pepper

Juice of 1 lime
½ cup sumac powder
2 tablespoons olive oil

1. Wash the fish and pat dry with a paper towel. Rub it well with 1 teaspoon salt and ¼ teaspoon pepper. Place it in a baking dish.

2. Squeeze lime juice over fish. Sprinkle both sides of the fillets with sumac powder to completely cover. Let stand, covered, in refrigerator for 3 hours.

3. Preheat the broiler. Uncover the fish and put 2 tablespoons of oil on the top of it. Broil in the upper level of the broiler for 5 to 7 minutes, or grill the fish over hot coals for approximately 6 to 10 minutes on both sides.

4. Serve with plain rice (*chelow*). *Nush-e Jan!*

Smoked White Fish

Makes 6 servings
Preparation time: 10 minutes
Cooking time: 1 hour

ماهی دودی

Mahi-ye doodi

3 whole bulbs garlic with the skin
½ cup olive oil
½ teaspoon salt
¼ teaspoon pepper
3 sprigs of thyme
1 whole Canadian smoked white fish, between 4–5 pounds

3 cloves garlic, peeled and crushed
4 fresh limes or Seville oranges (2 for juicing, 2 cut in half for garnish)

1. Place the garlic bulbs in a terra cotta garlic roaster or any baking dish. Sprinkle with olive oil, salt, pepper, and thyme. Cover and cook in a 300°F preheated oven for one hour. Remove from the oven and set aside.

2. Preheat oven to 350°F. Place the fish on a baking dish and stuff the fish with crushed garlic and the juice of two limes or Seville oranges.

3. Cover the fish. Place the baking dish in the preheated oven and bake for 30 minutes.

4. Remove fish from oven and gently transfer to a serving dish. Garnish with whole garlic and the limes or Seville oranges. *Nush-e Jan!*

Grilled Fish with Seville Orange

4 thick fillets of red snapper, swordfish, or salmon, cut into 2-inch
   cubes
1 onion, peeled and thinly sliced
5 cloves garlic, peeled and crushed
⅓ cup olive oil
½ cup Seville orange juice, or mixture of ½ cup orange juice and 2
   tablespoons lime juice
1 teaspoon salt
¼ teaspoon freshly ground
   black pepper

Makes 4 servings
Preparation time: 10 minutes
plus 3 hours' marinating time
Cooking time: 5 to 7 minutes

Kabab-e mahi ba narenj

1. Wash the fish and pat dry with a paper towel. Place it in a baking dish.

2. Mix all the remaining ingredients and pour over the fish. Marinate for a mini-mum of 3 hours in the refrigerator.

3. Preheat the broiler, and spear fish cubes onto skewers.

4. Broil the fish in the upper level of the broiler for 5 to 7 minutes, or grill it over hot coals for approximately 6 to 10 minutes, on both sides.

5. Serve with saffron-flavored rice (*chelow*), fresh herbs, and Persian pickles (*tor-shi*). *Nush-e Jan!*

Sauteed Fish with Garlic and Seville Orange

Makes 4 servings
Preparation time: 10 minutes
Cooking time: 30 minutes

Mahi-e sir-dagh
ba narenj

4 thick fillets of trout, red snapper, orange roughy, rockfish, or salmon
2 tablespoons all-purpose flour
1 teaspoon salt
10 cloves garlic, peeled
¼ cup olive oil
1 teaspoon ground turmeric or ½ teaspoon saffron dissolved in 2 tablespoons hot water

¼ teaspoon freshly ground black pepper
1 cup Seville orange juice or mixture of ½ cup fresh squeezed orange juice and ½ cup lime juice
½ cup fish stock

1. Wash and pat fish dry. Dust with 1 tablespoon flour and 1 teaspoon salt.

2. Saute fish on both sides with garlic in ¼ cup olive oil in a large non-stick skillet over medium heat.

3. Add the turmeric or saffron water and pepper; fry for a few minutes, until golden brown.

4. Dissolve 1 tablespoon flour in the Seville orange juice; add this to the skillet. Add ½ cup fish stock. Adjust salt and pepper.

5. Cover and simmer for another 5–10 minutes or until fish is tender.

6. Remove from heat; place the fish in a serving platter. Pour the sauce over it and serve with *chelow*, saffron-steamed rice and fresh herbs, and Persian pickles. *Nush-e Jan!*

Note: You may also place the fish in an ovenproof baking dish, pour the Seville orange juice mixture over it, and cover and bake in a preheated 400°F oven for 10–15 minutes.

Fish Stuffed with Fresh Herbs

Makes 6 servings
Preparation time: 30 minutes
Cooking time: 30–45 minutes, depending on the size of fish

ماهی تو پر با سبزی

Mahi-ye tu por ba sabzi

1 large fish (sea bass, salmon, rock-fish) or 6 thick fillets of flounder or orange roughy, about 6 pounds total, cleaned and scaled
2 teaspoons salt
½ cup butter or olive oil
2 cloves garlic, peeled and crushed
½ cup chopped fresh parsley
2 tablespoons chopped fresh tarragon
4 scallions, chopped
1 tablespoon chopped fresh coriander
¼ cup chopped fresh mint or 2 tablespoons dried mint

1 cup finely ground walnuts
¼ cup dried barberries, cleaned, soaked for 20 minutes in water and drained
¼ cup raisins
¼ cup fresh lime juice
¼ teaspoon freshly ground black pepper
¼ teaspoon ground saffron dissolved in 2 tablespoons hot water

Garnish
Barberries
Lime or Seville orange halves

1. Rinse fish in cold water. Pat dry with paper towel and rub inside and out with 1 teaspoon salt.

2. Heat half the butter or oil in a skillet and saute garlic, parsley, tarragon, scallions, coriander, and mint; add walnuts, barberries, raisins, lime juice, 1 teaspoon salt, and pepper. Mix well.

3. Preheat oven to 400°F. Fill the fish with the herb stuffing; sew or pin cavity shut. Lay the fish in a buttered baking dish. Dot the fish with the remaining butter or oil and saffron water.

4. Place in the oven and bake for 20–30 minutes (depending on the size of the fish), until the fish flakes easily with a fork. Baste occasionally with pan juices.

5. Arrange the fish on a serving platter and garnish with barberries and lime or Seville orange.

6. Serve with saffron-steamed plain rice and fresh herbs. *Nush-e Jan!*

Notes: If using fish fillets, place the stuffing in the center of a greased baking dish. Cover it with fish and pour the saffron wate and butter or oil over the fish. Continue with step 4.

Barberries are available from Iranian specialty food stores.

Clean sand from dried barberries (*zereshk*) by removing their stems and placing barberries in a colander. Place colander in a large container full of cold water and allow barberries to soak for 20 minutes. The sand will settle to the bottom of the container. Take the colander out of the container and run cold water over the barberries; drain and set aside. If using fresh barberries, remove stems and rinse with cold water.

Stuffed Sweet and Sour Fish

Makes 4 servings
Preparation time: 15 minutes
Cooking time: 45 minutes

*Mahi-ye tu por-e
torsh-o shirin*

1 large fish (sea bass, salmon, rock-fish) or 6 thick fillets of flounder or orange roughy, cleaned and scaled
2 teaspoons salt
½ cup olive oil or butter
½ cup finely chopped scallions
2 cloves garlic, peeled and crushed
¼ cup pitted and chopped dates
¼ cup finely chopped dried apricots
⅓ cup slivered pistachios
⅓ cup slivered blanched almonds

1 tablespoon slivered candied orange peel, page 380
Juice of 2 limes
½ teaspoon ground cinnamon
¼ teaspoon freshly ground black pepper
¼ teaspoon ground saffron dissolved in 2 tablespoons hot water

Garnish
2 tablespoons toasted slivered almonds and pistachios

1. Rinse fish in cold water. Pat dry with paper towel and rub inside and out with 1 teaspoon salt.

2. Heat half the butter or oil in a large frying pan and saute scallions and garlic. Add dates, apricots, pistachios, almonds, orange peel, juice of 1 lime, cinnamon, 1 teaspoon salt, and pepper. Mix well. Cook for 3 minutes.

3. Preheat the oven to 400°F. Stuff the fish with the mixture from step 2 and pin or sew the cavity shut. Lay the fish in a buttered baking dish. Pour the saffron water and the rest of the oil or butter and lime juice over the fish.

4. Place in the oven and bake for 15–25 minutes, until the fish flakes easily with a fork, basting from time to time with the pan juices.

5. Arrange the fish on a serving platter or serve from the baking dish; sprinkle a few toasted slivered almonds and pistachios over it. Pour the juices from the baking dish over the fish.

6. Serve with saffron-steamed plain rice. *Nush-e Jan!*

Note: If using fish fillets, place the stuffing in the center of a greased baking dish. Cover it with fish and pour the saffron water, oil or butter, and lime juice over the fish. Continue with step 4.

The Travels of Jean Chardin, 1686

They served up the dinner after this manner: There were spread before all the company, cloths of gold brocade, and upon them, all along, there was bread of three or four sorts, very good, and well made; this done, they immediately brought eleven great basins of that sort of food called *pilau*, which is rice baked with meat: There was of it, of all colors, and of all sorts of tastes, with sugar, with the juice of pomegranates, the juice of citrons, and with saffron: each dish weighed above fourscore pounds, and had alone been sufficient to satisfy the whole assembly. The four first had twelve fowls in each; the four next had a lamb in each; in the others there was only some mutton: with these basins, were served up four flat kettles, so large and heavy, that it was necessary to help to unload those that brought them. One of them was full of eggs made into a pudding; another of soup with herbs; another was filled with herbage and hashed meat; and the last with fried fish. All this being served upon the table, a porringer was set before each person, which was four times deeper than ours, filled with sherbet of a tartish sweet taste, and a plate of winter and summer sallets: After which, the carvers began to serve all the company out of each dish, in china plates. As for us Frenchmen, who were habituated to the country of Persia, we ate heartily at this feast, but the freshcomers fed upon the admiration of the magnificence of this service, which as all of fine gold, and which (for certain) was worth above a million.

Falcon hunt by Reza Abbasi, circa 1650

RICE

The Food of the Cloak

Mulla Nasruddin heard that there was a party being held in the nearby town, and that everyone was invited. He made his way there as quickly as he could. When the master of ceremonies saw him in his ragged cloak, he seated him in the most inconspicuous place, far from the great table where the most important people were being waited on hand and foot.

Mulla saw that it would be at least an hour before the waiters reached the place where he was sitting. So he got up, went home and dressed himself in a magnificent sable cloak and turban and returned to the feast. As soon as his host's heralds saw this splendid sight they started to beat the drum of welcome and sound the trumpets in a manner consistent with a visitor of high rank.

The Chamberlain himself came out of the palace, and conducted the magnificent Nasruddin to a place almost next to the Emir. A dish of wonderful food was immediately placed before him. Without a pause, Nasruddin began to rub handfuls of it into his turban and cloak.

"Your Eminence," said the prince, "I am curious as to your eating habits, which are new to me."

"Nothing special," said Mulla, "the cloak got me in here. Surely it deserves its share!"

R i c e

History

According to ancient Chinese writings, the Chinese began to grow rice about seven thousand years ago, during the New Stone Age. The Persian word for rice, *berenj*, comes from the Sanskrit *vrihi*. Rice was probably brought to Iran from southeast Asia or the Indian subcontinent and first cultivated in the Caspian area around the fourth century B.C.E. The best Persian rice still comes from Gilan, by the Caspian, where it is also the diet staple, eaten for breakfast, lunch, and dinner.

Types Of Rice

There are five major varieties of rice in Iran: *champa* (short and thick, probably from the ancient Indonesian kingdom of Champa), *rasmi* (longer and wider), *anbarbu, mowla'i,* and *sadri* (a variety brought to Gilan from Peshawar in 1850 by the grand vazir, Mirza Aqa Khan Nuri Sadr-e A'zam). Other varieties similarly have names based on their shape, perfume, or taste: *khanjari,* dagger shaped; *'anbarbu,* amber perfumed; *shekari,* sweet. Today in the West, basmati rice from India is readily available and is close to Persian rice. When basmati rice is cooked, it fills the air with a delightful aroma similar to that of flowers. Other kinds of long-grain rice may also be used for Persian rice dishes, but never the so-called converted rice (Uncle Ben's brand, for example).

Cooked Rice

Rice is eaten in great quantities in the Caspian region, but elsewhere in Iran bread is the main staple and rice is considered a luxury by the peasants or the urban poor and is eaten by them only on special occasions or served to guests. There are three major types of cooked rice in Iran: *kateh, chelow,* and *polow.* Though various *polows* were first mentioned in Persian literature by 'Obeyed e Zakani in his *Mush-o Gorbeh* in the 1300s, the present refined versions were probably developed in the 1800s during the Qajar period.

Kateh is the traditional dish of Gilan, and is the simplest way of cooking Persian rice. Rice, water, and salt are cooked until the water is absorbed. Butter is added, the pot is covered, and the rice is allowed to cook. The rice becomes compact with a crusty surface. In the Caspian region *kateh* is eaten for breakfast heated with milk and jam, or cold with cheese and garlic. For lunch and dinner it is eaten with meat, fowl, fish, or *khoresh* (stew).

Damy is a type of *kateh* cooked with herbs and vegetables. It is similar to *kateh* except that the heat is reduced immediately after the rice starts to boil. The pot is then covered with a dish towel (*dam-koney*) or 2 layers of paper towels wrapped around the lid to prevent steam from escaping. After 40 minutes remove the cover, pour oil or butter on top of the rice, recover, and continue cooking for another 20 minutes.

To Make Chelow
1. Pick over the rice.
2. Wash the rice.
3. Parboil the rice.
4. Drain through a large, fine-mesh colander.
5. Steam the rice.

Chelow has the same ingredients as *kateh* except that more care is taken in the cooking process, including presoaking, parboiling, and steaming. This results in a fluffy rice with each grain separate, and the bottom of the pot has a crisp golden brown crust, *tah dig. Tah dig* should be a golden color, never scorched or dark brown. The reputation of Iranian cooks rests on the quality of their *tah dig*, or golden crust. *Chelow* is then eaten with *khoresht*, called *chelow-khoresht*, or with *kabab*, called *chelow-kabab*.

Polow is first cooked in the same way as *chelow*. The meat, fruit, and vegetables are fried together and then arranged in alternating layers with the rice; they are then steamed together.

Rice is, of course, also used in many other dishes in Persian cuisine, including soups, *ashes,* meatballs, *kufte-berenji*, stuffed vegetables, and *dolmeh*. There are also many sweets and cookies made using rice flour: *halva, fereni, shirberenj,* and *nan-e berenji.* It is also used as a type of popcorn, by roasting, *berenj-e budadeh* or *berenjak,* and deep-fried as a candy, *reshteh bereshteh.*

A Note on Cleaning, Washing and Soaking Rice

Basmati rice contains many small, solid particles. This grit must be removed by picking over the rice carefully by hand. Then the rice is washed thoroughly in cold water. Place the rice in a large pot and cover with cold water. Agitate gently with your hand without breaking the rice, then pour off the water. Repeat 5 times until the rice is completely clean. If you use an ordinary colander to drain your rice, you may lose some rice through the holes. A fine-mesh, free-standing strainer or sieve is needed so the water can drain from the rice. When washed rice is cooked, it gives off a delightful perfume that unwashed rice can never have. In Gilan rice would often be soaked in salt water in large quantities and used for cooking as needed. Soaking and cooking in salt water seems to help firm up the rice, lengthen it, and keep it separated and fluffy after the cooking process.

Throughout this book I have used cooking times for basmati rice, which I recommend. However, if you use American long-grain rice it is not necessary to wash the rice 5 times.

Pots for Cooking Rice

A deep, non-stick pot must be used for the rice grains to swell properly and a good *tah dig* to form without sticking. Rice cookers are a wonderful invention for cooking rice Persian style because the nonstick coated mold allows for a golden crust (*tah dig*) and, as the temperature does not vary, it allows for consistently good rice. However, each type of rice cooker seems to have its own temperature setting; therefore the timing must be experimented with to get the best results. Step-by-step instructions are given for Steamed Plain Rice and Rice with Lentils using the National Delux electric rice cooker. Other rice recipes can be carried out similarly. Electric rice cookers and nonstick pots are available at specialty food stores.

A note on storing rice

Basmati rice is readily available in the United States these days. There are, however, several U.S. distributors, including: A&A Food Products Division of Richter Brothers, Inc., Carlstadt, NJ 07072; House of Spices, 76-17 Broadway, Jackson Heights, NY 11373; and E&I International, 5609 Fisher's Lane, #9A, Rockville, MD 20852, (301) 984-8287. I find it convenient to buy the large 55-pound sack and store the rice in a big popcorn tin with a cover. The rice should be mixed first with 1 pound of salt to repel bugs and keep mold from forming. Basmati rice is also sold in 11-pound sacks and 5-pound plastic bags. An exceptionally good variety is *lal quilla.* The rice should always be well-cleaned and washed before cooking.

Opening rice bag

Washing rice

Draining and rinsing rice

Prepared rice Chelow

Saffron Steamed Plain Basmati Rice

3 cups long-grain basmati rice
8 cups water
2 tablespoons salt
2 tablespoons plain yogurt
1 teaspoon ground saffron dissolved
   in 4 tablespoons hot water
¾ cup butter or *ghee* (page 147)

Makes 6 servings
Preparation time: 15 minutes
Cooking time: 1 hour 10 minutes

Chelow

Saffron consists of the dried stamens of a crocus. It was used in ancient times as a medicine, for dyeing clothes and to enhance the color and flavor of dishes.

1. Pick over the rice. Basmati rice like any other old rice contains many small solid particles. This grit must be removed by picking over the rice carefully by hand.

2. Wash the rice by placing it in a large container and covering it with *lukewarm water*. Agitate briskly with your hand, then pour off the water. Repeat five times until the rice is completely clean. When washed rice is cooked it gives off a delightful perfume that unwashed rice does not have. **If using long-grain American or Texmati rice, it is not necessary to soak or wash five times.** Once will suffice.

3. After washing the rice it is then desirable but not essential to soak it in 8 cups of water with 2 tablespoons of salt for 2 to 24 hours. Soaking and cooking rice in a lot of salt firms it up to support the long cooking time and prevents the rice from breaking up. The grains swell individually without sticking together. The result is light and fluffy rice called Pearls of Persian Cuisine.

4. Bring 8 cups of water with 2 tablespoons salt to a boil in a large non-stick pot. Pour the washed and drained rice into the pot. Boil briskly for 6 to 10 minutes, gently stirring twice with a wooden spoon to loosen any grains that may have stuck to the bottom. Bite a few grains. If the rice feels soft, it is ready. Drain rice in a large, fine-mesh colander and rinse in 2 or 3 cups of lukewarm water.

5. In a bowl, mix 2 spatulas of rice, the yogurt, and a few drops of dissolved saffron water.

6. In the pot, heat ½ cup butter and 2 tablespoons hot water; spread the yogurt-rice mixture over the bottom of the pot. This will help to create a tender golden crust (*tah dig*) when rice is cooked.

7. Take one spatula full of drained rice at a time and gently place it on top of the yogurt and rice mixture, gradually shaping the rice into a pyramid. This shape leaves room for the rice to expand and enlarge. Poke one or two holes in the rice pyramid with the handle of a wooden spatula.

8. Cover and cook rice for 10–15 minutes over medium heat in order to form a golden crust.

9. Dissolve the remaining butter in ½ cup hot water and pour over the rice pyramid. Place a clean dish towel or 2 layers of paper towels over the pot and cover firmly with the lid to prevent steam from escaping. Cook for 40–50 minutes longer over low heat.

10. Remove the pot from heat. Allow to cool on a damp surface for 5 minutes without uncovering it. This helps to free the crust from the bottom of the pot. Then put 2 tablespoons of rice in a dish, mix with remaining saffron water, and set aside for garnish.

11. Gently taking one spatula full of rice at a time, place it on a serving platter without disturbing the crust. Mound the rice into a cone. Sprinkle the saffron rice garnish over the top.

12. Detach the layer of crust from the bottom using a wooden spatula. Place into a small platter and serve on the side or arrange it around the rice. *Nush-e Jan!*

Clarified Unsalted Butter *(Ghee) (Roghan-e kareh)*—In a saucepan, bring 1 pound unsalted butter to a boil, cover, and simmer over low heat for 15–20 minutes until most of the froth subsides. Remove from heat and allow to cool for 5 minutes. Strain the liquid through a fine muslin cloth or three layers of cheesecloth to separate the clear butter fat from the milk solid. Seal and keep in your refrigerator. *Ghee,* a staple for the Persian kitchen, is used for cooking rice and pastries and has a wonderful flavor.

Painting by Kamal-ol Molk. Naseredin Shah's private musicians

Iraj Mirza on Friday Eve in the Company of Haj Amin, 1930

چه صال خوبی دش جمعه خوشی دیدیم   چه خوش بود اگر هر جمعه حال ما این بود

تمام حرف وفا دلبری و صفا در چشم   نه در سری هوسی بد نه در دلی کین بود

انار و سیب و به و نارنج و نارنگی   کباب بس خوب و شراب قزوین بود

معاشران همه خوش روی و مهربان بودند   نکی نبود که بدخوی و زشت آیین بود

بتول شور به مجلس فکند با ویلن   قمر مقابل او در غنا شیرین بود

What good cheer! What a pleasant Friday eve it was!
Oh, if every Friday eve would find it so!
Only friendly words held sway, and glances of good will,
No mind was unfaithful, nor spiteful any heart.
There were pomegranates and apples, quinces and oranges and tangerines.
There was sumptuous lamb kabab and the wine of Qazvin.
Our companions were all personable and gentle;
Not one present was ill-disposed or disagreeable.
Batul and her violin raised a clamor in the crowd.
While Qamar, sitting across, sweetly crooned.

Saffron Steamed Plain Rice: Rice Cooker Method

3 cups long-grain basmati rice
3½ cups water*
1 tablespoon salt
¼ cup oil
½ cup butter or *ghee* (page 147)
¼ teaspoon ground saffron dissolved in 1 tablespoon hot water

Makes 6 servings
Preparation time: 10 minutes
Cooking time: 1 hour 30 minutes

چلو با پُلوپَز

Chelow ba polow paz

1. Clean and wash 3 cups of rice 5 times in warm water.*

2. Combine all the ingredients except the saffron water in the rice cooker; gently stir with a wooden spoon and start the cooker.

3. After 1½ hours, pour saffron water on top of rice. Unplug rice cooker.

4. Allow to cool for 10 minutes without uncovering the pot.

5. Remove lid and place a round serving dish over the pot. Hold the dish and the pot tightly together and turn them over to unmold rice. The rice will be like a cake. Cut into wedges and serve. *Nush-e Jan!*

Note: These cooking times are for the National Delux rice cooker. The cooking time for rice may vary according to different brands of rice cookers. It is desirable but not essential to soak the rice in 8 cups water with 2 tablespoons salt for 2 to 24 hours. This is especially good for an older rice such as basmati.

Among other long-grained types of rice, choose those that are long, thick, and sleek at the tip.

*Note: For American long-grain rice, as opposed to basmati, use only 3 cups of water and wash the rice once.

Saffron consists of the dried stamens of a crocus. It was used in ancient times as a medicine, for dyeing clothes and to enhance the color and flavor of dishes.

Smothered Rice

3 cups long-grain basmati rice
1 tablespoon salt
6 cups water
½ cup butter or *ghee* **(page 147)**
2 tablespoons oil

Makes 6 servings
Preparation time: 5 minutes
Cooking time: 1 hour

Kateh

1. Clean and wash 3 cups of rice 5 times in warm water.

2. Place rice, salt, and water in a deep non-stick pot. Bring to a boil over high heat, then reduce heat and simmer for 20 minutes over medium heat (do not cover the rice). Gently stir the rice with a wooden spoon a few times while it boils.

3. When the rice has absorbed all the water, put the butter or margarine and oil on top of it. Reduce heat.

4. Place a clean dish towel or paper towel over pot and cover firmly with lid to prevent steam from escaping. Cook 40 minutes over low heat. Remove the pot from heat and allow to cool for 5 minutes on a damp surface without uncovering it.

5. Gently taking one skimmer or spatula full of rice at a time, place it on a serving platter without disturbing the crust. Mound rice in shape of a cone.

6. Detach the crust from the bottom of the pot using a wooden spatula. Place onto a small platter and serve on side. *Nush-e Jan!*

Oven-Baked Rice

Makes 6 servings
Preparation time: 1 hour
40 minutes
Cooking time: 2 hours
30 minutes

Shirazi polow-ye qalebi

3 cups long-grain basmati rice
1 chicken, about 2 pounds, with
    excess fat removed
3 large onions, peeled and thinly
    sliced
1 teaspoon ground saffron dissolved
    in 2 tablespoons hot water
3 medium-size eggplants
5 tablespoons oil

1 cup dried barberries (*zereshk*),
    page 379, or dried cranberries
1 cup *ghee* (clarified butter, page 147)
    or butter or oil
2 tablespoons sugar
2 cups yogurt
4 egg yolks
1 teaspoon ground cumin seed
    (optional)

1. Clean and wash 3 cups of rice 5 times in warm water. It is then desirable but not essential to soak the rice in 8 cups of water with 2 tablespoons of salt for at least 2 hours.

2. Place the chicken and 1 sliced onion in a saucepan. Do not add water. Cover and simmer for 1 hour over low heat. Bone the chicken and cut into pieces. Sprinkle 1 tablespoon of the saffron water over the chicken. Set aside, reserving juices.

3. Peel and cut eggplants lengthwise in ½-inch-thick slices. Place slices in a colander and sprinkle with water and salt to remove bitterness. Let stand for 20 minutes, then wash and pat dry. Brown slices in 5 tablespoons hot oil in a nonstick skillet, remove eggplant from skillet, and then brown the remaining onions in the same skillet. Set aside a few slices of the eggplant for garnish.

4. Clean sand from barberries (see Cleaning Dried Barberries, page 379).

5. In a skillet, saute cleaned barberries in 2 tablespoons of the butter for 1 minute. Do not overcook the barberries. Remove from heat, add the sugar and set aside. Set aside 2 tablespoons of the berries for garnish.

6. Bring 8 cups water and 2 tablespoons salt to a boil in a large non-stick pot. Pour the washed and drained rice into the pot. Boil briskly for 6 to 10 minutes, gently stirring twice to loosen any grains that may have stuck to the bottom. Bite a few grains. If the rice feels soft, it is ready. Drain rice in a large, fine-mesh colander and rinse in 2 or 3 cups lukewarm water.

7. Preheat oven to 350°F.

8. Melt ½ cup of the butter in a deep ovenproof dish.

9. Take 4 spatulas full of rice and combine with yogurt, egg yolks, and remaining saffron water. Place this rice mixture in the ovenproof dish. Arrange chicken pieces on top. Spread the barberry mixture over the chicken. Arrange a few slices of eggplant-onion mixture on top, and cover with remaining rice. Sprinkle the

cumin over the rice and pack it down into dish, using a spoon. Pour remaining butter and chicken juice over the top of the rice.

10. Place lid on the ovenproof dish to prevent steam from escaping, or cover with aluminum foil. Bake in the oven for 2 to 2½ hours, or until the crust is golden brown.

11. Remove the dish from oven and allow to cool for 15 minutes (do not uncover) on a damp surface. Loosen the rice around the edges of the dish with the point of a knife. Place a large serving platter on top of the dish. Hold the dish and platter firmly together and turn over to unmold the rice. Garnish with the reserved eggplant slices and spoon barberries on top of the rice. Serve hot. *Nush-e Jan!*

Rice with Lentils

Makes 6 servings
Preparation time: 35 minutes
Cooking time: 3 hours

Adas polow

3 cups long-grain basmati rice
3 onions, peeled and thinly sliced
5 cloves of garlic, peeled and crushed
2 pounds leg, shoulder, or shank of lamb, or 2 Cornish game hens
1½ teaspoons salt
¼ teaspoon freshly ground black pepper
½ teaspoon turmeric
1 teaspoon ground cinnamon
2 teaspoons Persian allspice (*rice advieh*), page 376

1 teaspoon ground saffron dissolved in 4 tablespoons hot water
1½ cup lentils
2 tablespoons oil
1 cup raisins
2 cups pitted dates
2 tablespoons slivered orange peel with bitterness removed (page 378)
1 cup melted clarified butter (*ghee*, page 147) or oil
2 tablespoons yogurt

1. Clean and wash 3 cups of rice 5 times in warm water.

2. Place 2 of the onions, garlic, and the meat or game hens in a baking dish. Season with salt, pepper, turmeric, cinnamon, and 1 teaspoon Persian allspice. Cover and bake for 2½ to 3 hours in a 350°F oven. Add 2 tablespoons of the saffron water and set aside.

3. Cook lentils about 10 minutes in 3 cups water and ½ teaspoon salt. Drain. In a non-stick frying pan, saute the remaining onions in 2 tablespoons oil. Add raisins, dates, and slivered orange peel. Mix well and set aside.

4. Bring 8 cups of water and 2 tablespoons salt to a boil in a large non-stick pot. Pour the washed and drained rice into the pot. Boil briskly for 6 to 10 minutes, gently stirring twice to loosen any grains that may have stuck to the bottom. Bite a few grains. If the rice feels soft, it is ready to be drained. Drain rice in a large, fine-mesh colander and rinse in 2 or 3 cups lukewarm water.

5. In the same pot, heat half the butter.

6. In a bowl, mix 2 spatulas full of rice, the yogurt, and a few drops of saffron water and spread the mixture over the bottom of the pot. This will help create a golden crust (*tah dig*).

7. Place 2 spatulas full of rice in the pot. Sprinkle with some of the Persian allspice. Add a spatula full of lentils, then raisins and dates. Repeat, mounding the ingredients in the shape of a pyramid.

8. Cover and cook the rice pyramid for 10 minutes over medium heat. Pour the remaining butter, ½ cup of water, and the remaining saffron water over the pyramid. Place a clean dish towel or paper towel over the pot and cover firmly with the lid to prevent steam from escaping. Cook for 50 minutes longer over low heat.

9. Remove the pot from heat and allow to cool for 5 minutes on a damp surface without uncovering it. This will help to free the crust from the bottom of the pot.

10. Open the pot, take out 2 tablespoons of the saffron-flavored rice, and set aside for garnishing.

11. Gently taking 1 spatula full of rice at a time, place it on a serving platter without disturbing the crust. Mound the rice in the shape of a cone. Arrange meat around rice. Decorate with saffron-flavored rice.

12. Detach the crust from the bottom of pot using a wooden spatula. Unmold onto a small platter and serve on the side with Persian pickles (*torshi*) and fresh herbs. *Nush-e Jan!*

Variation: Cook lentils for 15 to 20 minutes in 3 cups water and ½ teaspoon salt until tender. Drain and set aside. Chop and saute 1 onion, mixed with raisins, dates and orange peel, until golden brown and set aside. Make the rice as directed without adding the lentils. Before serving, place a spatula of rice on a serving platter, then alternate with layers of lentils, onion, raisins, dates, slivered orange peel and rice.

Rice with Lentils: Rice Cooker Method

Makes 6 servings
Preparation time: 20 minutes
Cooking time: 2 hours

Adas polow ba polow paz

3 cups long-grain basmati rice
3 onions, peeled and thinly sliced
5 cloves of garlic, peeled and crushed
½ cup oil
2 pounds leg, shoulder, or shank of lamb (optional)
1 teaspoon plus 1 tablespoon salt
¼ teaspoon freshly ground black pepper
1 teaspoon ground cinnamon
½ teaspoon turmeric

3 cups water
½ teaspoon ground saffron dissolved in 2 tablespoons hot water
½ cup clarified butter (*ghee*, page 147) or oil
1 cup lentils
½ cup raisins
2 cups pitted dates, halved
2 tablespoons slivered orange peel with bitterness removed (page 378)
1 teaspoon Persian allspice (rice *advieh*), page 376

1. Clean and wash 3 cups of rice 5 times in warm water.

2. In a pot, saute 2 of the onions and the garlic in 3 tablespoons oil, then add the meat. Season with 1 teaspoon salt, pepper, cinnamon, and turmeric. Add 3 cups water, bring to a boil, reduce heat, and cover and simmer for 2 to 3 hours over low heat. Add more water if necessary. Add a drop of saffron water. Keep warm.

3. In an electric rice cooker, combine 3½ cups of water, 3 cups washed and drained rice, 1 tablespoon salt, and 2 tablespoons oil.

4. Start the electric rice cooker. Cover and let cook for 15 minutes.

5. Clean and wash lentils and boil in 3 cups water and ½ teaspoon salt for 15 minutes over high heat. Drain.

6. Hollow out the middle of the rice mound and add the lentils.

7. In a skillet, brown the one onion in 4 tablespoons oil. Add raisins, dates, and slivered orange peel. Mix well. Add them to the rice, sprinkle the Persian allspice over the rice, and add the butter and saffron water.

8. Cover and cook for 60 minutes longer, then unplug cooker and let stand for 10 minutes without uncovering it.

9. Remove lid and place a large serving dish on top of the rice cooker mold. Grasp them together firmly and turn pot upside down to unmold rice onto the dish. Cut into wedges to serve with the cooked lamb. *Nush-e Jan!*

Rice with Dried Yellow Fava Beans

Makes 6 servings
Preparation time: 45 minutes, plus 2 hours' soaking time for the beans
Cooking time: 1 hour

Dampokhtak

3 cups long-grain basmati rice
3 large onions, peeled and thinly sliced
½ cup oil
1 tablespoon turmeric
2 cups dried yellow fava beans, cleaned, washed, soaked in 2 cups water for 2 hours, and drained
1 tablespoon salt

¼ teaspoon freshly ground black pepper
½ teaspoon ground cinnamon
1 teaspoon Persian allspice (*advieh*, page 376)
½ cup clarified butter (*ghee*, page 147) or oil

Garnish (optional)
½ cup raisins
½ cup pitted dates, cut in half
2 eggs, fried sunny-side-up

1. Clean and wash 3 cups of rice 5 times in warm water.

2. In a deep non-stick pot, brown the onions in the oil. Add turmeric, beans, 7 cups of warm water, salt, pepper, and cinnamon. Bring to a boil, reduce heat, cover and simmer over medium heat for 45 minutes.

3. Add the rice to the pot, cover and simmer 20 minutes over medium heat. As soon as the water has evaporated, sprinkle 1 teaspoon *advieh* and pour butter on top of the rice.

4. Place a clean dish towel or paper towel over the pot and cover firmly with the lid to prevent steam from escaping. Cook 50 minutes over low heat. Remove the pot from heat and allow to cool for 5 minutes on a damp surface without uncovering it.

5. Gently taking 1 skimmer or spatula full at a time, place rice in a serving platter without disturbing the crust. Mound the rice in the shape of a cone. Garnish with raisins, dates, and sunny-side-up fried eggs.

6. Using a wooden spatula, detach the crust from the bottom of the pot. Unmold onto a small platter and serve on the side.

7. Serve immediately with Persian pickles (*torshi*) and fresh vegetables and herbs (*sabzi-khordan*). *Nush-e Jan!*

Rice with Noodles

Makes 6 servings
Preparation time: 15 minutes
Cooking time: 3 hours

رشته پلو

Reshteh polow

3 cups long-grain basmati rice
3 onions, peeled and thinly sliced
3 tablespoons oil
1½ pounds leg, shoulder, lamb, deboned and cut into 1-inch cubes, or 2 Cornish game hens
1 teaspoon salt
¼ teaspoon freshly ground black pepper
½ teaspoon turmeric
2 teaspoons Persian allspice (*advieh*), page 376

1 teaspoon ground saffron dissolved in 4 tablespoons hot water
½ pound toasted Persian noodles (*reshteh*), cut into 1-inch lengths
½ cup raisins
2 tablespoons slivered orange peel with the bitterness removed (page 378)
2 cups pitted dates, cut in half
1 cup clarified melted butter (*ghee*, page 147) or oil
2 tablespoons yogurt

1. Clean and wash 3 cups of rice 5 times in warm water. It is then desirable but not essential to soak the rice in 8 cups water with 2 tablespoons of salt for at least 2 hours.

2. In a pot, saute 2 of the onions in 3 tablespoons oil; add meat. Season with salt, pepper, turmeric, and 1 teaspoon Persian allspice. Pour in 1½ cups water. Cover and simmer for 1½ to 2 hours over low heat. Add a few drops of saffron water and set aside.

3. If they are not already toasted, toast noodles in a large skillet for few minutes until golden brown.

4. In a non-stick skillet, brown the remaining onion, raisins, orange peel and dates. Set aside.

5. Bring 10 cups of water and 2 tablespoons salt to boil in a large non-stick pot. Pour the washed and drained rice into the pot. Add the noodles. Boil briskly for 6 to 10 minutes, gently stirring twice to loosen any grains that may have stuck to the bottom. Bite a few grains. If the rice feels soft it is ready to be drained. Drain rice in a large, fine-mesh colander and rinse in 2 to 3 cups lukewarm water.

6. In the same pot, heat half the butter.

7. In a bowl, mix 2 spatulas full of rice, the yogurt, and 2 tablespoons saffron water and spread the mixture over the bottom of the pot to create a golden crust (*tah dig*).

8. Place 2 spatulas full of the rice and noodle mixture in the pot. Sprinkle with some of the Persian allspice. Add a spatula of the raisins, orange peel and the dates. Repeat, arranging the rice in the shape of a pyramid.

9. Cover and cook rice for 10 minutes over medium heat. Pour the mixture of the remaining butter, ¼ cup water, and the remaining saffron water over the pyramid. Place a clean dish towel or paper towel over the pot and cover firmly with lid to prevent steam from escaping. Cook 50 minutes longer over low heat.

10. Remove rice from heat and allow to cool for 5 minutes on a damp surface without uncovering. This helps free the crust from the bottom of the pot.

11. Open the pot, take out 2 tablespoons of the saffron-flavored rice, and set aside for garnishing.

12. Gently taking 1 spatula full of rice at a time, place it on a serving platter without disturbing the crust. Mound the rice in the shape of a cone. Arrange meat around rice. Decorate with saffron-flavored rice.

13. Detach the crust from the bottom of the pot using a wooden spatula. Unmold onto a small platter and serve on the side with Persian pickles (*torshi*) and fresh herbs. *Nush-e Jan!*

Variation: Cook toasted Persian noodles (*reshteh*) for 10 to 15 minutes until tender in 3 cups water and ½ teaspoon salt until tender. Drain and set aside. Thinly slice 1 onion and, mixed with the raisins, orange peel and dates, saute until golden brown. Set aside. Make your rice as directed without adding the noodles. Before serving, place a spatula of rice on a serving platter, then alternate with layers of noodles, the mixture of browned onion, raisins, orange peel, and dates, and rice.

You may substitute the meat with Cornish game hen. Place chicken and 2 thinly sliced onions in a baking dish. Add 1 teaspoon salt and ½ teaspoon saffron water. Cover and bake for 1½ hours in a 350°F oven.

Rice with Apricots

Makes 6 servings
Preparation time: 15 minutes
Cooking time: 3 hours

Gheisi polow

3 cups long-grain basmati rice
2 onions, peeled and thinly sliced
1½ pounds leg or shoulder of lamb, deboned and cut into 1-inch cubes
⅔ cup clarified butter (*ghee*, page 147) or oil
½ cup raisins
2¼ cups dried apricots, quartered
1 teaspoon salt

¼ teaspoon freshly ground black pepper
½ cup pitted dates
¼ teaspoon ground saffron dissolved in 2 tablespoons hot water
2 tablespoons yogurt
1 teaspoon Persian allspice (*advieh*), page 376

1. Clean and wash 3 cups of rice 5 times in warm water. It is then desirable but not essential to soak the rice in 8 cups of water with 2 tablespoons of salt for at least 2 hours.

2. In a saucepan brown the onions and meat in 3 tablespoons butter; add the raisons and apricots and season with salt and pepper. Pour in 1½ cups water. Cover and simmer for 1 hour over low heat until the meat is tender, then add the dates and a third of the saffron water. Set aside.

3. Bring 8 cups water and 2 tablespoons salt to a boil in a large non-stick pot. Pour the washed and drained rice into the pot. Boil briskly for 6 to 10 minutes, stirring gently twice to loosen any grains that may have stuck to the bottom. Bite a few grains. If the rice feels soft, it is ready. Drain rice in a large, fine-mesh colander and rinse in 2 to 3 cups lukewarm water.

4. In the same pot, heat 4 tablespoons of the butter.

5. In a bowl, combine 2 spatulas full of rice, the yogurt, and a third of the saffron water and spread the mixture over the bottom of the pot to create a golden crust (*tah dig*).

6. Place 2 spatulas full of rice in the pot. Add 1 spatula full of the meat, raisin, apricot, and date mixture. Sprinkle half the Persian allspice on the rice. Repeat, alternating the rice with the meat and fruit mixture in the shape of a pyramid, and sprinkle the remaining Persian allspice on top.

7. Cover and cook for 10 minutes over medium heat.

8. Mix the remaining melted butter and saffron water and pour over the rice.

9. Place a clean dish towel or two layers of paper towel over the pot and cover firmly with lid to prevent steam from escaping. Cook another 50 minutes over

low heat. Remove from heat and allow to cool for 5 minutes on a damp surface without uncovering.

10. Uncover the pot, remove 2 tablespoons of the saffron-flavored rice and set aside for garnishing

11. Gently taking 1 spatula full at a time, place rice on an oval serving platter without disturbing the crust. Place the meat on the platter. Mound the rice in the shape of a cone. Decorate with the saffron-flavored rice. For even tastier rice melt two tablespoons of butter or *ghee* and drizzle it over the rice.

12. Detach the crust from the bottom of the pot using a wooden spatula. Unmold onto a small platter and serve on the side. Serve hot with fresh herbs and salad. *Nush-e Jan!*

Note: Ready-made Persian allspice is available at food specialty stores.

Rice with Fresh Fava Beans

Makes 6 servings
Preparation time: 20 minutes
Cooking time: 3 hours

Baqala polow

3 pounds leg or shank of lamb or 2 Cornish game hens
2 large onions, peeled and thinly sliced
4 cloves garlic, peeled and chopped
6 cups fresh dill weed, finely chopped
1 teaspoon salt
¼ teaspoon ground black pepper
½ teaspoon Persian allspice (*advieh*), page 376
1½ teaspoons ground saffron, dissolved in 2 tablespoons hot water

2 tablespoons fresh lime juice
2 pounds fresh or 1 pound frozen fava beans, shelled
3 cups long-grain basmati rice
½ teaspoon turmeric
2 tablespoons yogurt
¾ cup clarified butter (*ghee*, page 147) or oil
2 teaspoons ground cinnamon

1. In a baking dish, combine the meat, onions, 2 cloves of the garlic, and 2 tablespoons of the fresh chopped dill weed. Add ½ cup water, 1 teaspoon salt, pepper, ½ teaspoon Persian allspice, 2 tablespoons saffron water, and lime juice. Cover and bake for 2–3 hours in a 350°F oven, until the meat is tender.

2. Shell beans and remove outer layer of skin. If using frozen fava beans, soak in warm water for a few minutes, then peel.

3. Clean and wash 3 cups basmati rice 5 times in warm water.

4. Bring 10 cups of water and 2 tablespoons salt to a boil in a large, non-stick pot. Pour the washed and drained rice into the pot. Add the fava beans and turmeric to the pot while water is boiling (turmeric helps to keep the green color).

5. Boil briskly for 6 to 10 minutes, stirring gently with a wooden spoon to loosen any stuck grains. Bite a few grains. If rice feels soft, it is ready to be drained. Remove from heat and drain in a large, fine-mesh colander; rinse in 2 or 3 cups lukewarm water.

6. To form a tender golden crust (*tah dig*), mix 2 spatulas full of rice, the yogurt and a few drops of saffron water in a bowl. Heat ½ cup of the butter in the non-stick pot and spread the rice-yogurt mixture over the bottom.

7. Taking a spatula full of rice and beans, begin to form a pyramid by alternating layers of rice with dill, the rest of the garlic, and cinnamon. Repeat these layers. Cover and cook over medium heat for 10 minutes. This shape helps a golden crust (*tah dig*) to form.

8. Mix the remaining butter, saffron water, and ½ cup warm water and pour over the rice pyramid.

9. Place a clean dish towel or paper towel over the pot; cover the pot tightly to prevent steam from escaping. Cook 50 minutes longer over low heat. Remove pot from heat; allow to cool on a damp surface without uncovering it.

10. Remove lid and take out 2 tablespoons of the saffron-flavored rice and set aside for garnish.

11. Gently taking 1 spatula of rice at a time, mound the rice in the shape of a pyramid. Arrange the meat around the rice and garnish with saffron-flavored rice.

12. Detach the crust from the bottom of the pot with a wooden spatula. Unmold onto a small platter. Serve this rice with yogurt or Persian pickles (*torshi*) and sometimes with potato stew. *Nush-e Jan!*

Variation: Braised Leg of Lamb (*Run-e bareh*). This is a substitute for step 1—a trimmed leg of lamb (about 6–7 pounds) baked in the oven. Rinse and pat dry. Using the point of a small knife, make 10 slits all over the leg of lamb and insert a peeled clove of garlic in each slit. Peel and thinly slice 2 onions and spread them in a deep baking dish. Place leg of lamb on the onions. Sprinkle 2 tablespoons salt, ½ teaspoon pepper, 2 tablespoons Persian allspice, 2 tablespoons candied orange peel, and 1 teaspoon saffron dissolved in ¼ cup hot water all over the lamb. Add ¼ cup fresh lime juice in baking dish around the lamb. Cover the lamb with foil and roast it in a preheated 350°F oven for 3–3½ hours, uncovering it for the last half hour of cooking. Check your lamb. A well-done lamb tends to be more tender. When it is done, place it on a board and slice and serve along with your rice.

Note: You may substitute lima beans for fava beans. If using baby lima beans, you do not have to remove outer layer of skin.

Kaykhosrow's court, coffeehouse-style painting by Bolukifar, 1940

A Thousand and One Nights
The Story of the Barber's Sixth Brother

In the stories from the *Thousand and One Nights*, the *khalifeh* takes a girl each evening and then has her killed in the morning, until Shahrzad the noble daughter of the Vazir agrees to be the *khalifeh*'s wife for one night but devises a plan of starting a story each evening, refusing to finish it until the next night. Her plan is successful and the *khalifeh* ultimately abandons his murderous way with women.

In the story of the Barber's Sixth Brother, the barber's poor brother visits the mansion of a rich man with a sense of humor. The rich man treats the poor brother to a magnificent make-believe feast. While no food is actually served, the rich man describes a host of exotic dishes on the table in elaborate detail, beginning with all kinds of appetizers and then going on to rice with candied orange peel, carrots garnished with slivered pistachios and almonds, and lamb stuffed with pistachios.

By this time the poor brother is almost dead with hunger, but the rich man, who does not do anything in half measures, continues with khoreshes of meat, fruit, vegetables and nuts flavored with *advieh*, cloves, nutmeg, ginger, pepper and sweet herbs.

Finally come the desserts of date cake, almond cookies, chick-pea cookies, and honey almonds.

The poor brother is also a man of some wit and pretends to go along with all this while getting drunk on the make-believe wine. Then, pretending to have lost his senses, he gives the rich man a heavy blow. The rich man, a little upset at first, eventually catches on and, in appreciation of the poor brother's sense of humor, makes him his right hand man.

Sweet Rice with Candied Orange Peel, Pistachio and Almond Slivers

Makes 6 servings
Preparation time: 40 minutes
Cooking time: 2 hours

Shirin polow

3 cups long-grain basmati rice
2 cornish game hens or 1 frying
   chicken, about 3 pounds
1 onion, peeled and thinly sliced
2 cloves of garlic, peeled
¼ teaspoon salt
¼ teaspoon freshly ground
   black pepper
1 teaspoon ground saffron dissolved
   in 3 tablespoons hot water
3 cups slivered orange peel

4 cups carrots, peeled and cut into
   thin strips
⅔ cup clarified butter (*ghee*, page
   147) or oil
3 cups sugar
1½ cups slivered pistachios
1½ cups slivered almonds
2 tablespoons yogurt
1 teaspoon Persian allspice (*rice
   advieh*), page 376
1 teaspoon ground cardamom

1. Clean and wash 3 cups of rice 5 times in warm water. It is then desirable but not essential to soak the rice in 8 cups of water with 2 tablespoons of salt for at least 2 hours.

2. Stuff the hens or chicken with onion and 2 cloves of garlic. Place in a baking dish, sprinkle with salt, pepper, and some of the saffron water, and cover and bake for 1½ hours in a preheated 350°F oven.

3. Boil the slivered orange peel in 6 cups of water for 10 minutes over high heat and drain. Rinse with cold water.

4. Saute the thin strips of carrots in 3 tablespoons of the butter for 5 minutes and set aside.

5. In a saucepan, place the orange peel, sugar, carrots, and 3 cups water and bring to boil. Reduce heat and simmer over medium heat for 10 minutes. Drain. Add pistachios and almonds to the orange-carrot mixture and set aside.

6. Bring 8 cups water and 2 tablespoons salt to a boil in a large non-stick pot. Pour the washed and drained rice into the pot. Boil briskly for 6 to 10 minutes, gently stirring twice to loosen any grains that may have stuck to the bottom. Bite a few grains. If the rice feels soft, it is ready. Drain rice in a large, fine-mesh colander and rinse in 2 to 3 cups lukewarm water.

7. In a bowl, mix 2 spatulas full of rice, the yogurt, and a few drops of saffron water.

8. In the same pot, heat ¼ cup of the butter. Spread the yogurt-rice mixture over the bottom of the pot to create a golden crust (*tah-dig*).

9. Place 2 spatulas full of rice in the pot, then add 1 spatula of the candied orange peel and carrot mixture. Repeat these steps, arranging the rice in the shape of a pyramid. Sprinkle the Persian allspice and cardamom between layers of rice.

10. Cover and cook rice for 10 minutes over medium heat in order to form a golden crust.

11. Mix the remaining melted butter, saffron water, and ¼ cup water and pour over the rice. Place a clean dish towel or paper towel over the pot and cover firmly with lid to prevent steam from escaping. Cook for 50 minutes longer over low heat. Remove the pot from heat and allow to cool for 5 minutes on a damp surface without uncovering it.

12. Remove lid and take out 2 tablespoons of saffron-flavored rice and set aside for use as a garnish.

13. Place the chicken on a serving platter. Gently taking 1 spatula full of rice at a time, place it on the serving platter. Be careful not to disturb the crust on the bottom of the pot. Mound the rice in the shape of a cone. Garnish with saffron-flavored rice and the mixture of candied orange peel, carrot, pistachios, and almonds.

14. Detach the crust from the bottom of the pot using a wooden spatula. Unmold onto a small platter and serve on the side. Serve this rice presentation with fresh herbs and yogurt. *Nush-e Jan!*

Note: You may use ground meatballs in place of the chicken by combining 1 pound ground meat with 1 peeled and grated onion. Season with ¼ teaspoon salt and ¼ teaspoon pepper. Knead well and form the mixture into meatballs the size of hazelnuts. Brown in a non-stick skillet in 2 tablespoons butter and set aside. If using meatballs, serve on a serving platter along with the rice.

Advieh is available at Persian food specialty shops.

Rice with Green Peas

Makes 6 servings
Preparation time: 1 hour plus 2 hours' soaking time (optional)
Cooking time: 1 hour

Nokhod polow

3 cups long-grain basmati rice
2 pounds stew meat or chicken, cut into 1-inch cubes
½ cup clarified butter (*ghee*, page 147) or oil
1 onion, peeled and thinly sliced
½ teaspoon salt
¼ teaspoon freshly ground black pepper
1 pound whole canned tomatoes, drained, or 6 large fresh tomatoes

2 pounds fresh or frozen peas, shelled
1 teaspoon ground saffron dissolved in 4 tablespoons hot water
2 tablespoons yogurt
2 teaspoons Persian allspice (*rice advieh*), page 376

1. Clean and wash 3 cups of rice 5 times in warm water.

2. Brown the meat or chicken in 3 tablespoons butter in a pot with the onion and add the salt, pepper, and tomatoes. Cover and simmer for 20 minutes over low heat. (If using canned tomatoes, make sure they are completely drained.)

3. Add peas and cook for another 10 minutes.

4. Bring 8 cups water and 2 tablespoons salt to a boil in a large non-stick pot. Pour the washed and drained rice into the pot. Boil briskly for 6 to 10 minutes, gently stirring twice to loosen any grains that may have stuck to the bottom. Bite a few grains. If the rice feels soft, it is ready. Drain rice in a large, fine-mesh colander and rinse in 2 or 3 cups lukewarm water.

5. In the same pot, heat half the butter.

6. Combine 2 spatulas of rice, a drop of saffron water, and yogurt. Spread the mixture over the bottom of the pot to create a golden crust (*tah-dig*).

7. Place 2 spatulas full of rice in the pot, then add some of the meat mixture. Sprinkle with ½ teaspoon Persian allspice. Repeat, alternating the rice with the meat and Persian allspice to form a pyramid.

8. Cover and cook rice for 10 minutes over medium heat in order to form a golden crust.

9. Mix the remaining butter and saffron water and pour over the rice pyramid. Place a clean dish towel or paper towel over the pot and cover firmly with the lid to prevent steam from escaping. Cook for another 50 minutes over low heat. Remove rice pot from heat and allow to cool for 5 minutes on a damp surface without uncovering it.

10. Remove lid, take out 2 tablespoons of saffron-flavored rice and set aside for garnishing.

11. Gently taking 1 skimmer or spatula full of rice at a time, place it on an oval serving platter without disturbing the crust. Mound the rice in the shape of a cone. Garnish with the saffron-flavored rice.

12. Detach the crust from the bottom of the pot using a wooden spatula. Unmold onto a small platter and serve on the side.

13. Serve with Persian pickles (*torshi*) and fresh vegetables and herbs (*sabzi-khor-dan*). *Nush-e Jan!*

Barberry Rice

Makes 6 servings
Preparation time: 40 minutes
Cooking time: 2 hours 5 minutes

زرشک پلو

Zereshk polow

3 cups long-grain basmati rice
1 frying chicken, about 3 pounds, or
   2 Cornish game hens
2 peeled onions, 1 whole and 1
   thinly sliced
2 cloves of garlic, peeled
½ teaspoon salt
¼ teaspoon freshly ground
   black pepper
1 teaspoon ground saffron dissolved
   in 4 tablespoons hot water

2 cups dried barberries (*zereshk*),
   cleaned, washed, and drained
⅔ cup clarified butter (*ghee*, page
   147) or oil
4 tablespoons sugar
2 tablespoons yogurt
1 teaspoon Persian allspice (rice
   advieh), page 376 or 1 teaspoon
   ground cumin seed
2 tablespoons slivered almonds
2 tablespoons slivered pistachios

1. Clean and wash 3 cups of rice 5 times in warm water.

2. Place the whole chicken in a baking dish. Stuff the bird with one of the whole onions, the garlic, and sprinkle with salt, pepper, and 1 teaspoon saffron water. Cover and bake in a 350°F oven for 1½–2 hours.

3. Clean the barberries by removing their stems and placing the berries in a colander. Place colander in a large container full of cold water and allow barberries to soak for 20 minutes. The sand will settle to the bottom. Take the colander out of the container and run cold water over the barberries; drain and set aside.

4. Saute 1 sliced onion in 2 tablespoons butter, add barberries and saute for just 1 minute over low heat because barberries burn very easily. Add 4 tablespoons sugar, mix well, and set aside.

5. Bring 8 cups water and 2 tablespoons salt to a boil in a large, non-stick pot. Pour the washed and drained rice into the pot. Boil briskly for 6 to 10 minutes, gently stirring twice to loosen any grains that may have stuck to the bottom. Bite a few grains; if the rice feels soft, it is ready to be drained. Drain rice in a large, fine-mesh colander and rinse in 2 or 3 cups lukewarm water.

6. In the same pot heat 4 tablespoons butter.

7. In a bowl, mix 2 spatulas of rice, the yogurt, and a few drops of saffron water and spread the mixture over the bottom of the pot to form a tender crust (*tah-dig*).

8. Place 2 spatulas full of rice in the pot, then sprinkle ½ teaspoon Persian allspice or cumin over the rice. Repeat these steps, arranging the rice in the shape of a pyramid. This shape allows room for the rice to expand and enlarge. Cover and cook for 10 minutes over medium heat.

9. Mix the remaining melted butter and saffron water with ¼ cup of water and pour over the pyramid. Place a clean dish towel or paper towel over the pot; cover firmly with the lid to prevent steam from escaping. Cook for 50 minutes longer over low heat.

10. Remove the pot from heat and allow to cool, covered, for 5 minutes on a damp surface to free crust from the bottom of the pot.

11. Remove lid and take out 2 tablespoons of saffron-flavored rice and set aside for use as garnish.

12. Then, gently taking 1 spatula full of rice at a time, place rice on a serving platter in alternating layers with the barberry mixture. Mound the rice in the shape of a cone. Arrange the chicken around the platter. Finally, decorate the top of the mound with the saffron-flavored rice, some of the barberry mixture, and almonds and pistachios. *Nush-e Jan!*

Note: You may place the barberries in the rice and steam them together but the color of barberries will not be as red as when you layer them with the rice at the last minute.

If using fresh barberries, clean by removing the stems and rinse with cold water.

Jeweled Rice

Makes 6 servings
Preparation time: 40 minutes
Cooking time: 2 hours 5 minutes

جواهر پلو

Javaher polow

3 cups long-grain basmati rice
1 frying chicken, about 3 pounds, cut up, or 2 Cornish game hens
2 peeled onions, 1 whole and 1 thinly sliced
2 cloves of garlic, peeled
½ teaspoon salt
1 teaspoon ground saffron dissolved in 4 tablespoons hot water
1 cup very finely slivered Seville orange peel
2 large carrots, peeled and cut into thin strips

1 cup sugar
1 cup dried barberries (*zereshk*), cleaned, washed, and drained
½ cup clarified butter (*ghee*, page 147) or oil
½ cup raisins
2 tablespoons yogurt
1 teaspoon Persian allspice (rice *advieh*), page 376
2 tablespoons slivered almonds
2 tablespoons slivered pistachios

Considered the King of Persian dishes, Javaher Polow *is made of orange peel, almonds, sugar, barberries, and pistachios, as a wedding dish representing rubies and emeralds.*

1. Clean and wash 3 cups of rice 5 times in warm water.

2. Stuff the chicken with 1 whole onion and 2 cloves garlic and place it in a baking dish. Sprinkle with 1 teaspoon salt and ½ teaspoon saffron water, cover, and bake for 1½ hours in a 350°F oven.

3. Place the slivered orange peel in a saucepan and cover with water. Bring to a boil, then drain to remove bitter taste. Place the orange peel, carrot strips, 1 cup sugar, and 1 cup water in a saucepan and boil for 10 minutes. Drain and set aside.

4. Clean barberries by removing their stems and placing the berries in a colander. Place colander in a large container full of cold water and allow barberries to soak for 20 minutes. The sand will settle to the bottom. Take the colander out of the container and run cold water over the barberries; drain and set aside.

5. Fry the sliced onion in 2 tablespoons butter, add drained barberries and raisins, and cook for just 1 minute because barberries burn very easily. Remove from heat and set aside.

6. Bring 8 cups water and 2 tablespoons salt to a boil in a large, non-stick pot. Pour the washed and drained rice into the pot. Boil briskly for 6 to 10 minutes, gently stirring twice to loosen any grains that may have stuck to the bottom. Bite a few grains of rice. If the rice feels soft it is ready to be drained. Drain rice in a large, fine-mesh colander and rinse in 2 or 3 cups lukewarm water.

7. In the same pot heat 4 tablespoons butter.

The name pistachio comes from the Persian word Pesteh.

8. In a bowl, mix 2 spatulas of rice, the yogurt and a few drops of saffron water and spread the mixture over the bottom of pot to form a tender crust (*tah-dig*).

9. Place 2 spatulas full of rice in the pot, then add 1 spatula of orange peel and carrots. Sprinkle ½ teaspoon Persian allspice over the rice. Repeat these steps, arranging the rice and orange-carrot mixture in layers in the shape of a pyramid. This shape allows room for the rice to expand and enlarge. Sprinkle ½ teaspoon Persian allspice over the rice. Cover and cook for 15 minutes over medium heat.

10. Mix the rest of the melted butter, saffron water, and ¼ cup water and pour over the pyramid.

11. Place a clean dish towel or paper towel over the pot and cover firmly with the lid to prevent steam from escaping. Cook for 50 minutes longer over low heat.

12. Remove the pot from heat and allow to cool for 5 minutes on a damp surface, without uncovering it, to free crust from the bottom of the pot.

13. Remove lid and take out 2 tablespoons of saffron-flavored rice and set aside for use as garnish.

14. Then, gently taking 1 spatula full of rice at a time, place rice on a serving platter in alternating layers with the barberry mixture. Mound the rice in the shape of a cone. Arrange the chicken around the platter. Finally, decorate the top of the mound with the saffron-flavored rice, some of the barberry mixture, and almonds and pistachios.

15. Detach the crust from the bottom of the pot using a wooden spatula. Unmold onto a small platter and serve on the side. *Nush-e Jan!*

Note: You may cook steamed plain rice and mix in all the ingredients at the last moment, decorating in different-colored strips according to your fancy.

Rice with Yellow Split Peas

Makes 6 servings
Preparation time: 55 minutes
Cooking time: 1 hour

Qeymeh polow

3 cups long-grain basmati rice
3 onions, peeled and thinly sliced
2 pounds stew meat—lamb, veal, or beef—cut into ½-inch pieces
5 tablespoons oil
½ cup yellow split peas
1 teaspoon salt
¼ teaspoon freshly ground black pepper
2 cups fresh tomato juice
1 tablespoon dried Persian lime powder (powdered *limu-omani*)

2 tablespoons slivered orange peel with bitterness removed (page 378)
½ cup clarified butter (*ghee*, page 147) or oil
2 teaspoons ground saffron dissolved in 6 tablespoons hot water
2 tablespoons yogurt
2 teaspoons Persian allspice (rice *advieh*), page 376

1. Clean and wash 3 cups of rice 5 times in warm water. It is then desirable but not essential to soak the rice in 8 cups of water with 2 tablespoons of salt for at least 2 hours.

2. In a pot, brown the onions and meat in 5 tablespoons oil. Add split peas and saute for a minute. Add the salt, pepper, and tomato juice. Bring to a boil, cover, and simmer over medium heat for 20 minutes. Add lime powder and slivered orange peel. Cover and simmer for 10 to 20 minutes longer over low heat (split peas must be cooked). Set aside.

3. Bring 8 cups water and 2 tablespoons salt to a boil in a large non-stick pot. Pour the washed and drained rice into the pot. Boil briskly for 6 to 10 minutes, gently stirring twice to loosen any grains that may have stuck to the bottom. Bite a few grains. If the rice feels soft, it is ready. Drain rice in a large, fine-mesh colander and rinse in 2 or 3 cups lukewarm water.

4. In a pot, heat half the butter.

5. In a bowl, combine a drop of saffron water, yogurt, and 2 spatulas full of rice; mix well and spread the mixture over the bottom of the pot to create a golden crust (*tah-dig*).

6. Place 2 spatulas full of rice in the pot, then add some meat and split pea mixture. Repeat these steps, arranging the layers in the shape of a pyramid. Sprinkle the Persian allspice between each layer.

7. Mix the remaining butter, saffron water, and ¼ cup of water and pour over the rice. Cover and cook rice for 10 minutes over medium heat in order to form a golden crust.

8. Place a clean dish towel or paper towel over the pot and cover firmly with the lid to prevent steam from escaping. Cook for 50 minutes longer over low heat. Remove the pot from heat and allow to cool for 5 minutes on a damp surface without uncovering.

9. Remove lid and take out 2 tablespoons of saffron-flavored rice and set aside for use as a garnish.

10. Then, gently taking 1 skimmer or spatula full of rice at a time, place rice on an oval serving platter without disturbing the crust. Mound the rice in the shape of a cone and garnish with saffron-flavored rice.

11. Detach the crust from the bottom of the pot using a wooden spatula. Unmold onto a small platter and serve on the side with fresh herbs, yogurt, and Persian pickles (*torshi*). *Nush-e Jan!*

Note: Persian split peas need more time for cooking than American split peas. If using Persian split peas, let them cook longer in step 2, until they are almost tender.

Persian allspice is available at Persian specialty food shops.

Make your own dried lime powder by cutting open a whole dried lime and removing the seeds, then grinding it in the food processor. The powder available in the U.S. is usually bitter because the seeds have not been removed before grinding.

Rice with Green Cabbage

Makes 6 servings
Preparation time: 30 minutes
Cooking time: 1 hour

Kalam polow

3 cups long-grain basmati rice
1 pound stewing meat, veal or beef, cut into 1-inch cubes
1 onion, peeled and sliced
5 tablespoons oil
½ teaspoon salt
¼ teaspoon freshly ground black pepper
1 tablespoon ground cumin seed
6 medium-size fresh tomatoes, peeled and chopped

1 large head green cabbage, washed and cut into 1-inch pieces
½ cup clarified butter (*ghee*, page 147) or oil
2 tablespoons yogurt
1 teaspoon ground saffron dissolved in 2 tablespoons hot water
1 tablespoon Persian allspice (rice *advieh*), page 376

1. Clean and wash 3 cups of rice 5 times in warm water.

2. In a pot, brown the meat and onion in 3 tablespoons oil. Add salt, pepper, and the fresh tomato. Cover and simmer for 30 minutes over medium heat.

3. Brown the cabbage in 2 tablespoons oil in a non-stick skillet, stirring constantly to prevent burning. Add it to the meat and cook for 10 minutes longer. Remove from heat.

4. Bring 8 cups water and 2 tablespoons salt to a boil in a large non-stick pot. Pour the washed and drained rice into the pot. Boil briskly for 6 to 10 minutes, stirring gently twice to loosen any grains that may have stuck to the bottom. Bite a few grains. If the rice feels soft, it is ready. Drain rice in a large, fine-mesh colander and rinse in 2 or 3 cups lukewarm water.

5. In the same pot, heat ¼ cup of the butter.

6. In a bowl, combine 2 tablespoons yogurt, ½ tablespoon saffron water, and 2 spatulas full of rice. Spread the mixture over the bottom of the pot to create a golden crust (*tah dig*).

7. Place 2 spatulas full of rice in the pot, then add a layer of the cabbage and meat mixture. Repeat, alternating layers in the shape of a pyramid. Sprinkle **the** cumin between the layers.

8. Cover and cook rice for 10 minutes over medium heat in order to form a golden crust.

9. Mix the remaining butter and saffron water and pour over the pyramid. Sprinkle with Persian allspice. Place a clean dish towel or 2 layers of paper towels over the pot and cover firmly with the lid to prevent steam from escaping. Cover and cook 50 minutes longer over low heat. Remove the pot from heat and allow to cool for 5 minutes on a damp surface without uncovering it.

10. Remove the lid and take out 2 tablespoons of saffron-flavored rice for use as a garnish. Then, gently taking 1 spatula full at a time, place rice on an oval serving platter without disturbing the crust. Mound the rice in the shape of a cone. Garnish with the saffroned rice.

11. Detach the crust from the bottom of the pot using a wooden spatula. Unmold onto a small platter and serve on the side. *Nush-e Jan!*

Note: Persian allspice is available at food specialty stores.

Variation: You may replace the stewing meat with 1 pound ground meat made into meatballs. Combine meat with ½ teaspoon salt, ¼ teaspoon pepper and 1 grated onion. Knead well with damp hands to form meatballs the size of hazelnuts (known as sparrow heads, a reference to a meatball, cabbage and saffron dish from 16th-century Persia). Brown in a non-stick skillet in 3 tablespoons oil, then add the cabbage and tomato. Or stuff a chicken with onion and bake in a baking dish for 2 hours at 350°F. Serve with rice.

Rice with Green Beans

Makes 6 servings
Preparation time: 45 minutes
Cooking time: 1 hour

Lubia polow

3 cups long-grain basmati rice
1 large onion, peeled and thinly sliced
2 cloves garlic, peeled and crushed
2 pounds stew meat (veal or beef), cut into ½-inch cubes, or 1 pound ground meat
5 tablespoons oil
1 pound sliced, peeled, canned tomatoes, drained, or 6 large fresh tomatoes, peeled and sliced
1½ pounds fresh green beans, cleaned and cut into ½-inch pieces

1 teaspoon ground cinnamon
1½ teaspoons salt
¼ teaspoon freshly ground black pepper
1 teaspoon Persian allspice (rice *advieh*), page 376
1 teaspoon dried Persian lime powder (powdered *limu-omani*), page 382
½ cup clarified butter (*ghee*, page 147) or oil
2 tablespoons yogurt
½ teaspoon ground saffron dissolved in 2 tablespoons hot water

1. Clean and wash 3 cups of rice 5 times in warm water. It is then desirable but not essential to soak the rice in 8 cups water with 2 tablespoons of salt for at least 2 hours.

2. In a saucepan, brown the onion, garlic, and meat in 3 tablespoons oil. Add tomatoes, green beans, cinnamon, 1 teaspoon salt, ¼ teaspoon pepper, half of the Persian allspice, and half of the dried Persian lime powder. If using canned tomatoes, make sure they are completely drained. They must not have any sauce left. Cover and simmer over low heat for 40 minutes.

3. Bring 8 cups of water and 2 tablespoons salt to a boil in a large non-stick pot. Pour the washed and drained rice into the pot. Boil briskly for 6 to 10 minutes over high heat, gently stirring twice to loosen any grains that may have stuck to the bottom. Bite a few grains. If the rice feels soft it is ready to be drained. Drain rice in a large, fine-mesh colander and rinse in 2 or 3 cups lukewarm water.

4. In the same pot, heat half the butter.

5. In a bowl, combine yogurt, 2 spatulas of rice, and a drop of saffron water. Spread over the bottom of the pot to create a golden crust (*tah-dig*).

6. Place 2 spatulas full of rice in the pot, then add a layer of the green-bean-and-meat mixture. Repeat, alternating layers in the shape of a pyramid. Sprinkle the remaining Persian allspice and dried lime powder over the pyramid. Cover and cook for 10 minutes over medium heat.

7. Pour the remaining butter and saffron water over the rice. Place a clean dish towel or 2 layers of paper towels over the pot and cover firmly with the lid to prevent steam from escaping. Cook 50 minutes longer over low heat. Remove the pot from heat and allow to cool for 5 minutes on a damp surface without uncovering it, to free the crust from the bottom of the pot.

8. Open the pot, take out 2 tablespoons of the saffron-flavored rice and set aside for garnishing.

9. Gently taking 1 spatula full of rice at a time, place it on a serving platter without disturbing the crust. Mound the rice in the shape of a cone. Decorate with saffron-flavored rice.

10. Detach the crust from the bottom of the pot using a wooden spatula. Unmold onto a small platter and serve on the side. Serve rice with fresh scallions, basil, and Persian pickles (*torshi*). *Nush-e Jan!*

Chelow Kabab (Rice with Meat Kabab)

Chelow Kabab is Iran's national dish, the equivalent of steak and potatoes in the United States. It is served everywhere, from palaces to roadside stalls, but the best *chelow kababs* are probably those sold in the bazaars, where it is served with a tin cloche covering the rice to keep it warm. The *kabab*s are brought to the table by the waiter, who holds five or ten skewers in his left hand and a piece of bread in his right hand. He places a skewer of *kabab* directly on the rice and, holding it down with the bread, dramatically pulls out the skewer, leaving the sizzling kababs behind.

Chelow kabab consists of *chelow* (steamed rice) and *kabab*, skewers of lamb, veal, or beef cubes or ground meat marinated in saffron, onions, yogurt, and lime juice. Grilled tomatoes and raw onions are also an integral part of *chelow kabab*. The traditional way to serve *chelow kabab* is as follows:

Heap a pyramid of *chelow* on each plate. Add a dab of butter and sprinkle with a teaspoon of powdered sumac. Mix well.

Place the kababs (*kabab-e kubideh, kabab-e barg* or a combination of both, called *sultani,* which literally means kingly) and the grilled tomatoes on the rice.

Serve hot with trimmings such as *sabzi-khordan* (fresh herbs and scallions), *mast-o khiar* (yogurt and cucumber), *mast-o musir* (yogurt and shallots), and *torshi* (Persian pickles). *Chelow kabab* is often washed down with *dugh,* a yogurt drink with mint, but a Pepsi with *chelow kabab* on Fridays for lunch was the treat of our childhood.

The prudent cook should always keep some meat marinating in the refrigerator at home to serve to unexpected guests and hungry members of the family. Then while the *chelow* is cooking, the fire can be started and the kababs prepared. This is truly convenience cooking—simple, yet nutritious and delicious. Children too love *chelow kabab*.

Chelow kabab

Rice with Ground Meat Kababs and Trimmings
Chelow kabab
Recipe page 180

181

Rice with Tomato Sauce

Makes 6 servings
Preparation time: 20 minutes
Cooking time: 1 hour

Eslamboli polow

3 cups long-grain basmati rice
1 large onion, peeled and thinly
  sliced
2 pounds stew meat (lamb, veal, or
  beef, or deboned chicken), cut
  into ½-inch cubes
5 tablespoons oil
3 tablespoons tomato paste
10 large, fresh tomatoes, peeled and
  sliced, or 1 12-ounce can whole
  tomatoes, drained and sliced
1 cup tomato sauce

¼ teaspoon turmeric
½ teaspoon ground cinnamon
1 teaspoon salt
¼ teaspoon freshly ground
  black pepper
½ cup clarified butter (*ghee*, page
  147) or oil
¼ teaspoon ground saffron dissolved in 2 tablespoons hot water

1. Clean and wash 3 cups of rice 5 times in warm water.

2. In a deep saucepan, brown the onion and meat in 5 tablespoons oil. Add tomato paste, fresh tomatoes, tomato sauce, turmeric, cinnamon, salt, and pepper. Cover and simmer over low heat for about 40 minutes.

3. Bring 8 cups water and 2 tablespoons salt to a boil in a large non-stick pot. Pour the washed and drained rice into the pot. Boil briskly for 6 to 10 minutes, gently stirring twice to loosen any grains that may have stuck to the bottom. Bite a few grains. If the rice feels soft, it is ready. Drain rice in a large, fine-mesh colander and rinse in 2 or 3 cups lukewarm water.

4. In a pot, heat half the butter.

5. Mix 2 spatulas full of rice and a few drops of saffron water and spread over the bottom of the pot to create a golden crust (*tah-dig*).

6. Place 2 spatulas full of rice in the pot; then add a layer of the meat-and-tomato mixture. Repeat, alternating layers in the shape of a pyramid. Cover and cook rice for 10 minutes over medium heat in order to form a golden crust.

7. Pour the remaining butter and saffron water over the rice. Place a clean dish towel or paper towel over the pot and cover firmly with lid to prevent steam from escaping. Cook 50 minutes longer over low heat.

8. Remove the pot from heat and allow to cool for 5 minutes on a damp surface without uncovering it.

9. Gently taking 1 skimmer or spatula full at a time, place rice on an oval serving platter without disturbing the crust. Mound the rice in the shape of a cone.

10. Detach the crust from the bottom of the pot using a wooden spatula. Unmold onto a small platter and serve on the side.

11. Serve immediately with Persian pickles (*torshi*) and fresh vegetables and herbs (*sabzi-khordan*). *Nush-e Jan!*

Variation: In a non-stick pot or a rice cooker, brown the onion and 1 pound ground meat. Add turmeric, cinnamon, 1 tablespoon salt, and ¼ teaspoon pepper. Add 4 cups tomato juice and tomato paste, bring to a boil, and reduce heat. When the water evaporates, pour the remaining butter and saffron water over the rice, cover firmly, and let cook over low heat for about 45 minutes longer. Before serving, if desired, pour 2 tablespoons melted butter over the rice.

Baked Saffron Yogurt Rice with Lamb

Makes 6 servings
Preparation time: 1 hour 10 minutes plus 2 hours' marinating
Cooking time: 3 to 3 hours 30 minutes

Tah chin-e barreh

2 large onions, peeled and thinly sliced
2 cloves garlic, peeled and crushed
1 teaspoon salt
¼ teaspoon freshly ground black pepper
½ teaspoon turmeric
2 pounds boned leg or shoulder of lamb, cut in 2-inch cubes
2 cups yogurt
2 egg yolks, beaten

2 teaspoons ground saffron dissolved in 4 tablespoons hot water
1 tablespoon slivered orange peel with bitterness removed (page 378)
3 cups long-grain basmati rice
¾ cup clarified butter (*ghee*, page 147) or oil
½ teaspoon ground cumin seed
1 teaspoon Persian allspice (rice *advieh*), page 376

1. Preheat the oven to 350°F. Place one onion, garlic, salt, pepper, turmeric, and meat in an ovenproof baking dish. Cover and bake for 1 hour, drain and allow to cool.

2. In a bowl, combine the yogurt, egg yolks, half the saffron water, the slivered orange peel, and one thinly sliced onion. Add salt to taste and marinate meat in this mixture for at least 8 hours and up to 24 hours.

3. Clean and wash 3 cups of rice 5 times in warm water.

4. Bring 8 cups water and 2 tablespoons salt to a boil in a large non-stick pot. Pour the washed and drained rice into the pot. Boil briskly for 6 to 10 minutes, gently stirring twice to loosen any grains that may have stuck to the bottom. Bite a few grains. If the rice feels soft, it is ready. Drain in a large, fine-mesh colander and rinse in 2 to 3 cups lukewarm water.

5. Preheat oven to 350°F. Remove meat from the marinade. Add 4 spatulas of rice to half of the marinade and mix well.

6. Heat half the butter in a Pyrex baking dish in the oven. Add the mixture of rice and marinade, spreading it across the bottom and up the sides of the baking dish. Place half of the meat pieces on top and cover with layers of rice and the rest of the yogurt marinade. Sprinkle with the ground cumin and Persian allspice. Pour the remaining saffron water and butter over the rice. Pack firmly using a wooden spoon and cover with oiled aluminum foil.

7. Place baking dish in the oven and bake 1½ to 2 hours, until the bottom turns golden brown.

8. Remove baking dish from oven. Allow to cool on a damp surface for 10 to 15 minutes (do not uncover). Then loosen the rice around the edges of the baking dish with the point of a knife. Place a large serving dish over the baking dish. Hold both dishes firmly together with two hands and turn them upside down.

9. Serve hot with fresh herbs, yogurt, and Persian pickles (*torshi*). *Nush-e Jan!*

Baked Saffron Yogurt Rice with Chicken

Tah chin-e morgh

Rice with chicken can be made the same way as Baked Saffron Yogurt Rice with Lamb. Simply replace the lamb with a whole large chicken and follow the recipe as directed. Be sure to debone the chicken before marinating.

Baked Saffron Yogurt Rice with Spinach

Makes 6 servings
Preparation time: 1 hour
30 minutes
Cooking time: 2 hours
30 minutes

تَه چین اِسفناج

Tah chin-e esfenaj

1 pound boned leg or shoulder of
   lamb, cut in 2-inch pieces, or 1
   large frying chicken, cut up
3 large onions, peeled and thinly
   sliced
1 teaspoon salt
½ teaspoon turmeric
½ teaspoon freshly ground
   black pepper
2 cloves garlic, peeled and crushed
1½ cups plain yogurt

1 egg yolk
½ teaspoon saffron dissolved in ¼
   cup hot water
3 pounds fresh spinach, cleaned and
   washed, or 1½ pounds frozen
   chopped spinach
1 cup clarified butter (*ghee*, page 147)
   or oil
3 cups pitted prunes
2 cups long-grain basmati rice

1. Preheat the oven to 350°F. In a large ovenproof baking dish, combine the meat with one sliced onion, ½ teaspoon salt, turmeric, ¼ teaspoon pepper, and garlic. Cover and bake for 1 hour; remove from heat, drain and allow to cool.

2. In a bowl, beat the yogurt, egg yolk, half the saffron water, ½ teaspoon salt, and ¼ teaspoon pepper. Marinate the meat in this mixture in a refrigerator for at least 8 hours, or up to 24 hours.

3. Chop the cleaned and washed spinach into large pieces. Steam the spinach in a steamer for 20 minutes (to remove bitterness) and set aside. If using frozen spinach, follow package instructions.

4. In a large skillet, brown 2 onions in 3 tablespoons butter, add the spinach and prunes, and simmer for 3 minutes over low heat.

5. Clean and wash 2 cups of rice 5 times in warm water.

6. Bring 8 cups of water and 2 tablespoons salt to a boil in a large non-stick pot. Pour the rice into the pot. Boil briskly for 6 minutes, gently stirring twice to loosen any grains that may have stuck to the bottom. Bite a few grains. If the rice feels soft, it is ready. Drain rice in a large, fine-mesh colander and rinse in 2 or 3 cups lukewarm water.

7. Remove the meat from the yogurt marinade. Add 4 spatulas of rice to the marinade and mix well.

8. Preheat oven to 350°F.

9. Heat ½ cup of the butter in a large deep ovenproof Pyrex baking dish in the oven. Add the mixture of rice and marinade on top, spreading it across the bottom of the dish and up the sides. Place the pieces of meat on top and add a layer of spinach and prunes. Cover with rice. Pour the remaining saffron water and butter over the rice. Pack firmly with a wooden spoon and cover with the lid or oiled aluminum foil.

10. Place the baking dish in the oven and bake for 1½ to 2 hours or until the crust is golden brown.

11. Remove baking dish from oven. To unmold, keep it covered and allow to cool on a damp surface for 10 to 15 minutes. Then loosen the rice around the edge of the baking dish with the point of a knife. Place a large serving dish over the baking dish. Hold both dishes firmly together with your hands and turn them upside down. Serve hot. *Nush-e jan!*

Rice with Fresh Herbs and Fish

Makes 6 servings
Preparation time: 45 minutes
Cooking time: 1 hour

3 cups long-grain basmati rice
½ cup chopped fresh chives or scallions
2 cups coarsely chopped fresh dill
2½ cups coarsely chopped fresh parsley
2 cups chopped fresh coriander
3 cloves garlic, peeled and crushed
½ cup clarified butter (*ghee*, page 147) or oil
2 tablespoons yogurt
1 teaspoon ground saffron dissolved in 4 tablespoons hot water

2 cloves whole green garlic, washed thoroughly and trimmed
1 teaspoon ground cinnamon
1 large white-fleshed fish (striped bass or sea bass), scaled and cleaned, about 3 pounds, or whole smoked white fish
½ cup flour combined with ½ teaspoon salt and ½ teaspoon ground cinnamon for dredging the fish
4 tablespoons olive oil
Juice of 2 Seville oranges, if available, or juice of 2 limes

Sabzi polow ba mahi

This dish is associated with the New Year celebration.

1. Clean and wash 3 cups of rice 5 times in warm water. It is then desirable but not essential to soak the rice in 8 cups water with 2 tablespoons of salt for at least 2 hours.

2. Bring 8 cups of water and 2 tablespoons salt to a boil in a large non-stick pot. Pour the washed and drained rice into the pot. Boil briskly for 6 to 10 minutes, gently stirring twice to loosen any grains that may have stuck to the bottom. Bite a few grains. If the rice feels soft it is ready to be drained. Drain rice in a large, fine-mesh colander and rinse in 2 or 3 cups lukewarm water.

3. In a bowl, mix cleaned, washed, chopped herbs and crushed garlic.

4. In the same pot, heat half the butter.

5. In a bowl, combine 2 spatulas full of rice, yogurt, and one drop of saffron water and spread the mixture evenly over the bottom of the pot to create a golden crust (*tah-dig*).

6. Place 2 spatulas full of rice in the pot, then add one spatula full of herbs and the whole green garlic cloves. Repeat, alternating layers of the rice and herbs in the shape of a pyramid, and sprinkle the cinnamon between the layers. This shape allows room for the rice to expand and enlarge. Cover and cook for 10 minutes over medium heat.

7. Pour the remaining butter and saffron water and ½ cup hot water over this pyramid.

8. Place a clean dish towel or 2 layers of paper towels over the pot and cover firmly with the lid to prevent steam from escaping. Cook 50 minutes longer over low heat.

Note: If using dried herbs, reduce the amount used to ¼ of the fresh herbs. Place a sieve in a bowl of lukewarm water and soak the dried herbs for 20 minutes. Remove the sieve from the bowl and use the herbs.

9. While the rice is cooking, cut the fresh fish down the center lengthwise without removing the backbone. Slice across into 6 pieces.

10. Wash and pat fish pieces dry. Dust them in the seasoned flour.

11. Just before serving, brown fish pieces on both sides in 4 tablespoons oil in a skillet over medium heat. Add more oil if necessary. Sprinkle the fish with the Seville orange or lime juice.

12. Remove rice pot from heat and allow to cool for 5 minutes on a damp surface without uncovering it. This frees the crust from the bottom of the pot.

13. Remove 2 tablespoons of saffron-flavored rice and set aside for garnish. Gently taking 1 spatula full of rice at a time, place it on a serving platter without disturbing the crust. Mound the rice in the shape of a cone. Decorate with saffron-flavored rice.

14. Detach the crust from the bottom of the pot using a wooden spatula. Unmold onto a small platter and serve on the side.

Variation: This rice is also excellent with Smoked White Fish (page 135).

15. Arrange fish on a serving platter and pour the remaining saffron water over it. Serve hot with fresh herbs. *Nush-e Jan!*

Rice with Sour Cherries

Makes 6 servings
Prep time: 35 minutes
Cooking time: 1 hour

آلبالو پُلو

Albalu polow

2 Cornish game hens or 1 frying chicken, about 3 pounds total
2 large peeled onions
1¼ teaspoons salt
1 teaspoon ground saffron dissolved in 2 tablespoons hot water
3 jars, 1 pound each, red pitted sour or morello cherries in light syrup, or 3 cups dried pitted tart cherries
1 cup sugar

½ cup clarified butter (*ghee*, page 147) or oil
3 cups long-grain basmati rice
2 tablespoons plain yogurt

Garnish
1 tablespoon slivered almonds
2 tablespoons slivered pistachios
2 tablespoons melted butter
¼ cup cherry syrup

1. Stuff the hens with the whole onions and 1 teaspoon salt. Add a few drops of the saffron water and cook in a covered baking dish in a 350°F oven for 2 hours.

2. Drain the cherries. Place cherries and sugar in a saucepan. Cook for 35 minutes over high heat. (If using dried cherries, add ¼ cup water and 3 tablespoons sugar for 3 cups dried cherries and cook over medium heat for 5 to 10 minutes, then drain.) Strain the cherries over a bowl until no syrup remains. Save the syrup. Add 2 tablespoons butter to the cherries and set aside.

3. Clean and wash 3 cups of rice 5 times in warm water.

4. Bring 8 cups water and 2 tablespoons salt to a boil in a large, non-stick pot. Pour the rice into the pot. Boil briskly for 6 to 10 minutes, gently stirring twice with a wooden spoon to loosen grains stuck together. Bite a few grains. If the rice is soft, it is ready to be drained. Drain in a large, fine-mesh colander and rinse with 2 or 3 cups lukewarm water.

5. In the same pot, heat ¼ cup butter and a few drops of saffron water.

6. In a bowl, combine 2 spatulas full of rice and the yogurt. Spread the mixture evenly over the bottom of the pot with the back of a spoon to create a golden crust (*tah-dig*).

7. Place 2 spatulas of rice in the pot, then add 1 spatula of cherries. **Do not add syrup**. Set aside 2 spatulas of cherries for garnish.

8. Repeat, alternating layers of rice and cherries in the shape of a pyramid.

9. Cover and cook over medium heat for 10 minutes. This will help form a golden crust on the bottom of the pan. Pour the remaining butter and saffron water over the pyramid.

10. Place a clean dish towel or 2 layers of paper towels over the pot; cover firmly with the lid to prevent steam from escaping. Cook 50 minutes longer over low heat.

11. Remove the pot from heat and allow to cool on a damp surface for 5 minutes without uncovering it. Take out 2 tablespoons of saffron-flavored rice and set

aside with the rest of the garnish.

12. Gently taking 1 spatula at a time, place the rice on a platter without disturbing the crust. Place the hens or chicken around the rice. Mound rice in the shape of a pyramid. Garnish with the saffron rice, cherries, almonds, and pistachios. Pour ¼ cup hot cherry syrup and 2 tablespoons melted butter over the rice. Detach crust from the bottom of the pot with a wooden spatula and serve on the side. *Nush-e Jan!*

Note: If using fresh or frozen cherries, use ⅔ cup sugar to each pound of pitted sour cherries. Cook over high heat for 35 minutes, then drain.

If using sour cherries in heavy syrup, do not add sugar. Do not cook the sour cherries; first drain them and then add ½ cup hot water to dilute the syrup, then drain again for further use because the syrup is too sweet to use on its own.

Variation: You may substitute the chicken with meatballs. In a bowl, combine 1 pound ground meat with one grated onion. Add salt and pepper, and knead well to form into tiny balls the size of hazelnuts. Brown in a skillet in 2 tablespoons oil. Add 2 tablespoons cherry syrup to it and set aside.

Rice with Fresh Fava Beans
Baqala polow
Recipe page 162

Rice with Lentils
Adas polow
Recipe page 154

Saffron Steamed Plain Rice: Rice Cooker Method
Chelow ba polow paz
Recipe page 150

194

From the Ni'matnameh, circa 1500

Saffron Steamed Plain Basmati Rice
Chelow
Recipe page 146

Jeweled Rice
Javaher polow
Recipe page 172

Braised Leg of Lamb
Run-e bareh
Recipe page 163

بوی کورد بوی ککری کل چنبیلی بوی برک ترنج

بوی تیلیه عنبر اشهب کل چنبه بوی کل جائی جویی

بوی برک لیمو بوی بدهل بوی پوست کرنده سلارس

بوی بالا

قرنفل

بوی

موز

کل ترنج

بوی صندل دیکر انواع دتهاره دتهاره روهن

دتهاره اسیر دتهاره بالا دتهاره تلسی وازیرک تخان

From the Niʿmatnameh, *circa 1500*

Rice Meatballs
Kufteh berenji
Recipe page 128

200

Tongue with Tomato Sauce
Khorak-e zaban
Recipe page 131

201

1. *Placing ground beef on wide, flat skewers*
2. *Skewering chicken kababs*

3. *Different kababs with all the trimmings*
4. *Grilling kababs on charcoal*

5. *Basting kababs with saffron and lime juice*
6. *Removing kababs from skewers with* lavash *bread*

Detail from Ferdowsi Encounters the Three Poets of Ghazna, from the Shah Tahmasp Shahnameh, *painted by Aqa-Mirak*

Ground Meat and Lamb Kababs
Kabab-e kubideh va kabab-e barg
Recipes pages and 115 and 130

204

Detail from the Divan of Anvari, *"Firing Up the Poet's Kettle," 16th century*

Shahnameh of Ferdowsi, 1010 C.E.
The Devil, Disguised as a Cook,
Ensnares Zahhak

بدو داد دستور فرمانروا   کلید خورش خانه‌ی پادشا

بدانست کاری بایک زمان تندرست   خورش زرده‌ی خایه داد و شتخست

بسی زید و آمد دلش پرامید   خورش‌های کبک و تذرو سپید

بیاراست خوان از خورش کبیره   سه دیگر به مرغ و کبابی بره

خورش کو از پشت گاو و جوان   به روز چهارم چو بنهاد خوان

همان سالخورده می و مشک ناب   بدوی اندرون زعفران و گلاب

Iblis, the devil, presents himself to King Zahhak disguised as a charming young gourmet cook. Up to that time people had been vegetarians and killing for food was unknown. The cook prepares a series of dishes to ensnare the royal epicure. The feasts begin simply but increase in delicacy day by day.

The first night he cooks egg-yolk dishes to give the king vigorous health in a short time. The king thanks the cook for the delicacy of this food.

The second night the cook prepares a meal with partridge, gray pheasant, and quail.

The third night he serves a dish with chicken and lamb kabab mixed together.

The fourth night he sets a glamorous table and serves fillet of veal cooked in saffron, rose water, old wine, and pure musk.

By this time the king is literally eating out of the devil's hands and asks how he might express his gratitude. The reply seems innocent, even flattering; the cook wanted only to lay his face and eyes upon the king's shoulder. Zahhak grants the request. Iblis kisses him and vanishes. Suddenly, two ravenous black snakes sprout from Zahhak's shoulders.

Zahhak Ensnared by the Devil through Cooking, from Shahnameh Shah Tahmasp. *Painting by Sultan Mohammad*

Peach Khoresh
Khoresh-e hulu
Recipe page 242

KHORESH

If a Pot Can Multiply

One day Mulla lent his cooking pots to a neighbor, who was giving a feast. The neighbor returned them, together with an extra one—a very tiny pot.

"What is this?" asked Mulla.

"According to law, I have given you the offspring of your property which was born when the pots were in my care," said the joker.

Shortly afterwards Mulla borrowed his neighbor's pots, but did not return them.

The man came round to get them back.

"Alas!" said Mulla Nasruddin, "They are dead. We have established, have we not, that pots are mortal?"

Khoresh

Khoresh is a delicate and refined stew. It is a combination of either meats (lamb, beef, or veal), poultry, or fish with vegetables; fresh or dried fruits; and beans, grains, and sometimes nuts. It is seasoned subtly with fresh herbs and spices, then simmered for a long time over low heat. To achieve the slow fusing of flavors that characterizes *khoresh,* it is best to cook it in a heavy pot, cast iron if possible. I recommend a classic Dutch oven, but any heavy stew pot will do.

Khoresh can be made in advance and reheated just before serving; in fact, it often improves after sitting for a while. To obtain a wonderful *khoresh,* brown your meat and onion very well. Don't use too much water, and cook for a long time over low heat.

The good Persian cook always uses whatever vegetables and fruits are in season when preparing *khoresh,* not only because it is more economical to do so, but because their freshness enhances the flavor of the dish. For every recipe, I have simply specified stew meat. However, for exceptionally good results, in the case of lamb use the leg or shanks; for veal or beef use eye round; and carefully monitor the cooking period.

Khoresh is always served with *chelow,* saffron-steamed rice, which is heaped on each dinner plate with the *khoresh* served on top. In Iran this is called *chelow khoresh.*

Okra Khoresh

2 medium size onions, peeled and
   thinly sliced
2 cloves garlic, peeled and crushed
1 pound stew meat (lamb or beef),
   cut into 1-inch cubes, or 2 pounds
   veal shank, or 2 pounds chicken
   legs, cut up
3 tablespoons oil
1¼ teaspoons salt
½ teaspoon freshly ground
   black pepper

1 teaspoon turmeric
3 tablespoons tomato paste
1 tomato, peeled and chopped
½ red pepper, chopped (optional)
Juice of 1 lime
1 pound fresh or frozen okra

Makes 4 servings
Preparation time: 30 minutes
Cooking time: 2 hours

Khoresh-e bamieh

1. In a non-stick Dutch oven, brown onion, garlic, and meat or chicken in 3 table-spoons oil. Sprinkle with salt, pepper, and turmeric. Add the tomato paste, fresh tomato and red pepper. Pour in water—2 cups for meat and 1½ cups for chicken. Cover and simmer over low heat for 2 hours for meat or 1½ hours for chicken, until the meat is tender, stirring occasionally.

2. While meat is cooking, wash okra. Boil it in salted water for 10 minutes and drain. If using frozen okra, follow package instructions.

3. When the meat is tender, add lime juice and okra. Simmer, uncovered, for 5 to 10 minutes over low heat. Check to see if the okra is tender. Taste the stew and adjust the seasoning.

4. Transfer the stew to a deep casserole. Cover and place in a warm oven until serving time. Serve hot with *chelow*, saffron-steamed rice. *Nush-e Jan!*

Mushroom Khoresh

Makes 6 servings
Preparation time: 30 minutes
Cooking time: 2 hours

Khoresh-e qarch

2 large onions, peeled and thinly sliced
2 cloves of garlic, peeled and crushed
2 pounds chicken legs, cut up, or 1 pound stew meat (lamb, veal, or beef), cut into 1-inch cubes
6 tablespoons oil
½ teaspoon salt
¼ teaspoon freshly ground black pepper
1 pound fresh mushrooms
2 tablespoons flour

2 tablespoons chopped fresh parsley
2 tablespoons fresh lime juice
¼ teaspoon ground saffron dissolved in 1 tablespoon hot water
2 egg yolks, beaten
1 teaspoon ground cumin (optional)

1. In a Dutch oven, brown onions, garlic, and meat or chicken in 3 tablespoons oil. Add salt and pepper. Pour in water—1½ cups for meat, ½ cup for chicken. Cover and simmer over low heat for about 1½ hours for meat or 45 minutes for chicken, stirring occasionally.

2. Clean mushrooms, cut off stems and slice. Sprinkle with flour and parsley and saute in 3 tablespoons oil.

3. Add mushrooms, lime juice, and saffron water to the meat. Cover and simmer 35 minutes over low heat.

4. Taste the stew and adjust seasoning. Add beaten egg yolks and cumin if desired. Simmer 5 minutes over low heat, gently stirring.

5. Transfer the stew to an ovenproof casserole. Cover and place in a warm oven until ready to serve. Serve hot from the same dish with *chelow*, saffron-steamed rice. *Nush-e Jan!*

Carrot and Prune Khoresh

Makes 6 servings
Preparation time: 20 minutes
Cooking time: 2 hours 10 minutes

2 large onions, peeled and thinly sliced
1 clove garlic, peeled and crushed
2 pounds chicken legs, cut up, or 1 pound stew meat (lamb, veal, or beef), cut into 1-inch cubes, or 2 pounds veal shank
½ cup oil
1 teaspoon salt
¼ teaspoon freshly ground black pepper

1 teaspoon ground cinnamon
¼ teaspoon ground saffron dissolved in 1 tablespoon hot water
¼ teaspoon ground cardamom
1 pound carrots, scraped and sliced
1½ cups freshly squeezed orange juice
2 cups pitted prunes* or golden plums (*alu zarb*)
2 tablespoons sugar

Khoresh-e havij-o alu

1. In a Dutch oven, brown the onions, garlic, and meat or chicken in 3 tablespoons oil. Add salt, pepper, cinnamon, saffron water, and cardamom. Pour in water—1½ cups for meat, ½ cup for chicken. Cover and simmer over low heat for about 1 hour 15 minutes for meat or 40 minutes for chicken, stirring occasionally.

2. Saute the carrots in 2 tablespoons oil and add to the chicken or meat; add orange juice, prunes, and 2 tablespoons sugar. Cover and simmer for 1 hour 15 minutes longer over low heat.

3. Check to see if meat and prunes are tender. Taste the stew and adjust seasoning. Transfer to a deep ovenproof casserole. Cover and place in a warm oven until ready to serve.

4. Serve hot with *chelow*, saffron-steamed rice. *Nush-e Jan!*

*Note: If using prunes, add 2 tablespoons fresh squeezed lime juice.

Butternut Squash and Prune Khoresh

Makes 6 servings
Preparation time: 35 minutes
Cooking time: 2 hours 40 minutes

خورش کدو حلوایی و آلو

Khoresh-e kadu halvai-o alu

2 large onions, peeled and thinly sliced
1 pound stew meat (lamb or beef), cut up, or 2 pounds veal shanks, or 2 pounds chicken legs, cut up
⅓ cup oil
1 teaspoon salt
¼ teaspoon freshly ground black pepper
1 teaspoon ground cinnamon
2 pounds fresh butternut squash
2–4 tablespoons sugar
¼ cup fresh lime juice
¼ teaspoon ground saffron dissolved in 1 tablespoon hot water
2 cups pitted dried prunes or dried golden plums (*alu zard*)

1. In a Dutch oven, brown onions and meat or chicken in 3 tablespoons oil. Add salt, pepper, and cinnamon. Pour in water—2 cups for meat, 1½ cups for chicken. Cover and simmer over low heat for about 55 minutes for meat or 30 minutes for chicken, stirring occasionally.

2. Meanwhile, peel and cut the squash into 3-inch cubes. In the remaining oil brown squash in a skillet on all sides for 15–20 minutes over medium heat.

3. When the meat or chicken is tender, add the sugar, lime juice, saffron water, prunes or plums, and butternut squash cubes. Cover and simmer 30–55 minutes over low heat.

4. Check the taste of the stew and adjust seasoning. Add more lime juice or sugar according to your taste.

5. Transfer the *khoresh* to a deep casserole, carefully arrange first the butternut squash, then the meat, and spoon in the broth. Cover and place in a warm oven until ready to serve. Serve hot from the same dish with *chelow*, saffron-steamed rice. *Nush-e Jan!*

Note: Dried golden plums (*alu zard*) are available in Iranian specialty stores.

Cardoon or Artichoke Khoresh

Makes 6 servings
Preparation time: 35 minutes
Cooking time: 2 hours

Khoresh-e kangar

1 pound fresh cardoon stalks, or 2 packages frozen (9 oz. each) artichoke hearts
1 teaspoon vinegar
2 large onions, peeled and thinly sliced
1 pound stew meat, (lamb, veal, or beef), cut into 1-inch cubes, or 2 pounds veal shank, or 2 pounds chicken legs, cut up
⅓ cup oil

1 teaspoon salt
¼ teaspoon freshly ground black pepper
¼ teaspoon turmeric
3 cups chopped fresh parsley
½ cup chopped fresh mint
4 tablespoons fresh lime juice or ½ cup sour grape juice (*ab ghureh*)
¼ teaspoon ground saffron, dissolved in 1 tablespoon hot water

1. Carefully remove and discard prickly parts of cardoon stalks after removing leafy heads. Be sure to remove strings by lifting them with the tip of a knife and peeling them off. Cut into pieces 2 inches long. To prevent them from discoloring and to keep them tender, soak peeled cardoon pieces in a bowl of water with a splash of vinegar until ready to use. If using frozen artichoke hearts, there is no need to soak them in water.

2. In a Dutch oven, brown onions and meat or chicken in 3 tablespoons oil. Add salt, pepper, and turmeric. Pour in water—2 cups for meat, 1½ cups for chicken. Cover and simmer over low heat for about 55 minutes for meat or 30 minutes for chicken, stirring occasionally.

3. If using cardoon, drain the cardoon. In a skillet, saute the cardoon pieces in the remaining oil. Add parsley and mint and fry for 10 minutes longer.

4. When the meat is done, add lime juice, saffron water, and the cardoon. Cover and simmer for 1 hour over low heat. If using artichokes, add them to the stew in the last 40–55 minutes of cooking.

5. Check to see if the cardoon or artichoke hearts are tender. Taste the *khoresh* and adjust seasoning. Transfer it to a deep casserole. Cover and place in a warm oven until ready to serve.

6. Serve hot from the same dish with *chelow*, saffron-steamed rice. *Nush-e Jan!*

Note: Cardoon is a vegetable from the artichoke family. Cardoon and sour grape juice (*ab ghureh*) are available at Iranian specialty stores.

Celery Khoresh

Makes 6 servings
Preparation time: 30 minutes
Cooking time: 2 hours 25 minutes

Khoresh-e karafs

2 large onions, peeled and thinly sliced
1 pound stew meat (lamb, veal or beef), cut in 1-inch cubes, or 2 pounds veal shank, or 2 pounds chicken legs, cut up
⅓ cup oil
1 teaspoon salt
½ teaspoon freshly ground black pepper
½ teaspoon turmeric

5 stalks celery, washed and chopped into 1-inch lengths (4 cups, chopped)
3 cups chopped fresh parsley
½ cup chopped fresh mint, or 2 tablespoons dried
⅓ cup fresh squeezed lime juice or 1 cup unripe plums (*gojeh sabz*), or 4 whole dried Persian limes, pierced
½ teaspoon ground saffron dissolved in 2 tablespoons hot water

1. In a Dutch oven, brown onions and meat or chicken in 3 tablespoons oil. Add salt, pepper, and turmeric. Pour in water—2 cups for meat, 1½ cups for chicken. Cover, and simmer over low heat for about 30 minutes for meat or 10 minutes for chicken.

2. In a non-stick frying pan, fry the chopped celery in 3 tablespoons oil for 10 minutes, stirring occasionally. Add chopped herbs and fry for 10 minutes longer.

3. Add the mixture of celery and herbs, the lime juice, and the saffron water to the meat. Cover and simmer over low heat for 1½ hours longer, or until the meat and celery are tender.

4. Taste the stew and adjust seasoning accordingly. Transfer it to a deep casserole; cover and place in a warm oven until ready to serve.

5. Serve hot from the same dish with *chelow*, saffron-steamed rice. *Nush-e Jan!*

Note: Unripe plums (*gojeh sabz*) in season are available in Iranian specialty shops.

Green Bean Khoresh

1 pound stew meat (lamb, veal, or beef), cut into 1-inch cubes, or 2 pounds chicken legs, cut up
2 onions, peeled and thinly sliced
⅓ cup oil
1 teaspoon salt
¼ teaspoon freshly ground black pepper

½ teaspoon ground cinnamon
¼ teaspoon turmeric
1 pound fresh or frozen green beans
2 tablespoons fresh lime juice
3 tablespoons tomato paste
1 medium fresh tomato, peeled and sliced

Makes 6 servings
Preparation time: 30 minutes
Cooking time: 2 hours 30 minutes

Khoresh-e lubia sabz

1. In a Dutch oven, brown the meat or chicken and onions in 3 tablespoons oil. Add salt, pepper, cinnamon, and turmeric. Pour in water—2 cups for meat, 1½ cups for chicken. Cover and cook for about 45 minutes for meat or 20 minutes for chicken over low heat, stirring occasionally.

2. Remove strings, if any, from beans. Cut into 1-inch pieces. Saute in a skillet in the remaining oil.

3. Add green beans to the meat. Add lime juice, tomato paste, and fresh tomato. Cover and simmer 1¼ hours over low heat.

4. Taste and correct seasoning. Transfer the stew to an ovenproof casserole, cover, and place in a warm oven until ready to serve.

5. Serve hot from the same dish with *chelow*, saffron-steamed rice. *Nush-e Jan!*

Spinach and Prune Khoresh

Makes 6 servings
Preparation time: 20 minutes
Cooking time: 2 hours 35 minutes

Khoresh-e esfenaj-o alu

3 large onions, peeled and thinly sliced
1 pound stew meat (lamb, veal or beef), cut into 1-inch cubes, or 2 pounds veal shank, or 2 pounds chicken legs, cut up
⅓ cup oil
1½ teaspoons salt
¼ teaspoon freshly ground black pepper

¼ teaspoon turmeric
6 pounds fresh spinach, washed and coarsely chopped, or 2 pounds frozen chopped spinach
3 cups pitted prunes* or golden dried plums (*alu zard*)
1 tablespoon sugar (optional)
3 tablespoons Seville orange juice or ¼ cup fresh orange juice and 2 tablespoons fresh lime juice

1. In a Dutch oven, brown 2 of the onions and meat or chicken in 3 tablespoons oil. Add salt, pepper, and turmeric. Pour in water—2½ cups for meat, 1½ cups for chicken. Cover and simmer 45 minutes for meat or 20 minutes for chicken over low heat.

2. Steam the spinach in a steamer for 10 to 15 minutes. If using frozen spinach, follow package instructions.

3. In a skillet, brown the remaining onion, then add the spinach and saute for another 2 minutes.

4. Add the spinach and onion mixture, prunes, sugar, and orange juice to the pot. Cover and simmer 1½ hours longer over low heat.

5. Check to see that meat is cooked. Taste the stew and adjust seasoning. Transfer the stew to a deep casserole. Cover and place in a warm oven until ready to serve.

6. Serve hot from the same dish with *chelow*, saffron-steamed rice. *Nush-e Jan!*

*Note: If using plums, cook them separately and add to the stew with spinach in step 4.

Seville orange juice is available at Iranian specialty shops.

Pomegranate Khoresh with Chicken

Makes 6 servings
Preparation time: 30 minutes
Cooking time: 2 hours

خورش فسنجان با جوجه

*Khoresh-e fesenjan
ba jujeh*

2 large onions, peeled and thinly sliced
2 pounds chicken legs with skin removed, cut up
3 tablespoons oil or butter
1 teaspoon salt
½ cup pomegranate paste dissolved in 1½ cups water, or 2½ cups fresh squeezed pomegranate juice

½ pound or 2 cups shelled walnuts, very finely ground in a food processor
2 tablespoons sugar
¼ teaspoon ground saffron dissolved in 1 tablespoon hot water
1 cup peeled and chopped butternut squash
2 tablespoons fresh pomegranate seeds (for garnish)

1. In a Dutch oven, brown onions and chicken in the oil. Add salt and diluted pomegranate paste.

2. Add the ground walnuts, sugar, saffron water, and butternut squash to the Dutch oven, stirring gently. Cover and simmer for 2 hours, stirring occasionally with a wooden spoon to prevent the nuts from burning.

3. If the stew is too thick, add warm water to thin it. Taste the sauce and adjust for seasoning and thickness. The stew should be sweet and sour according to your taste. Add pomegranate paste to sour the taste of the stew or sugar to sweeten it.

4. Transfer the stew from the Dutch oven to a deep ovenproof casserole. For decoration, sprinkle 2 tablespoons fresh pomegranate seeds. Cover and place in a warm oven until ready to serve with *chelow*, saffron-steamed rice. *Nush-e Jan!*

Variation: As an alternative to chicken, you may use 2 pounds of ground meat mixed with 1 grated onion and ½ teaspoon salt. Make small meatballs the size of hazelnuts, fry the meatballs in 3 tablespoons of oil in a frying pan, and add to the Dutch oven in step 2.

Pomegranate Khoresh with Duck

Makes 6 servings
Preparation time: 30 minutes
Cooking time: 3 hours

خورش فسنجان بازغابی

Khoresh-e fesenjan ba morghabi

1 large duck, 4 to 5 pounds
3 whole spring onions
3 cloves garlic, peeled
1 teaspoon salt
1 pound shelled walnuts, ground very fine in a food processor
1 cup pomegranate paste diluted in 2½ cups water, or 2½ cups fresh squeezed pomegranate juice
1 cup peeled and chopped butternut squash

2 tablespoons sugar
½ teaspoon ground saffron dissolved in 2 tablespoons hot water
2 large onions, peeled and thinly sliced
½ teaspoon Persian allspice (*advieh*), page 376

1. Preheat the oven to 350°F. Rinse the duck in cold water and pat dry. Salt generously on all sides. Stuff the duck with 3 whole spring onions, 3 cloves whole garlic, and 1 teaspoon salt. Place the duck on a large baking pan. Place on rack in the center of oven and cook for 2 to 3 hours (basting the duck with the duck juices), or until the meat separates easily from the bone and duck is brown and crispy.

2. In a Dutch oven, mix the ground walnuts with the diluted pomegranate paste and let it cook over low heat for 20 minutes. It is important to keep the heat low and to stir occasionally with a wooden spoon to prevent the nuts from burning.

3. Add butternut squash, sugar, 1 teaspoon salt, and saffron water to Dutch oven. Cover and simmer for another 20 minutes over low heat, stirring occasionally.

4. After 1½ hours of cooking, remove the duck from the oven and pour the juices from the duck into a container. Turn the duck over, return it to the oven and cook until crisp.

5. In a frying pan, brown the onions in 3 tablespoons duck juice until golden brown. Add to the Dutch oven. Add ½ teaspoon Persian allspice, cover, and simmer for 35 minutes over low heat, stirring occasionally.

6. Taste the stew and adjust the seasoning. If the stew is too thick, add pomegranate juice to thin it. The stew should be sweet and sour according to your taste. Add pomegranate paste to make it sour or sugar to sweeten it.

7. Ten minutes before serving, transfer the stew from the Dutch oven to a deep ovenproof casserole. Cut up the duck and arrange the pieces in the casserole dish; cover and place in a warm oven until ready to serve. Serve with *chelow*, saffron-steamed rice. *Nush-e Jan!*

Note: As an alternative, you may cut up the duck and arrange it on a serving platter. Pour the stew around it just before serving. Or baste the duck with duck juices, serving it whole with the stew. Sprinkle 2 tablespoons fresh pomegranate seeds around it. It is always a treat to see a whole roast duck on the dinner table, especially if you serve it with Jeweled Rice, page 172.

Spinach and Orange Khoresh

Makes 6 servings
Preparation time: 30 minutes
Cooking time: 1 hour 30 minutes

1 pound ground meat (lamb, veal, or beef) or 2 pounds chicken legs, cut up
2 onions, 1 peeled and grated, 1 peeled and thinly sliced
1 teaspoon salt
¼ teaspoon freshly ground black pepper
⅓ cup oil or butter
3 pounds fresh spinach, washed and chopped, or 1 pound frozen chopped spinach

2 cloves garlic, peeled and crushed
1 cup chopped fresh parsley
¼ teaspoon turmeric
1½ cups freshly squeezed orange juice
4 tablespoons fresh lime juice
1 tablespoon rice flour
¼ teaspoon ground saffron dissolved in 1 tablespoon hot water

Esfenaj-o-porteqal (Saak)

1. Combine the meat, grated onion, ½ teaspoon salt, and a pinch of pepper in a bowl. Shape into small meatballs the size of hazelnuts. Brown in a skillet in 3 tablespoons oil or butter and set aside. If using chicken, brown legs with onion, salt, and pepper.

2. Steam the spinach for 10 to 15 minutes in a steamer. If using frozen spinach, follow package instructions.

3. In a Dutch oven, brown the sliced onion and garlic in 2 tablespoons oil, add spinach and parsley, and saute for another 2 minutes. Add ½ teaspoon salt, ¼ teaspoon pepper, and turmeric. Add 1 cup of the orange juice and the meatballs or chicken. Cover and cook over low heat for about 30 minutes.

4. In a bowl, combine the rest of the orange juice, lime juice, rice flour, and saffron water. Add this mixture to Dutch oven. Cover and simmer for 1 hour over low heat.

5. Check to see if the stew is done. Taste it and adjust seasoning. Transfer it to a deep ovenproof casserole. Cover and place in a warm oven until ready to serve.

6. Serve hot from the same dish with *chelow*, saffron-steamed rice. *Nush-e Jan!*

It is He Who sends down
Rain from the skies:
With it We produce
Vegetation of all kinds:
Out of which
We produce grain,
Heaped up at harvest;
Out of the date-palm
And its sheaths
Come clusters of dates
Hanging low and near:
And then there are gardens
Of grapes and olives,
And pomegranates,
Each similar in kind
Yet different in variety:
When they begin to bear fruit,
Feast your eye with the fruit,
And the ripeness thereof.
Behold! In these things
There are Signs for people
Who believe.

Koran, Sura VI, The Cattle, Verse 99

Orange Khoresh

Makes 6 servings
Preparation time: 30 minutes
Cooking time: 2 hours

Khoresh-e porteqal

2 large onions, peeled and thinly
  sliced
2 pounds chicken legs, cut up
⅓ cup oil
1 tablespoon flour
2 tablespoons slivered orange or
  tangerine peel with bitterness
  removed, page 378
1 teaspoon Persian allspice (*advieh*),
  page 376
1 teaspoon salt
¼ teaspoon freshly ground
  black pepper
1½ cups freshly squeezed
  orange juice

2 large carrots
4 oranges
2 tablespoons vinegar
¼ cup fresh lime juice
½ cup sugar
¼ teaspoon ground saffron dissolved in 1 tablespoon hot water

Garnish
2 teaspoons slivered pistachios
2 teaspoons slivered almonds

1. In a Dutch oven, brown onions and chicken pieces in 3 tablespoons oil, sprinkle in 1 tablespoon flour and mix well. Add orange or tangerine peel, Persian allspice, salt, and pepper. Pour in the orange juice. Cover and simmer for 35 minutes.

2. Scrape the carrots and slice into thin slivers. Saute in 2 tablespoons oil for a few minutes. Add the carrot to the chicken, cover, and simmer for 1 hour.

3. Peel the oranges, separate them into segments, and peel the membrane from each segment.

4. In a saucepan, combine the vinegar, lime juice, sugar, and saffron water. Mix well and simmer for 10 minutes over low heat. Remove from heat and add the orange segments and set aside to macerate for 10 minutes.

5. Transfer the *khoresh* to a deep ovenproof casserole, carefully arrange the orange segments with the sauce on the top, cover and place in an warm oven until ready to serve.

6. Check to see if the chicken is tender. Taste and adjust seasoning. Add more sugar or lime juice according to your taste.

7. Just before serving, sprinkle the stew with slivered pistachios and almonds. Serve hot from same dish with *chelow*, saffron-steamed rice. *Nush-e Jan!*

Variations: Canned orange segments or tangerines in syrup may be substituted for fresh oranges and sugar. This dish may also be made without carrots.

Orange Khoresh
Khoresh-e porteqal
Recipe page 224

225

T h e   H a f t   P a i k a r   b y   N i z a m i ,   1 2 t h   C .
T h e   T u r q u o i s e - B l u e   D o m e

سیب پرخون طبع های رحمت ... نار بشکفته درج های عقیق

به چه کویی برآکنیده به مشک ... پسته یا خنده برز لب خشک

رنگ شقتالو از شمایی شاخ ... کرده یاقوتی سرخ و زرد فراخ

The Haft Paikar describes in verse the life and adventures of King Bahram and his seven princesses. Each princess comes from a different region of the world and represents the climes into which the habitable world is divided. Each lives in a separate symbolically colored dome and palace that Bahram has had built for her. Bahram then visits them on seven successive nights.

Here is a section from the story told by the princess from the turquoise-blue dome of mercury, visited by Bahram on Wednesday night.

Mahan enlarged the hole and put his head through it, there he saw a garden, not an earthly one, but a part of paradise, a garden of Eram.

Its fruit trees were bent to the ground in adoration. There were apples like goblets filled with ruby-red wine, pomegranates like jewel-boxes made of agate; the quinces looked like balls stuffed with musk and the pistachio nuts smiled with juice. Then there were peaches, like red hyacinths on one side, like yellow suns on the other. Next to them bananas, dates, pears and figs—a vine, wearing its cap of leaves askew, was watching over its subordinates, light ones and dark ones—a sight of unparalleled splendor. Soon the memory of yesterday's hell faded. Mahan walked around quietly—plucking a rose here, picking an apple there, tasting peaches and cracking nuts.

In this paradise Mahan encounters an old man who loves him as a son from first sight. And then Mahan is tempted by a band of beautiful girls who prepare a banquet for him.

A pomegranate *khoresh* flavored with saffron, sugar and honey, scented with musk, aloe and rose-water served with saffron flavored rice

And range chicken *kabab* with plenty of circular *lavash* bread loaves, soft and tender like the backs and breasts of the girls who unwrapped them.

And finally the sweets: *halva* in candied sugar and a thousand different types of pastries and cookies.

City Dweller Desecrates Garden, from the Haft Awrang of Jami, *attributed to 'Abd-ul 'Aziz of Kashan, 1550 C.E.*

Pomegranate Khoresh with Duck
Khoresh-e fesenjan ba ordak
Recipe page 221

228

Roast Duck with Fresh Pomegranate Seeds in Pomegranate Khoresh
Khoresh-e fesenjan ba anar-e dun kardeh ba ordak
Recipe page 221

229

Celery Khoresh
Khoresh-e karafs
Recipe page 217

230

Artichoke Khoresh
Khoresh-e kangar
Recipe page 216

231

Okra Khoresh
Khoresh-e bamieh
Recipe page 212

232

Eggplant Khoresh
Khoresh-e bademjan
Recipe page 247

233

Fresh Herb Khoresh
Khoresh-e qormeh sabzi
Recipe page 246

234

Butternut Squash and Prune Khoresh
Khoresh-e kadu halvai-o alu
Recipe page 215

235

Potato Khoresh
Khoresh-e qeymeh
Recipe page 248

236

Spinach and Prune Khoresh
Khoresh-e esfenaj-o alu
Recipe page 219

237

Painting from Habib Al-Sayar, *1579*

Apple Khoresh
Khoresh-e sib
Recipe page 244

239

Rhubarb Khoresh
Khoresh-e rivas
Recipe page 241

240

Rhubarb Khoresh

Makes 6 servings
Preparation time: 30 minutes
Cooking time: 2 hour 15 minutes

Khoresh-e rivas

2 onions, peeled and thinly sliced
1 pound stew meat (lamb, veal, or beef) cut into 1-inch cubes or 2 pounds veal shank, or 2 pounds chicken legs, cut up
⅓ cup oil
1½ teaspoons salt
¼ teaspoon freshly ground black pepper
¼ teaspoon turmeric
3 cups chopped fresh parsley

½ cup chopped fresh mint or 2 tablespoons dried
¼ teaspoon ground saffron dissolved in 1 tablespoon hot water
1 tablespoon tomato paste
2 tablespoons fresh lime juice
1 pound fresh rhubarb, cut into 1-inch pieces

1. In a Dutch oven, brown onions and meat or chicken in 3 tablespoons oil. Add salt, pepper, and turmeric. Pour in water—2½ cups for meat and 1½ cups for chicken. Cover and cook for about 1 hour for meat and 15 minutes for chicken over low heat, stirring occasionally.

2. In a skillet, fry parsley and mint in remaining oil for 10–15 minutes.

3. Add parsley and mint, saffron water, tomato paste, and lime juice to the meat. Cover and simmer 55 minutes longer over low heat.

4. Preheat oven to 350°F. Transfer the stew to a deep ovenproof casserole. Arrange the rhubarb on the top and cover the casserole with aluminum foil. Pierce several holes in the foil and place the serving dish in the oven; cook for 25 to 35 minutes or until the rhubarb is tender.

5. Adjust seasoning. If the stew is too sour, add 1 tablespoon sugar. If the rhubarb needs more cooking, continue until done. Remember, rhubarb is fragile; the pieces must be cooked, but not to the point of dissolving or falling apart.

6. Serve hot from the same dish with *chelow*, saffron-steamed rice. *Nush-e Jan!*

From ancient times rhubarb has been known for its qualities for cleansing the blood and purifying the system.

Peach Khoresh

Makes 6 servings
Preparation time: 30 minutes
Cooking time: 2 hours

Khoresh-e hulu

2 large onions, peeled and thinly
  sliced
1 pound stew meat (lamb, veal, or
  beef), cut into 1-inch cubes, or 2
  pounds chicken legs, cut up
⅓ cup oil
1 teaspoon salt
¼ teaspoon freshly ground
  black pepper
1 teaspoon Persian allspice (*advieh*),
  page 376

½ cup fresh lime juice
½ cup sugar
¼ teaspoon ground saffron dissolved in 1 tablespoon hot water
5 firm, unripe peaches

1. In a Dutch oven, brown onions and meat or chicken in 3 tablespoons oil. Add salt, pepper, and Persian allspice. Pour in water—2 cups for meat, 1 cup for chicken. Cover and simmer over low heat for 1 hour for meat or 30 minutes for chicken.

2. Mix together the lime juice, sugar, and saffron water and stir the lime mixture into the meat. Cover and simmer 45 minutes longer over low heat.

3. To remove fuzz, wash the peaches well. Remove pits and cut peaches into ½-inch wedges. Brown in a skillet in 2 tablespoons oil until golden brown. Add the peaches to the Dutch oven, cover, and simmer 25 minutes longer

4. Check to see if meat or chicken and peaches are tender. Taste and adjust seasoning. Transfer the stew to a deep ovenproof casserole. Cover and place in a warm oven until ready to serve.

5. Serve hot from the same dish with *chelow*, saffron-steamed rice. *Nush-e Jan!*

Variation: You may use 3 cups sliced frozen peaches or 3 cups canned sliced peaches in heavy syrup in place of fresh peaches. Just eliminate the ½ cup sugar and add peaches, without the syrup, in the last 10 minutes of cooking. Or use 2 cups sliced dried peaches and add in step 2 with ½ cup water.

Note: Peaches originally came from ancient Persia, and many languages refer to them as Persian fruit. In French, *pêche*; in Russian, *persik*; in Italian, *pesca*; and in German, *pfirsich*.

Quince Khoresh

2 large onions, peeled and thinly
    sliced
1 pound stew meat (lamb, veal, or
    beef), cut into 1-inch cubes, or 2
    pounds chicken legs, cut up
½ cup oil
1 teaspoon salt
¼ teaspoon freshly ground
    black pepper

¼ teaspoon ground cinnamon
2 large quinces
½ cup sugar
¼ cup balsamic vinegar
¼ cup fresh lime juice
¼ teaspoon ground saffron dis-
    solved in 1 tablespoon hot water
⅓ cup yellow split peas

Makes 6 servings
Preparation time: 20 minutes
Cooking time: 2 hours

Khoresh-e beh

Quince is an ancient fruit used in Persian cooking.

1. In a Dutch oven, brown onions and meat or chicken in 3 tablespoons oil. Add salt, pepper, and cinnamon. Stir in water—3 cups for meat or 1½ cups for chicken. Cover and simmer for 1 hour for meat and 30 minutes for chicken over low heat, stirring occasionally.

2. Wash but do not peel the quinces. Core using an apple corer, cut into quarters, and remove seeds; cut into wedges.

3. Brown quince in the remaining oil in a skillet for about 10 to 15 minutes, until golden brown. Add it to the meat and simmer for 30 minutes.

4. Add the sugar, vinegar, lime juice, saffron water, and yellow split peas to the meat. Cover and simmer for 30–45 minutes longer over low heat (the cooking time depends on the type of yellow split peas).

5. Taste the stew and adjust seasoning. Transfer to a deep ovenproof casserole. Cover and place in a warm oven until ready to serve.

6. Serve hot with *chelow*, saffron-steamed rice. *Nush-e Jan!*

Apple Khoresh

Makes 4 servings
Preparation time: 20 minutes
Cooking time: 2 hours 35 minutes

Khoresh-e sib

2 large onions, peeled and thinly sliced
2 pounds chicken legs, cut up, or 1 pound stew meat (veal, lamb, or beef), cut into 1-inch pieces
⅓ cup oil
1 teaspoon salt
¼ teaspoon pepper
½ teaspoon ground cinnamon

⅓ cup yellow split peas
1 tablespoon tomato paste
3 tablespoons sugar
3 tablespoons vinegar
½ teaspoon ground saffron dissolved in 2 tablespoons hot water
5 tart cooking apples

1. In a Dutch oven, brown the onions with the chicken or the meat in 3 tablespoons oil. Sprinkle with salt, pepper, and cinnamon. Pour in 1½ cups water for chicken and 2 cups water for meat. Cover and simmer over low heat for 55 minutes for chicken and 1½ hours for meat.

2. Add yellow split peas, tomato paste, sugar, vinegar, and saffron water. Cover and simmer for 15 minutes longer.

3. Core and peel the apples and cut into wedges. Saute in remaining oil for 10 to 15 minutes, until golden brown.

4. Taste the stew and correct seasoning. Add either more sugar or vinegar if necessary. The stew should be sweet and sour.

5. Preheat oven to 350°F. Transfer the stew to a deep casserole and arrange the apples on the top. Cover and place in the oven. Cook for 45 minutes longer. Serve from the same dish with *chelow*, saffron steamed rice. *Nush-e Jan!*

Fresh Almond Khoresh

Makes 6 servings
Preparation time: 30 minutes
Cooking time: 2 hours 30 minutes

خورش چغاله با دلم

Khoresh-e chaghaleh badam

2 onions, peeled and thinly sliced
1 pound stew meat (lamb, veal, or beef), cut up into 1-inch cubes, or 2 pounds veal shank, or 2 pounds chicken legs, cut up
⅓ cup oil
1 teaspoon salt
¼ teaspoon freshly ground black pepper
½ teaspoon turmeric

½ pound fresh unripe almonds
3 cups chopped fresh parsley
½ cup chopped fresh mint, or 2 tablespoons dried mint
⅓ cup fresh lime juice or ½ cup sour grape juice (*ab ghureh*)
1 tablespoon sugar
¼ teaspoon ground saffron dissolved in 1 tablespoon hot water

1. In a Dutch oven, brown onions and meat or chicken in 3 tablespoons oil. Add salt, pepper, and turmeric. Pour in water—2 cups for meat and 1½ cups for chicken. Bring to a boil; cover and simmer for about 1 hour for meat or ½ hour for chicken over low heat.

2. Saute the almonds, parsley, and mint for 10 minutes in the remaining oil.

3. Add the mixture of almonds and herbs, lime juice or sour grape juice, sugar, and saffron water to the meat. Cover and simmer over low heat 1 hour longer.

4. Check to see if the meat is tender. Taste and adjust seasoning. Transfer the stew to a deep casserole; cover and place in warm oven until time to serve.

5. Serve hot from the same dish with *chelow,* saffron-steamed rice. *Nush-e Jan!*

Note: Sour grape juice (*ab ghureh*) is available at Iranian specialty shops. You can also make stew of unripe plums (*gojeh sabz*) by just replacing the almonds with unripe plums and leaving out the lime juice.

Unripe almonds are available in the springtime in Iranian specialty food stores.

Fresh Herb Khoresh

Makes 6 servings
Preparation time: 25 minutes
Cooking time: 3 hours

خورش قرمه سبزی

Khoresh-e qormeh sabzi

Note: If using dried herbs, place a sieve in a bowl of lukewarm water and soak the herbs for 20 minutes. Remove the sieve from the bowl and use the herbs.

2 large onions, peeled and thinly sliced
2 pounds lamb shank or 1½ pounds deboned leg of lamb cut in 2-inch pieces, or 2 pounds chicken legs, cut up
½ cup oil
1½ teaspoons salt
¼ teaspoon freshly ground black pepper
½ teaspoon turmeric
⅓ cup dried kidney beans

4 whole dried Persian limes (*limu-omani*), pierced
4 cups finely chopped fresh parsley or 1 cup dried
1 cup finely chopped fresh chives or scallions or ¼ cup dried
1 cup finely chopped fresh coriander
1 cup chopped fresh fenugreek leaves or ¼ cup dried
2 tablespoons dried Persian lime powder (*limu-omani*) or 4 tablespoons fresh lime juice

1. In a Dutch oven, brown onions with meat or chicken in 3 tablespoons oil. Add salt, pepper, and turmeric. Pour in water—4 cups for meat or 2 cups for chicken. Add kidney beans and whole dried Persian limes. Bring to a boil, cover and simmer for about 30 minutes for meat or 10 minutes for chicken over low heat, stirring occasionally.

2. Meanwhile, fry the chopped parsley, chives or scallions, coriander, and fenugreek in the remaining oil over medium heat for 20 minutes, stirring constantly or until the aroma of frying herbs rises (this stage is very important to the taste of the stew).

3. Add the sauteed herbs and lime powder or juice to the pot. Cover and simmer for another 2½ hours for meat and 1½ hours for chicken over low heat, stirring occasionally.

4. Check to see if meat and beans are tender. Taste the stew and adjust seasoning. Transfer to a deep casserole; cover and place in a warm oven until ready to serve.

5. Serve hot from the same dish with *chelow*, saffron-steamed rice. *Nush-e Jan!*

Note: You can make your own dried Persian lime powder, powdered *limu-omani*, from a whole dried Persian lime (*limu*) by removing the seeds and grinding the remainder to a powder in a food processor. Fenugreek leaves and dried Persian limes are available in Iranian specialty shops.

A dried mixture of herb stew is available in Iranian specialty stores. Just add it in step 3.

Variation: 1 pound fish fillet may be substituted in the last 30 minutes of cooking in place of the meat, or 12 ounces cooked kidney beans with their water may be substituted in the last 15 minutes of cooking. In this case reduce the water to 2½ cups.

Eggplant Khoresh

Makes 6 servings
Preparation time: 20 minutes
Cooking time: 2 hours 15 minutes

خورش بادمجان

Khoresh-e bademjan

Variation: *Khoresh-e Gheimeh Bademjan*—Replace meat with 1 pound stew meat cut into ½-inch cubes. Brown with 2 onions until golden brown, add 2 cups water; 4 tomatoes, peeled and chopped; 4 whole pierced dried Persian limes (*limu-omani*); and Persian all-spice (*advieh*). Add ⅓ cup yellow split peas in 1½ cups water for 20 minutes, drain, and add them for the last 10 minutes of cooking. You may also substitute summer squash for the eggplant.

Note: Unripe grapes (*ghureh*) and Persian allspice (*advieh*) are all available at Iranian specialty shops.

2 large onions, peeled and thinly sliced
2 cloves garlic, peeled and crushed
2 pounds lamb shanks, or 2 pounds chicken legs with skin removed, cut up
½ cup oil
1 teaspoon salt
¼ teaspoon freshly ground black pepper
1 teaspoon turmeric
½ teaspoon ground saffron dissolved in 4 tablespoons hot water
2 cups fresh squeezed tomato juice
1 cup unripe grapes (*ghureh*)
4 tablespoons lime juice
3 medium or 9 slim eggplants
1 egg white
1 teaspoon Persian allspice (*advieh*), page 376 (optional)

Garnish
1 large onion, peeled and thinly sliced
1 large tomato, peeled and left whole
2 tablespoons oil

That food which I most cherish is the sour-grape, chicken, and eggplant dish

آن غذائی که مرا چون جان است   غوره و جوجه و بادمجان است

1. In a non-stick Dutch oven, brown the onions and garlic with meat or chicken in 3 tablespoons oil over medium heat. Add salt, pepper, turmeric, and saffron water.

2. Add 2 cups water for meat and no water for chicken, tomato juice, unripe grapes, and lime juice. Cover and simmer over low heat for 2½ hours for meat and 30 minutes for chicken.

3. Peel eggplants and cut lengthwise in quarters if they are large. Place in a colander, sprinkle both sides with water and 2 tablespoons salt, and set aside for 20 minutes to remove the bitter taste. Rinse and pat dry.

4. Brush each eggplant on all sides with egg white and brown the eggplant in a non-stick skillet in 3 tablespoons oil; set aside.

5. Add Persian allspice to the meat or chicken; mix well and adjust seasoning to your taste.

6. For the garnish, brown the onion and tomato in a non-stick skillet in 2 tablespoons oil; set aside.

7. Preheat the oven to 350°F. Transfer the chicken or meat and sauce into a deep ovenproof casserole; arrange the eggplant, then onion and tomato, on the top. Cover and bake for 30 minutes, then remove cover and bake another 15 minutes uncovered or until the eggplant is tender.

8. Serve immediately from the same dish or keep warm in the oven until ready to serve. Serve with saffron-steamed plain rice (*chelow*). *Nush-e Jan!*

Potato Khoresh

Makes 6 servings
Preparation time: 20 minutes
Cooking time: 2 hours 15 minutes

2 onions, peeled and thinly sliced
1 pound stew meat (lamb, veal, or beef) cut into ½-inch pieces
5 tablespoons oil
4 whole dried Persian limes (*limu-omani*), pierced
1 teaspoon salt
¼ teaspoon freshly ground black pepper
½ teaspoon turmeric
½ teaspoon Persian allspice (*advieh*), page 376 (optional)

1 large tomato, peeled and chopped
1 tablespoon tomato paste
1 tablespoon slivered orange or tangerine peel, with bitterness removed, page 378
½ teaspoon ground saffron dissolved in 2 tablespoons hot water
1 pound or 2 large potatoes, peeled and cut into sticks
1 cup oil for deep frying
⅓ cup yellow split peas

Khoresh-e qeymeh

1. In a non-stick Dutch oven, brown the onions and meat in 3 tablespoons oil. Add dried Persian limes, salt, pepper, and turmeric. Saute for 2 minutes longer. Pour in 1½ cups water and bring to a boil. Cover and simmer over low heat for 55 minutes, stirring occasionally.

2. Add Persian allspice, fresh tomato, tomato paste, orange or tangerine peel, and saffron water. Cover and cook for another 45 minutes.

3. During this time fry the potato sticks in the 1 cup of oil; drain on a paper towel and set aside.

4. Cook yellow split peas in 2½ cups of water and ¼ teaspoon salt for 30 minutes. Drain and add to the Dutch oven.

5. Check to see if meat and peas are tender. Taste the stew and correct seasoning. Transfer the *khoresh* to a deep ovenproof Pyrex dish, cover and place in a warm oven until ready to serve.

6. Just before serving arrange the french fries on top. Serve with *chelow*, saffron-steamed rice, Persian pickles (*torshi*) and fresh vegetables and herbs (*sabzi-khordan*) on the side. *Nush-e Jan!*

Note: Dried Persian limes (*limu-omani*), and Persian allspice (*advieh*) are available at Iranian specialty stores.

Rice with Fresh Fava Beans (*Baqali polow*), page 162, traditionally accompanies *Khoresh-e qeymeh* without potato.

Yogurt Khoresh

2 onions, peeled and thinly sliced
2 pounds chicken legs with skin
    removed, cut up
¼ cup chopped celery (2 stalks)
3 tablespoons oil
1 teaspoon salt
¼ teaspoon freshly ground
    black pepper

3 heaping tablespoons curry powder
1 tablespoon flour
2 tablespoons lime juice
2 cups yogurt, beaten

Garnish
⅓ cup slivered almonds
¼ cup raisins

Makes 6 servings
Preparation time: 15 minutes
Cooking time: 1 hour 40 minutes

Khoresh-e mast

1. In a Dutch oven, saute onions with the chicken and celery in 3 tablespoons oil. Sprinkle with salt, pepper, curry powder, and flour. Mix well. Do not add water since the chicken will produce its own juice. Add lime juice, cover, and simmer for about 1 hour 30 minutes over low heat, stirring occasionally.

2. In a bowl, beat the yogurt well with a fork.

3. When the chicken is cooked, stir in the yogurt mixture and simmer 5 minutes over low heat, occasionally stirring gently (do not boil the yogurt).

4. Check to see if the chicken is tender. Taste and adjust seasoning. Transfer the stew to a deep serving dish.

5. Garnish with almonds and raisins and serve hot with *chelow*, saffron-steamed rice. *Nush-e Jan!*

Variation: Curry powder and celery may be replaced with 1 teaspoon ground saffron dissolved in 4 tablespoons hot water and ½ cup candied orange peel (see page 380) in this recipe. Mix the saffron with the yogurt in step 2; add the candied orange peel in step 1.

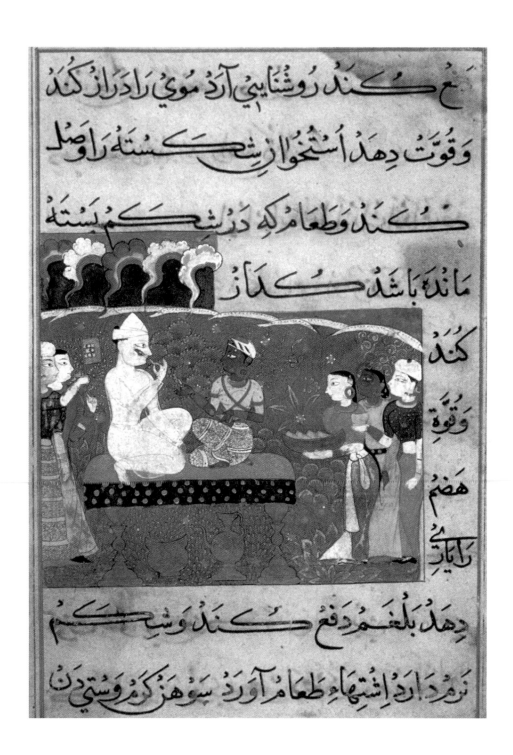

کند روشنایی آرد موی را دراز کند

وقوت دهد استخوان شکسته را وصل

کند وطعام که درشکم بسته

ماند باشد کذا سکه

کند

وقوة

هضم

رایات

دهد بلغم دفع کند و شکم

نرم و ارد اشتهاء طعام آورد سوهز کرم وستی دن

From the Ni'matnameh, circa 1500

250

PICKLES AND RELISHES

زیباترین اشیا، فشرخترین اعیان ازهرچه هست پیدا و زهرچه هست پنهان

ازمرغها مرغ زارست، ازوقتها محرکه ازفصلها بهارست، ازنوعها انسان

ازعهد شبابست، ازآبها شرابست ازنجم آفتابست، ازماهها نیسان

ازسنگها دل دوست، ازعیشها غم اوست ازتیغها ابرو، ازدشنهاست مژگان

اززیبها افسر، ازطیبها عنبر ازعضوها است دیده، ازخلقهاست جان

Of things most beautiful of hours most wonderful
Of all that is visible of all that is hidden

Of birds—the nightingale, of time—the dawn
Of seasons—the spring, of species—the human

Of Age it is youth, of liquids it is wine
Of planets our sun, of months the April rain

Of stones—a friend's heart, of pleasures—the pain
Of swords—the eyebrow, of daggers—the eyelash

Of jewels it is the Tiara, of fragrance it is amber
Of the senses it is sight, of qualities it is virtue.

Neshat

Pickles   and   Relishes

Whenever the *sofreh* or cloth is spread for a meal, you will find a variety of pickles and relishes, *torshis,* accompanying the main course. Most of these *torshis* consist of vegetables or fruits and spices preserved in vinegar. For this chapter, I have selected only a few of the many kinds of *torshi* made in Iran. All are simple, traditional recipes.

   Good *torshis* are made with fresh ingredients and good wine vinegar. The fruits, vegetables and herbs must be thoroughly washed and dried. Not a trace of water can remain if the *torshi* is to keep well. After the jars have been sealed, they should be stored in a cool, dark place for aging. Once they are opened, they should be kept in the refrigerator.

Mango Pickle

1 pound tamarind or 2 cups tama-
    rind paste
7 to 8 cups red wine vinegar
4 mangoes
1 tablespoon salt
1 tablespoon Persian allspice for
    pickle (*advieh-ye torshi*), page 377
½ teaspoon ground saffron
1 tablespoon confectioners' sugar

Makes 2 half-pints
Preparation and cooking time:
35 minutes
Storage time: 6 weeks
before using

Torshi-e anbeh

1. Bring to a boil tamarind in 4 cups vinegar and simmer over medium heat for 15 to 20 minutes. Add more vinegar if needed. Drain in a colander set over a bowl, and press with the back of a spoon to remove pits, pods, threads, etc. Keep the liquid. You may also buy ready-made tamarind paste.

2. Wash mangoes. Cut them up and remove the pits.

3. In a large laminated pot, place mangoes, tamarind liquid, and 3 cups of vinegar. Bring to a boil over high heat, then reduce heat and simmer for 15 minutes. Remove the pot from heat and let cool. The pickle should be of a thick consistency.

4. Add salt, Persian allspice, saffron, and the confectioners' sugar. Mix well. Add more salt or vinegar, according to your taste.

5. Sterilize canning jars in boiling water. Drain and dry thoroughly with a clean towel. Fill the jars within ½ inch of top, end with a bit of salt and splash of vinegar, and seal.

6. Store the jars in a cool, dark place for at least 6 weeks before using. *Nush-e Jan!*

Note: Persian allspice (*advieh*) is available at Iranian specialty stores.

Fruit Chutney

Makes about 4 pints
Preparation and cooking time:
3 hours
Storage time: 10 days
before using

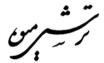

Torshi-e miveh

Persian Chutney Spice Mixture
(Advieh-ye Torshi)
2 teaspoons ground green cumin
1 teaspoon ground black cumin
3 teaspoons ground angelica
    powder (*gol-par*)
½ teaspoon freshly ground
    black pepper
½ teaspoon ground turmeric
3 teaspoons ground coriander seeds
2 teaspoons ground cinnamon
3 teaspoons ground ginger
1 teaspoon ground cardamom
1 tablespoon powdered dried
    Persian lime (*limu-omani*)

Fruit and Vegetables
1 pound apricots, chopped
½ pound fresh or dried tamarind*
2 pounds pitted dates, chopped, or 1
    cup honey or sugar
1 pound dried pitted prunes,
    finely chopped
1 pound seedless grapes,
    finely chopped

1 pound apples, cored
    and finely chopped
1 pound quinces, cored
    and finely chopped
1 pound persimmons,
    finely chopped
1 pound pitted sour cherries
2 red peppers, seeds removed and
    finely chopped
2 navel oranges, peeled, seeds
    removed and finely chopped
5 pounds peaches, peeled, pitted
    and finely chopped
1 bulb of fresh garlic, peeled
    and crushed
5 pounds mangoes, peeled
    and chopped
2 or more quarts apple vinegar

Seasoning
2 teaspoons ground saffron
2 tablespoons nigella seeds
    (*siah daneh*)
2 tablespoons salt

A food processor may be used to chop your fruit and vegetables.

1. Prepare the Persian chutney spice mixture (*advieh-ye torshi*) by placing all the ground spice ingredients in a bowl and mixing well. Set aside.

2. Place all the prepared fruit and vegetables in a large pot. Cover with the vinegar and simmer for 2 to 3 hours over low heat, stirring occasionally with a wooden spoon.

3. Remove the pot from heat. Add the Persian chutney spice mixture and the seasoning to the pot and mix well. Let stand uncovered for 24 hours. Adjust seasoning to taste; add more vinegar if necessary.

4. Sterilize canning jars in boiling water. Drain and dry thoroughly. Fill the jars to within ½ inch of the top with chutney, then end with a splash of vinegar and a bit of salt on top. Seal the jars.

5. Store the jars for at least 10 days in a cool, dark place before using. The result should be a healthful, sweet-and-sour chutney. *Nush-e Jan!*

*Note: If you are using dried tamarind, cover the fruit in vinegar overnight, then drain in a colander set over a bowl, and using the back of the spoon, press the tamarind to remove the seeds, threads, and pods.

For the best results both for flavors and for your budget, buy your fruit as it comes into season. Wash, prepare, and cook it with vinegar as in Step 2; then store it in airtight containers in a cool place. At the end of the year (or when you have collected and prepared all the fruit), place all the fruit in a large saucepan, add the spices, and continue from Step 3. The fresher your fruit, the better your *torshi!*

Seven-Spice Pickle

Makes 4 pints
Preparation and cooking
time: 1 hour 15 minutes
Storage time: 10 days
before using

Torshi-e haft-e bijar

¼ **pound dried Persian shallots**
    (*musir*) **or 1 pound dried**
2 **quarts wine vinegar**
4 **large or 10 small eggplants**
3 **teaspoons salt**
1 **teaspoon freshly ground**
    black pepper
½ **teaspoon red pepper, crushed**
3 **tablespoons angelica powder**
    or petals (*gol-par*)
2 **tablespoons nigella seeds**
    (*siah daneh*)
1 **tablespoon Persian allspice for**
    pickle (*advieh-ye torshi*), page 377
2 **bulbs of garlic, peeled and crushed**

1 **teaspoon peppercorns**
½ **cup chopped fresh mint leaves**
    or 2 tablespoons dried
½ **cup chopped fresh tarragon**
    leaves or 2 tablespoons dried
½ **cup chopped fresh basil leaves**
    or 2 tablespoons dried
½ **cup chopped fresh parsley or**
    2 tablespoons dried
½ **cup chopped fresh fenugreek**
    leaves or 2 tablespoons dried
½ **cup chopped fresh coriander**
    leaves or 2 tablespoons dried
½ **cup chopped fresh summer**
    savory or 2 tablespoons dried

1. Wash the *musir*, cover them with vinegar, and cook for 25 minutes over medium heat; drain and chop.

2. Wash eggplants and pat dry. Make a lengthwise incision in each eggplant and remove the stem, but do not peel. Place the whole eggplants in a saucepan and pour in enough vinegar so that they are covered. Cook over medium heat for 45 minutes, or until tender. Drain and set aside to cool.

3. Place the cooled eggplants on a wooden cutting board and chop into tiny pieces. In a large bowl, combine with salt, black and red pepper, angelica powder, nigella seeds, Persian allspice, garlic, *musir*, peppercorns, the chopped herbs, and 1 quart vinegar. Mix thoroughly with a wooden spoon. If necessary add more vinegar. Adjust seasoning to your taste with additional angelica powder or petals.

4. Sterilize canning jars in boiling water. Drain and dry thoroughly. Fill the jars to within ½ inch of the top with *torshi* mixture. Sprinkle with a bit of salt and a splash of vinegar. Seal the jars.

5. Store the jars for at least 10 days in a cool, dark place before using. *Nush-e Jan!*

Note: Powdered angelica (*gol-par*), nigella seeds (*siah daneh*), and Persian allspice (*advieh*) are available in Iranian specialty stores.

If herbs and vegetables are not quite dry, place them in a pot, cover with vinegar and boil for 10 minutes.

If using fresh *musir*, wash and peel them and cook in vinegar. Drain, chop, and cover.

Mixed Vegetable Pickle

Makes 4 pints
Preparation and cooking time: 2 hours 30 minutes
Storage time: 10 days before using

Torshi-e makhlut

¼ pound shallots
3 to 4 quarts wine vinegar
2 large eggplants
½ cup chopped fresh mint leaves
½ cup chopped fresh parsley
½ cup chopped fresh coriander leaves
½ cup chives, washed and chopped
½ cup chopped fresh tarragon
1 pound pickling cucumbers, washed, dried and chopped
2 green peppers, cut into small pieces
1 pound carrots, scraped and finely chopped
½ pound turnips, chopped
2 to 3 stalks celery, chopped
2 large potatoes, peeled and chopped

5 cloves garlic, peeled and chopped
1 pound pearl onions, peeled
½ head cauliflower, separated into florets
2 tablespoons salt
½ teaspoon freshly ground black pepper
4 tablespoons angelica powder (*gol-par*)
1 tablespoon Persian allspice for pickles (*advieh-ye torshi*), page 377
2 tablespoon nigella seeds (*siah daneh*)
¼ teaspoon cayenne pepper

1. Wash and peel the shallots. Cover them with vinegar and cook them for 15 minutes over high heat; drain and chop.

2. Prick the eggplants with a fork to prevent bursting and bake on oven rack for 1 hour at 350°F.

3. Wash the herbs and drain. Dry thoroughly, then chop.

4. Remove the eggplant from the oven. Place baked eggplant on wooden cutting board. Remove and discard the skin; chop the flesh into small pieces. Place in a colander and let stand for an hour.

5. Place all chopped herbs and vegetables in a large laminated container and cover with vinegar.

6. Add salt, pepper, angelica powder, Persian allspice, nigella seeds, and cayenne pepper. Mix well. Adjust seasoning to taste.

7. Sterilize canning jars in boiling water. Drain and dry thoroughly. Fill the jars to within ½ inch of the top with the mixture. Sprinkle with salt and a splash of vinegar. Seal the jars.

8. Store for at least 10 days in a cool, dark place before using. *Nush-e Jan!*

Note: Angelica powder (*gol-par*), nigella seeds (*siah daneh*), and Persian allspice (*advieh*) are available in Iranian specialty stores.

Onion Pickle

2 pounds pearl onions
1 tablespoon salt
1 quart wine vinegar or more
4 sprigs of fresh tarragon

Makes 2 pints
Preparation and cooking
time: 30 minutes
Storage time: 10 days
before using

Torshi-e piaz

1. Wash and drain the onions. Peel the onions and remove the roots at the bottom. With the point of a knife cut a cross mark in the bottom of each onion so it will absorb vinegar. Leave onion tops intact.

2. In a heavy pot bring salt and vinegar to a boil over high heat, remove from heat and set aside to cool.

3. Sterilize the canning jars in boiling water. Drain and dry thoroughly.

4. Fill the jars almost to the top by layering onions and sprigs of fresh tarragon. Fill to within ½ inch of the top with the vinegar mixture. Seal the jars.

5. Store the jars for at least 10 days in a cool, dark place before using. Serve as a relish with meats. *Nush-e Jan!*

Pickled Garlic

1 pound garlic bulbs
½ cup dried barberries, cleaned,
**   soaked for 20 minutes in cold**
**   water, and drained**
1 quart vinegar or more

Makes 2 pints
Preparation time: 20 minutes
Storage time: 6 weeks
before using

Torshi-e sir

1. Peel off just one outside layer of garlic bulbs.

2. Fill in the center of each bulb with 1 teaspoon barberries.

3. Sterilize canning jars in boiling water and dry thoroughly.

4. Fill the jars nearly to top with garlic bulbs. Fill the jar to within ½ inch of the top with vinegar. Add a bit of salt to the top. Seal the jars.

5. Store the jars in a cool, dark place for at least 6 weeks before using. Garlic pickle is at its best when 7 years old. It tastes sweet, like preserves. *Nush-e Jan!*

Vegetables in Brine

4 carrots
½ small head of cauliflower
1 stalk celery
4 turnips
2 red peppers
2 pounds small pickling cucumbers
10 pearl onions
5 cloves garlic, peeled
4 sprigs fresh dill

4 sprigs coriander
4 coriander leaves
4 bay leaves
4 fresh celery leaves
1 tablespoon salt for every
    4 cups of water
½ cup vinegar

Makes 4 pints
Preparation time: 40 minutes
Storage time: 6 weeks
before using

Torshi-e makhlut-e shur

1. Wash and drain the vegetables. Clean, wash and drain the herbs.

2. Peel carrots and clean the cauliflower, celery, turnips and red peppers. Cut into small (½ inch) pieces. Leave cucumbers, onions, and garlic whole. Combine these vegetables in a large bowl.

3. Sterilize canning jars in boiling water. Drain and dry thoroughly.

4. Fill each jar almost to the top with alternating layers of herbs and the vegetables.

5. Bring 2 tablespoons salt, 8 cups water, and ½ cup vinegar to a boil and fill each jar within ½ inch of the top with this hot liquid; seal jars immediately.

6. Store the jars for at least 6 weeks in a cool, dark place before using. *Nush-e Jan!*

Musir Pickle

**1 pound dried Persian shallots (*musir*)
   or 4 pounds fresh
4 cups vinegar
1 tablespoon salt**

*Makes 1 pint
Preparation and cooking time: 1
hour plus 24 hours' soaking time
Storage time: 4 weeks
before using*

ترشی موسیر

Torshi-e musir

1. Place *musir* in a saucepan and cover with vinegar. Bring to a boil and simmer over medium heat for 25 minutes or until tender. Add more vinegar if necessary.

2. Drain the *musir,* pat dry and chop.

3. Place the *musir* in a pot and pour in enough vinegar so that they are covered. Bring to a boil. Remove from heat and let cool.

4. Sterilize canning jars in boiling water. Drain and dry thoroughly. Fill each jar almost to the top with *musir*. Sprinkle the surface with salt and fill the jar to within ½ inch of the top with the rest of the vinegar. Seal the jars.

5. Store the jars in a cool, dark place for at least 4 weeks. *Nush-e jan!*

Note: If using fresh *musir*, wash and peel them and cook in vinegar. Drain, chop, and cover.

Sumac and Date Pickle

1 pound tamarind
1 pound sumac berries or powder
1 cup lime juice
1 clove garlic, peeled and crushed
1 tablespoon salt
2 tablespoons Persian allspice for
   pickle (*advieh-ye torshi*),
   page 377
2 pounds pitted dates

Makes 1 pint
Preparation and cooking
time: 2 hours
Storage time: 10 days
before using

تُرشی سماق وخرما

Torshi-e somaq o khorma

1. Prepare the tamarind by placing it in 4 cups water. Boil for 15 to 20 minutes over medium heat. Drain in a colander set over a bowl and press with the back of a spoon to keep the liquid and remove the seeds and pod.

2. In a saucepan, bring the sumac berries to a boil in 4 cups of water, reduce heat ad simmer over medium heat for 35 minutes. Drain through a strainer set over a bowl and keep the sumac water.

3. In a large laminated pot, place sumac water, tamarind juice, lime juice and garlic. Bring to a boil, reduce heat and cook for 15 minutes over low heat.

4. Remove from heat, add salt and Persian allspice, mix well and let cool. Adjust seasoning to taste.

5. Sterilize a large jar in boiling water; drain and dry thoroughly.

6. Fill jar nearly to the top with dates and cover with the sumac-tamarind-lime juice mixture up to ½ inch from the top. Sprinkle the top with a bit of salt.

7. Seal the jar. Keep in a cool, dark place.

8. Store the jar for at least 10 days before using. *Nush-e Jan!*

Sumac is made from the ground
berries of the sumac shrub.

Eggplant Pickle

20 small pickling eggplants (Italian)
1¼ quarts wine vinegar
2 tablespoons salt
2 cups chopped fresh mint
1 cup chopped fresh coriander or
    parsley
½ pound or 3 bulbs of garlic, sepa-
    rated into cloves, peeled, and
    finely chopped

Makes 2 pints
Preparation and cooking
time: 40 minutes
Storage time: 40 days
before using

Bademjan torshi

1. Wash the eggplants and remove the stems. Make a lengthwise slit on one side of each eggplant.

2. Place the eggplants in a laminated pot, cover with vinegar, bring to a boil and simmer over medium heat for 20 minutes, or until tender.

3. Drain the eggplant and let stand for a few hours until completely dry. In a saucepan, bring to a boil 2 tablespoons salt and 1 quart vinegar.

4. Mix 1 tablespoon salt, herbs, and garlic together. Stuff each of the eggplants with the herb mixture and press shut.

5. Sterilize the canning jars in boiling water. Drain and dry thoroughly. Fill them to within ½ inch of the top with stuffed eggplants. Cover with the salted vinegar. Seal the jars.

6. Store the jars in a cool, dark place for at least 40 days before using. *Nush-e Jan!*

Note: Autumn eggplants make excellent pickles.

جینج وآرد برنج پنڈالو وآرد برنج تیل رایی آرد جارولی

آرد نخود و جارولی منك وآرد بادام خرما وآرد برنج تمر

هندی وشكر تری وبرنج پویی وآرد برنج سونف

وآرد برنج

كشنین

قرنفل

مشك

پترج

ج سونف سوخته درتیل تیل درمیهی سوخته تیل زیره

تیل درهنك سوخته الایچی روغن كردگان وبرنج

From the Ni'matnameh, circa 1500

264

PRESERVES

Quince tree, circa 1200

Preserves

Persian preserve recipes are special because they combine fruit, flower, and spice to a perfect sweetness. Besides being eaten with bread and butter, which is most often the case, these preserves are good with yogurt, to sweeten tea, or to eat on their own as a dessert.

Golden Rules for Cooking Preserves

1. Use good-quality fruit at the peak of the season.

2. Fruit should not be overripe, and should have no bruises or blemishes.

3. For every 2 cups prepared fruit, you will need 1½ cups sugar.

4. Always store your preserves in a cool, dark place.

Golden-Plum Preserves

2 pounds golden plums
4 cups brown sugar
1 cup water
2 tablespoons lime juice
1 teaspoon ground cardamom or
    ¼ cup rose water (optional)

Makes 4 half-pint jars
Preparation time: 15 minutes
plus overnight macerating
Cooking time: 45 minutes

Moraba-ye alu zard

1. Do not remove stems from the plums; wash and peel them. (To peel plums more quickly, blanch them first for 1 minute in boiling water—the skin will come off easily.)

2. Place sugar and plums in a large saucepan. Macerate overnight. Remove the plums from the saucepan. Add 1 cup water. Bring to a boil. Reduce heat and let simmer over medium heat for 10 minutes.

3. Add the peeled plums and lime juice. Simmer uncovered for 30 to 35 minutes over medium heat, or until the syrup has thickened enough to coat the back of a spoon, stirring gently from time to time. Add cardamom or rose water.

4. Sterilize jelly jars in boiling water. Drain and dry thoroughly. Fill the jars with jam and seal them tightly. Store in a cool, dark place. *Nush-e Jan!*

Sour-Cherry Preserves

2 pounds pitted sour cherries
5 cups sugar
1 cup water
1 tablespoon lime juice
¼ teaspoon vanilla

Makes 4 half-pint jars
Preparation time: 1 hour plus
overnight macerating
Cooking time: 50 minutes

Moraba-ye albalu

1. Wash cherries and remove stems and pits. Place the cherries and sugar in large laminated pot and macerate overnight.

2. Add the water and the lime juice to the pot of cherries and bring to a boil over high heat. Skim the foam as it forms. Reduce heat and simmer for about 35 minutes over medium heat. Gently stir occasionally, to prevent burning, until the syrup has thickened. Add the vanilla. Remove from heat. If the syrup is still too thin at the end of the cooking time, remove the cherries and boil the syrup for a few minutes longer to thicken. Add cherries back to reduced syrup.

3. Sterilize jelly jars in boiling water. Drain and dry thoroughly. Fill the jars with hot preserves and seal them. Store in a cool, dark place. *Nush-e Jan!*

Note: If using sour cherries in light syrup, drain the cherries first. Use ⅓ cup sugar for every jar (one pound) of cherries. Cook for 35 minutes over medium to high heat.

Quince Preserves

2 pounds quince (3 medium size quince)
1½ cups water
4 cups sugar
¼ teaspoon vanilla extract or 1 cinnamon stick
4 tablespoons fresh lime juice

Makes 4 half-pint jars
Preparation time: 25 minutes
Cooking time: 2 hours 30 minutes

Moraba-ye beh

1. Quarter the quinces and remove the cores. Slice the quarters into wedges. Place in a container full of cold water and a splash of vinegar to prevent the quince from turning black. Wash and drain.

2. Place quince wedges and 1½ cups water in a pot. Bring to a boil over high heat, then reduce the heat, cover and let simmer over low heat for about 15 minutes. Add the sugar and the vanilla extract or cinnamon stick. Place a clean dish towel or 2 layers of paper towels over the pot and cover firmly with lid. Let simmer over low heat for 1 hour.

3. Add lime juice. Cover and simmer for 1¼–1½ hours more over low heat, stirring gently from time to time, until the syrup has thickened and the quince has turned red. Remove from heat and cool.

4. Sterilize jelly jars in boiling water and drain and let dry. Fill the jars with hot preserves and seal them. Store in a cool, dark place. *Nush-e Jan!*

Fig Preserves

2 pounds firm seedless fresh
    green figs
4 cups sugar
2 cups water
1 tablespoon lime juice
½ teaspoon ground cardamom or
    cinnamon

Makes 4 half-pint jars
Preparation time: 5 minutes plus
overnight macerating
Cooking time: 45 minutes

Moraba-ye anjir

1. Wash the figs.

2. Place the figs and sugar in a laminated pot. Cover and macerate overnight.

3. Add the water and lime juice to the pot, bring to a boil, and let simmer for about 30 minutes over medium heat, or until syrup has thickened enough to coat the back of a spoon. Add cardamom or cinnamon and remove the pan from the heat.

4. Sterilize jelly jars in boiling water; drain and dry. Fill the jars with hot preserves and seal them. Store in a cool, dark place. *Nush-e Jan!*

Carrot Preserves

2 pounds carrots
½ cup slivered orange peel
5 cups sugar
1½ cups water
½ cup fresh lime juice
½ teaspoon ground cardamom or
¼ cup rose water
½ cup slivered pistachios

Makes 4 half-pint jars
Preparation time: 15 minutes
Cooking time: 1 hour

Moraba-ye havij

1. Scrape, wash, drain, and sliver carrots; wash and drain.

2. Place the slivered orange peel in a saucepan with water. Boil for 10 minutes. Drain.

3. Combine the sugar, 1½ cups of water, orange peel, and carrots in a heavy saucepan. Bring to a boil over high heat, add the lime juice and cardamom or rose water. Reduce the heat and simmer for 35 minutes over medium heat, or until the syrup has thickened. Add pistachios. Remove the pot from the heat.

4. Sterilize jelly jars in boiling water and dry them. Fill the jars with the hot preserves and seal them. Store in a cool, dark place. *Nush-e Jan!*

Rose-Petal Preserves

1 pound fresh rose petals or
   3 oz. (100g) dried rose petals
2½ cups sugar
1½ cups water
1 cup slivered pistachios, shelled
¼ teaspoon lime juice
2 tablespoons rose water (if using
   dried rose petals)

Makes 2 half-pint jars
Preparation time: 35 minutes
Cooking time: 30 minutes

*Moraba-ye gol-e
Mohammadi*

1. Select fresh pink rose petals. Cut off the white ends of the petals and wash carefully. Place rose petals in a saucepan and cover with cool water. Let stand for 15 minutes. Drain and let dry. If using dried rose petals, place rose petals in a steamer and steam for 10 minutes. Pat dry. Toast the rose petals in a skillet for a few minutes over low heat, stirring constantly.

2. Place the sugar and the water in a laminated pot. Bring to a boil, reduce the heat, and let simmer for 20 minutes over medium heat, or until the syrup has thickened. Add the lime juice and rose petals. Mix well, and then add the slivered pistachios and rose water and simmer for 10 minutes. Remove the pot from the heat.

3. Sterilize jelly jars in boiling water; drain and dry. Fill the jars with the hot preserves and seal them. Store in a cool, dark place. *Nush-e Jan!*

Variation: You may boil the rose petals in water, then add sugar and cook over high heat for 20 minutes.

Orange Blossom Preserves

1 pound fresh orange blossoms or 3
    oz. (100g) dried orange blossoms
¼ cup pickling lime
2 cups sugar
1½ cups water
2 tablespoons fresh lime juice

Makes 1 half-pint jar
Preparation time: 35 minutes
plus 1 day's marination
Cooking time: 45 minutes

مربای بهار نارنج

Moraba-ye bahar narenj

1. Carefully wash the orange blossoms, separate the petals, and soak in a bowl of cold water. Set in refrigerator for a day, changing the water several times (to remove bitterness).

2. Place the pickling lime in 4 cups of water to dissolve. Let it stand for one hour so that the chalk settles to the bottom.

3. Place the orange blossom petals in a container and pour in the lime mixture carefully so that the sediment does not mix. Let stand for 1 hour, then drain and rinse.

4. Bring 3 cups of water to a boil in a laminated pan over high heat. Add the blossoms, reduce heat and simmer for 15 minutes; drain.

5. Place the blossoms in a container, cover with cold water, and then drain.

6. In a heavy saucepan bring the sugar and 1½ cups water to a boil, then reduce heat and simmer for 15 to 20 minutes over medium heat. Add orange blossom petals, and lime juice and simmer 15 minutes longer until the syrup has thickened enough to coat the back of a spoon. Remove the pan from the heat.

7. Sterilize jelly jars in boiling water; drain and dry. Fill the jars with the hot preserves and seal them. Store in a cool, dark place. *Nush-e Jan!*

Note: Pickling lime, or slaked lime, is labeled calcium hydroxide, U.S.P. It is available both in the grocery store and at the drugstore. It is used to make fruits crisp.

Orange blossoms may be special ordered through food specialty stores.

Plum-Paste Rolls (Fruit Roll-ups)

6 pounds ripe greengage plums
⅓ cup water
½ teaspoon salt

Preparation time: 10 minutes
Cooking time: 45 minutes
Drying time: 4 to 5 days

Lavashak

1. Wash plums and place in a large pot with the water. Cook over medium heat for 30 to 45 minutes, or until the flesh falls away from the pit. Stir occasionally to prevent the flesh from sticking to the bottom.

2. Transfer the fruit to a colander placed over a bowl. Press all the juice and flesh through with a masher; only the pits and skin will remain in the colander. The pulp should be smooth. Add salt and mix well.

3. Pour ¼-inch-thick layers into several cookie sheets lined with plastic wrap. Set out to dry in direct sunlight for 4 to 5 days. (If you use a dehydrator, the process of drying is reduced to few hours).

4. Roll up the fruit in the plastic wrap and store in the refrigerator. *Nush-e Jan!*

Note: Plum-paste rolls, *lavashak*, the original fruit roll-up, are a special treat that many Iranian children prefer to chocolate. This fruit paste can be prepared with many different fruits, such as apricots, berries, cherries, and any other kind of plum. It is particularly good, however, when made with greengage golden plums.

Variation: Puree the pitted fruit in a food processor. Add water and salt. Bring to a boil. Pass through a meshed colander over a bowl (the pulp should be smooth). Let it cool. Spread the puree as in Step 3.

Whole Apple Preserves

Makes 1 pint jar
Preparation time: 15 minutes
Cooking time: 45 minutes

مربای سیب

Moraba-ye sib

2 pounds Lady Apple apples with
   stems
1 cup water
3 cups sugar

½ teaspoon ground cardamom or
   ¼ cup rose water
¼ cup fresh lime juice

1. Wash and peel the apples (keep them whole and do not remove the stems), then core the apple from the bottom and place into a large container of water with 2 tablespoons vinegar for 2 minutes. Drain.

2. Place the apples in a laminated pot. Cover with 1 cup water. Bring to a boil, then reduce the heat. Simmer over medium heat for about 5 minutes, until the apples are tender.

3. With a skimmer, remove the apples from the pan.

4. Add the sugar to the pan and bring to a boil. Simmer for 5 minutes over low heat.

5. Return the apples to the pan, add cardamom or rose water and lime juice. Cook for 35 minutes over medium heat, or until the syrup has thickened enough to coat the back of a spoon. Stir gently from time to time. Remove the pan from the heat.

6. Sterilize jelly jars in boiling water; drain and dry. Fill the jars with hot preserves and seal them. Store in a cool, dark place. *Nush-e Jan!*

Watermelon Rind Preserves

Makes 1 pint jar
Preparation time: 20 minutes
Cooking time: 1 hour 45 minutes

Moraba-ye hendevaneh

2 cups watermelon rinds, cut into
   1-inch pieces
1 cup water
1½ cups sugar
1 tablespoon lime juice
5 cardamom pods, peeled

1. Place the watermelon rinds in a heavy pan and cover with water. Bring to a boil, reduce heat and simmer over low heat for 1¼ hours. Drain and set aside the rinds.

2. In the same pan, combine 1 cup water and 1½ cups sugar and bring to a boil.

3. Add the cardamom, watermelon rind, and lime juice to the pan. Boil for 10–15 minutes, then cover and remove from heat. Allow to set overnight.

4. The next day, reheat the pan and simmer over medium heat for 20 minutes or until the syrup has thickened.

5. Sterilize jelly jars in boiling water; drain and dry. Fill the jars with hot preserves and seal them. Store in a cool, dark place. *Nush-e Jan!*

Seville-Orange Preserves

6 Seville oranges
1 tablespoon Seville orange seeds
1 cup water
10 cups sugar

Makes 1 pint jar
Preparation time: 30 minutes
Cooking time: 1 hour

مربای نارنج

Moraba-ye narenj

1. Scrub orange skins thoroughly so that they are smooth. Make sure that any black spots on the skin are removed.

2. Quarter each orange without entirely separating it—leave about ¼ inch intact at the bottom. Remove the seeds.

3. Place 1 tablespoon orange seeds in a cheesecloth, tying the corners so that the seeds do not fall out. Soak in 1 cup water for 1 hour.

4. Bring 8 cups water to a boil over high heat. Place the oranges in the boiling water; boil for 5 to 10 minutes. Drain. Repeat the process. This step is essential as it removes all traces of bitterness.

5. Pour 1 cup water in a large laminated pot and arrange the oranges in the pot side by side.

6. Sprinkle the sugar all over the oranges.

7. Pour the water used to soak the seeds over the oranges. Bring to boil over high heat, then reduce the heat. Simmer for about 30 minutes until the syrup has thickened and become glossy.

8. Remove the oranges from the pot. If necessary, let the syrup cook longer to thicken. Remove from heat.

9. Sterilize jars in boiling water; drain and dry thoroughly. Fill jars with the hot oranges; ladle in the syrup.

10. Seal jars tightly. Store in a cool, dark place. *Nush-e Jan!*

Seville Orange Peel Jam

9 Seville oranges or 9 oranges and
   juice of five limes

1½ cups sugar
10 cardamom pods, peeled

Makes 1 pint jar
Preparation time: 30 minutes
Cooking time: 35 minutes

Moraba-ye khalal-e pust-e narenj

1. Wash and peel oranges with peeler. Place peels in a saucepan, cover with cold water, boil for 10 minutes and drain and rinse with cold water.

2. Squeeze the oranges. 9 oranges should produce about 3 cups juice.

3. Bring 3 cups orange juice and 1½ cups sugar to a boil and add the cardamom pods and orange peel. Simmer over low heat for 25 minutes until the mixture is transparent.

4. Fill sterilized jar with hot preserves. Seal tightly and store in a cool, dark place. *Nush-e Jan!*

Bergamot Preserves

2 large bergamots
2 cups pickling lime
4 cups water
6 pounds sugar
¼ teaspoon citric acid
½ teaspoon cardamom pods, peeled,
    or 2 tablespoons rose water

Makes 1 pint jar
Preparation time: 30 minutes
plus 48 hours' standing time
Cooking time: 1 hour 30 minutes

مربای بادرنگ

Moraba-ye baderang

1. Scrub the bergamots so that they are thoroughly clean and smooth.

2. Cut each bergamot into 4 lengthwise slices. Remove the seeds, but leave the skins on.

3. Cut the sliced bergamot into 4-inch pieces.

4. Place the bergamot pieces in a container, cover with cold water and set in the refrigerator for a day. Change the water several times. Drain.

5. Place pickling lime in a container and dissolve in 4 cups cold water. Let this stand for 1 hour so that the sediment settles to the bottom.

6. Place bergamot in a container and pour in the lime water carefully so that the sediment does not mix. Let stand for 1 hour.

7. Remove bergamot from lime water. Drain and rinse. Cover with cold water and place in refrigerator again for a day, changing the water several times. Drain.

8. Place bergamot in a pot and cover with cold water. Bring to a boil over high heat for 30 minutes. Drain. Pat dry with a paper towel.

9. Place 4 cups water, sugar, and citric acid in a laminated pot. Bring to a boil. Place bergamot in this syrup and simmer over low heat, uncovered, for about 30 minutes.

10. Remove the pot from heat and let stand uncovered for about 24 hours. Remove fruit from the pot. Add cardamom or rose water to the pot and boil for another 10 minutes over medium heat until syrup has thickened enough to coat the back of a spoon. Return fruit to the pot.

11. Remove the preserves from the heat. Place hot preserves in a sterilized jar.

12. Seal the jar. Store in a cool, dark place.

Note: *Balang is a fruit similar to baderang. Follow the same instructions to prepare the preserves. If you use balangs, peel them and cut the fruit into small pieces.*

Bergamots are available in specialty food sections of gourmet grocery stores. Pickling lime, or slaked lime, is labeled calcium hydroxide, U.S.P. It is available both in the grocery store and the drugstore. It is used to make fruit crisp.

PASTRIES AND BREADS

Poetic Discourse Between Malek-o Shoara Bahar and Iraj Mirza, 1928
A Friendly Complaint

ملکا با تو دگر دوستیم ما نشود بعد لگر شده ست، اباصلا نشود

دلم از طیب برپیب تو سخت گرفت تا کشایی بکنم از تو دلم وا نشود

اسم نان بردم و گفتی که نان کلان هیچ نانی که خورد حضرت دلدار نشود

نان نمی گویم خوب ست دلی بربم نیست همه خواهیم که بهتر شود اما نشود

ای که بودی دو سه ماه پیش در این ملک خراب نان نبود آنچه تو می خوردی حاش نشود

نان از این بهتر و خوبی تو شیرین تر نان سنگک که دلت سنگک و حلوا نشود

بس کن این سخن از نان در زبان کردی کار این ملک دنده یا شود یا نشود

My friendship with you, Malek, is possible no longer.
If it thrives later, so be it! But now its way is barred.
Your good-natured chariness has pained my heart,
Which, till I voice this complaint, will find no ease.
I happened to mention "bread," provoking your response:
"What others eat hardly compares to His Grace's bread."
The bread's not extraordinary, true, but neither is it bad;
We all hope it were better, but hoping won't make it so.
O you who sojourned in this wasteland two months ago or three!
It wasn't bread you ate then, that can't be denied.
What! Do you seek bread any crisper, sweeter, or finer than this?
Do you think sangak can turn into cotton candy or halva?

Iraj Mirza

Pastries and Breads

Iranian pastries were refined during the foodie Qajar era of the nineteenth century. Although these pastries are very delicate, the recipes that follow are simple and well worth trying. As for the bread, perhaps only the *parisienne baguette* can compete with *nan-e barbari*.

Detail of a 16th century bakery by Dust Mohammad

Rice Cookies

**1 egg yolk
1 cup confectioners' sugar
1 cup unsalted butter, melted
2 cups rice flour
1½ teaspoons cardamom powder
1 tablespoon poppy seeds**

*Makes 36 pieces
Preparation time: 30 minutes
plus 2 to 4 hours' resting time
Cooking time: 15 to 20 minutes*

Nan-e berenji

1. In a mixing bowl, beat the egg yolk with the sugar and the butter until creamy.

2. Add rice flour and cardamom to the mixture to produce a dough that does not stick to your hands. Place the dough in a plastic bag and leave in the refrigerator for 2 to 4 hours.

3. Remove the dough from the refrigerator. Knead well with your hands for 10 to 15 minutes.

4. Preheat the oven to 350°F. Grease a cookie sheet and line it with wax paper.

5. Take a spoonful of dough, roll it into a ball the size of a hazelnut, flatten slightly, and place on the cookie sheet. Repeat, leaving 2½ inches between each ball. With a fork or the open end of a thimble, draw geometric patterns on the cookies and sprinkle with poppy seeds.

6. Place the cookie sheet in the center of the preheated oven and bake the cookies 15 to 20 minutes. Keep in mind that the cookies should be white when they are done.

7. Remove cookies from the oven and allow to cool. These cookies crumble very easily; remove them carefully from the wax paper.

8. Arrange the cookies in a pyramid on a footed cake dish.

Note: Rice flour is available from Iranian specialty stores.

Chick-Pea Cookies

1 cup clarified unsalted butter or margarine
1 cup confectioners' sugar
2 teaspoons ground cardamom
3 cups roasted chick-pea flour
2 tablespoons unsalted slivered pistachios for garnish

Makes 36 pieces
Preparation time: 30 minutes
Cooking time: 10 to 15 minutes

Nan-e nokhodchi

1. For clarified butter, bring butter to a boil over very low heat. Simmer for 10 minutes. Remove foam as it rises, then remove from heat and let it stand until milk solid settles. Decant the clear yellow liquid from the top.

2. In a mixing bowl, combine the clarified butter, sugar, cardamom and flour, stirring constantly to produce a dough. Knead well with your hands, about 15 minutes, until the dough no longer sticks to your hands. Cover and set aside for 2 hours at room temperature.

3. Preheat the oven to 300°F. Roll the dough out to a ¼-inch thickness on a plate and cut out cookies with a tiny cloverleaf cookie cutter. Decorate each cookie with slivered pistachios. Line a greased cookie sheet with wax paper and place the cookies on the sheet, leaving 1 inch between pieces to allow them to spread.

4. Place the cookie sheet in the center of the oven and bake the cookies 10 to 15 minutes, until slightly golden. Remove the cookies from the oven and cool. Carefully lift cookies off the wax paper. These cookies crumble very easily.

5. Arrange the cookies in a pyramid on a platter. *Nush-e Jan!*

Note: Roasted chick-pea flour is available in Iranian specialty stores, health-food stores, and sometimes on the gourmet shelf of the supermarket.

Baklava

Makes 1 full sheet
Preparation time: 35 minutes
plus 1 hour for dough to rise and
24 hours to settle before serving
Cooking time: 35 minutes

Baqlava

Syrup
2½ cups sugar
1½ cups water
½ cup rose water

Filling
2 pounds of blanched almonds,
　ground
2 cups sugar
2 tablespoons ground cardamom

Dough
¼ cup milk
½ cup unsalted butter, melted
1 tablespoon syrup (prepared)
¼ cup rose water
1 egg
2 cups sifted all-purpose flour
½ cup corn oil or melted butter
　for baking
2 tablespoons chopped or ground
　pistachios for garnish

1. Prepare the syrup by combining the sugar and water in a saucepan. Bring to a boil, add the rose water, and set aside.

2. For the filling, finely grind the almonds, sugar, and cardamom in a food processor. Set aside.

3. For the dough, combine the milk, melted butter, syrup, rose water, and egg in a mixing bowl or dough maker. Add the flour and mix well for 5 to 10 minutes to form a dough that does not stick to your hands. Divide the dough into 2 balls of equal size and place in a bowl. Cover with a clean towel and let rise for ½ hour at room temperature.

4. When the dough has risen, grease a 17-by-11-by-1-inch sheet with ¼ cup oil and preheat the oven to 350°F.

5. Prepare a large, wide area for rolling out the dough. Cover the surface with a dusting of flour. Remove 1 ball of dough from bowl and roll out into a very thin rectangular layer with a thin wooden rolling pin (the rolled dough should be thinner than a pie crust). Roll dough from the center to the outside edge in all directions, giving it a quarter turn occasionally for an even thickness. The finished dough should be larger than the cookie sheet.

6. Roll the thin layer of dough around the wooden rolling pin. Place it on the greased cookie sheet and unroll the dough until it covers the whole cookie sheet. Do not cut off the excess dough; let the dough hang over the edge of the cookie sheet, 1 inch on all sides.

7. Evenly sprinkle all the almond-filling mixture on top of the dough. Spread and smooth the mixture on the dough with your hand.

8. Roll the second ball of dough out into a very thin rectangular layer as in step 5. Roll the layer around the rolling pin, place on top of the filling mixture in the cookie sheet, and unroll the dough to cover the mixture, allowing it to hang over all sides like the bottom layer. Press down on the dough evenly with your hands all over the surface of the dough.

9. Trace an outline of 1-inch diamond shapes on top of the baklava with a sharp knife. Guide the knife in a straight line, assuring that each piece will be of equal size. (See photos on pages 312–314.)

10. Fold and roll the overhanging dough from the top layer under the dough from the bottom layer. Press together and pinch the top and bottom edges together to seal like a pie, forming a rim around the edge of the cookie sheet.

11. Hold down the dough with one hand, pressing down with your palm while cutting the dough into diamond shapes with a sharp knife. With a brush, paint the dough with ¼ cup oil and place the baking pan in the middle of the pre-heated oven.

12. Bake for 20 to 35 minutes (depending on your oven). When the baklava is pink, remove it from the oven and pour half of the syrup all over the top.

13. Decorate the baklava with chopped or ground pistachio nuts. Cover the baklava tightly with aluminum foil and let stand for 24 hours until it settles.

14. Using a sharp knife, lift the diamond pieces out of the baking pan and carefully arrange on a serving dish.

15. Keep this pastry covered, in the refrigerator or freezer. *Nush-e Jan!*

Note: This sweet flaky pastry, filled with chopped nuts and topped with sugar syrup, has come to be known and enjoyed worldwide. The origins of the word are probably Persian, either from *pokhtan*, meaning cooking or from *balg*, meaning leaf. Persian *baqlava* uses a combination of chopped almonds and pistachios spiced with cardamom and a rose-water-scented syrup. It is a subtle, delicate blend of flavors and quite different from the *baqlava* of other Middle Eastern countries. While many Persians still make the thin dough at home, frozen filo pastry, which is ready to use, could be an acceptable alternative.

The dough can be divided into 3 layers with one layer of pistachios and one layer of almonds. You can also substitute honey for the syrup.

A thin, long dough roller or tool handle available at hardware stores makes a perfect rolling pin.

Walnut Cookies

5 egg yolks
¾ cup confectioners' sugar
¼ teaspoon vanilla extract
2 cups chopped walnuts
2 tablespoons ground pistachios
    for decoration

Makes 20 pieces
Preparation time: 30 minutes
Cooking time: 15 to 20 minutes

Nan-e gerdui

1. In a mixing bowl, beat egg yolks until creamy. Add the confectioners' sugar, vanilla, and walnuts. Beat thoroughly for a few minutes with a wooden spoon.

2. Preheat oven to 300°F. Grease a cookie sheet. Drop batter by the teaspoonful on the sheet, leaving about 2½ inches between cookies. Decorate each one with ground pistachios.

3. Bake 15 to 20 minutes in the center of the oven. Remove the cookies from the oven and cool. Lift the cookies off the sheet.

4. Arrange the cookies on a serving dish. *Nush-e Jan!*

Almond Cookies

Makes 20 pieces
Preparation time: 40 minutes
Cooking time: 10 to 15 minutes

Nan-e badami

Dough #1
1 pound blanched almonds
5 egg whites
1½ cups confectioners' sugar
½ teaspoon ground cardamom or
  2 tablespoons rose water
2 tablespoons unsalted slivered
  pistachios or toasted almond
  slices for decoration

Dough #2 (*Haji-badam*)*
1 pound blanched almonds, ground
2½ cups sugar
1 teaspoon baking soda
1 tablespoon ground cardamom
2 tablespoons rose water
5 egg yolks

1. In a food processor, grind almonds to produce almond powder.

2. In a mixing bowl, beat the egg whites until foamy. Gently mix in sugar, almond powder, and cardamom. Mix well for a second until a dough is formed.

3. Preheat oven to 350°F. Grease a cookie sheet.

4. Scoop out some of the dough with a teaspoon and roll it into a small ball the size of a hazelnut. Place it on the cookie sheet. Continue, leaving 2½ inches between each piece for expansion. Decorate each piece with a few slivered pistachios or toasted almond slices.

5. Place the cookie sheet in the center of the oven and bake for about 10 to 15 minutes, until the cookies are golden.

6. Remove the cookies from the oven and allow to cool. Remove the cookies from the cookie sheet. Keep them in a covered container.

7. When ready to serve, arrange the cookies in a pyramid on a footed cake dish. *Nush-e Jan!*

***Variation:** For dough #2, place all the ingredients in a mixing bowl. Mix well for a second until a dough forms. Continue at step 4 above, then bake the cookies in a preheated 250°F oven for 15 minutes. Reduce heat to 200°F, then bake for 5 minutes longer.

Yazdi Cupcakes

Makes 8 servings
Preparation time: 10 minutes
Cooking time: 35 minutes

کیک یزدی

Cake-e yazdi

3 eggs
1 cup sugar
1 cup unsalted butter, melted,
   or oil
1 cup yogurt
1 teaspoon baking powder and ½
   teaspoon baking soda
1 teaspoon ground cardamom
1 tablespoon rose water
2 cups sifted all-purpose flour
2 tablespoons ground pistachios
   for decoration

1. Preheat oven to 350°F.

2. Blend eggs and sugar in a stainless bowl set over simmering water and beat for 5 minutes until creamy.

3. Remove the bowl from the water and transfer the eggs into a mixing bowl. Beat the eggs at high speed until the mixture has more volume and cools.

4. Add melted butter, yogurt, baking powder, baking soda, cardamom, rose water, and flour; continue beating for another five minutes until a batter is formed.

5. Pour the batter into individual cupcake molds, greased or lined with papers.

6. Decorate each cupcake with the ground pistachios.

7. Place the cupcake pan in the center of the oven and bake for 20 to 35 minutes, or until golden.

8. Remove the cupcakes from the oven and allow to cool. Remove the cupcakes from the pan and cover them tightly with aluminum foil.

9. When ready to serve, arrange the cupcakes in a pyramid on a footed cake dish. *Nush-e Jan!*

Elephant Ears

Dough #1
3 eggs
¼ cup yogurt
¼ cup rose water
1 cup cornstarch
¼ teaspoon baking powder
2 cups sifted all-purpose flour
4 cups oil for frying

Dough #2
2 egg yolks
2 tablespoons oil
1–1½ cups all-purpose flour

Garnish
1 cup confectioners' sugar
1 teaspoon ground cardamom
2 tablespoons ground pistachios

Makes 25 pieces
Preparation time: 45 minutes
plus 3 hours for the dough to rise
Cooking time: 30 minutes

Gush-e fil

1. In a mixing bowl, beat the eggs until creamy. Add yogurt, rose water, cornstarch, and baking powder, and slowly blend in flour, stirring constantly. Knead well to produce a dough that does not stick to your hands. Cover the bowl with a clean towel or wrap the dough in plastic wrap and put it in the refrigerator for 3 hours.

2. For the garnish, mix the confectioners' sugar with cardamom and set aside.

3. Using a rolling pin, roll out the dough on a cool pastry board until paper thin. Cut the rolled dough into circles 3 inches in diameter, using a cookie cutter or the rim of a glass. Gather each circle around the middle with your fingers and pinch the center to make it hold its shape like a bow.

4. Heat the oil in a deep saucepan or deep-fat fryer over medium heat to 375°F.

5. To test the temperature of oil, drop a scrap of unshaped dough into the hot oil: if the dough rises to the top, the oil is hot enough.

6. Drop the bows into the hot oil and fry until lightly golden—about 30 seconds on each side.

7. Drain bows in a colander or on paper towels. When they are cool, sprinkle with the confectioners' sugar mixture. Garnish with ground pistachios.
Nush-e Jan!

Variation: For dough #2, place all the ingredients in a mixing bowl. Create a dough that does not stick to your hands, adding more flour if necessary. Continue with step 3.

Almond Delight

Makes 20 pieces
Preparation time: 1 hour plus 3 hours for dough to rise
Cooking time: 30 minutes

Qottab

Dough
½ cup unsalted butter, melted
¾ cup yogurt
2 cups sifted all-purpose flour

Filling
1 cup unsalted ground almonds or walnuts
½ cup sugar
½ teaspoon ground cardamom

4 cups oil for frying
½ cup confectioners' sugar for dusting
½ cup unsalted pistachios for decoration

1. For the dough, combine melted butter and yogurt in a food processor or mixing bowl. Slowly blend in flour, stirring constantly. Knead well to produce a dough that does not stick to your hands. Place the dough in a plastic bag and refrigerate for 3 hours.

2. Meanwhile, prepare the filling by mixing ground almonds and sugar together, then toasting this mixture in a skillet over medium heat for 10 minutes. Add cardamom, mix well, and set aside to cool.

3. On a cool floured pastry board, roll the dough out very thin with a rolling pin. Cut the dough into small circles, using the open end of a glass dipped in flour or a floured cookie cutter. Fill each circle with ½ teaspoon of almond mixture. Fold each circle to a crescent shape and, using a fork, press the dough around the filling to seal it.

4. Heat the oil in a deep saucepan or deep-fat fryer to 375°F.

5. To test the temperature of the oil, drop a scrap of unshaped dough into the hot oil: if the dough rises to the top the oil is ready for frying the dough.

6. Carefully slip the crescent shapes one by one into the hot oil. Do not crowd. Fry on both sides until golden brown, about 3 to 5 minutes over medium heat.

7. Drain pastries in a colander or on paper towels. When they cool, roll them in confectioners' sugar and sprinkle with pistachios.

8. Arrange the pastries in a pyramid on a serving platter and serve immediately, or cover and refrigerate. *Nush-e Jan!*

Sweet Fritters

Makes 10 pieces
Preparation time: 1 hour
Cooking time: 20 minutes

زولبیا

Zulbia

Ladyfingers (*Bamieh*)—In a saucepan, bring 1 cup water and ½ cup butter or oil to a boil. Reduce heat, blend in 1 cup flour, and mix well until smooth. Remove from heat and allow to cool. Add 3 eggs, one at a time, mixing thoroughly until creamy. Heat ½ cup corn oil in a deep fat fryer. Force the dough through a snowflake design disk of a cake decorator tool; scrape from the tool with a knife, and drop into the hot oil.

Syrup
2 cups water
4 cups sugar
1 tablespoon honey
2 tablespoons lime juice
¼ cup rose water

Batter #1
1 package or 1 tablespoon dry yeast
1 cup lukewarm water
1 cup sifted all-purpose flour
1 teaspoon fresh lime juice

Batter #2*
1½ cups cornstarch
1½ cups yogurt
1½ teaspoons baking powder

4 cups oil for frying

Zulbia is associated with the fast-breaking ceremony during the month of Ramazan.

1. To prepare batter #1, dissolve the yeast in 1 cup lukewarm water in a mixing bowl. Add flour and lime juice. Mix thoroughly until creamy and set aside for 30 to 45 minutes.

2. To make the syrup, place the water, sugar, and honey in a saucepan. Bring to a boil over high heat. Add lime juice and rose water. Reduce heat and keep warm over very low heat.

3. Fill several clean plastic squeeze bottles (like ketchup dispensers) or a disposable decorating bag with batter. Heat the oil in a deep-fat fryer to 375°F. To test the temperature of oil, drop a spoonful of the batter into the oil. If the batter rises to the top, the oil is ready for frying.

4. Hold the bottle perpendicularly over the fryer. Squeeze batter into pretzel shapes by turning clockwise directly into the oil. Fry until golden brown on all sides.

5. With a skimmer or slotted spoon, gently remove the fritters from the oil. Dip them in the syrup, covering the entire surface.

6. Using another clean skimmer, remove the fritters from the syrup and arrange on a serving platter. (It is helpful to have two people cooking at this point: one person to place the batter into the oil and the other to remove it). *Nush-e Jan!*

Note: These pretzel-shaped fritters can be made with either yeast or cornstarch. Either way, the result is a sweet, light, fluffy fritter.

*Variation: For batter #2, mix 1½ cups cornstarch with 1½ cups yogurt. Add baking powder. Beat with an electric mixer for 5 minutes on high speed. Follow Steps 2 through 6 for cooking the batter and preparing the syrup.

Window Cookies

Makes 30 cookies
Preparation time: 10 minutes
Cooking time: 30 minutes

نان پنجره ای

Nan-e panjerehi

Batter #1
4 eggs
¾ cup sifted all-purpose flour
¾ cup corn starch
¼ cup rose water

Batter #2
5 eggs
1 tablespoon all-purpose flour
1 cup corn starch
1 cup milk
1 tablespoon rose water

4 cups oil for frying

Garnish
1 cup confectioners' sugar
1 teaspoon ground cardamom
½ cup unsalted ground pistachios
   for decoration

Note: *It is important that the rosette iron (mold) be neither too hot nor too cold.*

1. For the garnish, combine the confectioners' sugar with the cardamom, mix well, and set aside.

2. In a mixing bowl, beat the eggs until creamy. Add flour, cornstarch, and rose water or milk, and beat well in order to create a smooth batter. The batter should have the consistency of pancake batter—if it is too runny, add more flour.

3. Heat 4 cups of oil in a deep saucepan or deep-fat fryer.

4. Heat a rosette iron (mold) by dipping it into the hot (375°F) oil. Shake the iron well and let the excess oil run off. Dip it immediately into the batter. It is essential to dip the mold into the batter to **just below the top edge**.

5. Plunge the batter-coated iron (mold) into the hot oil. Shake well: this will help the cookie separate from the iron and lift out easily. Repeat, and cook each cookie until golden. It is important to stir the batter frequently to maintain proper consistency. (It is helpful to have 2 people for cooking at this point: one person to place the cookies in the oil and one person to remove them.)

6. Remove the cookies from the oil with a fork. Place them on paper towels in a large tray and allow to cool. Repeat this process until all the batter is used up.

7. When the cookies have cooled, sprinkle both sides with the cardamom-flavored confectioners' sugar. Sprinkle with ground pistachios for decoration. The cookies should be crisp and golden. *Nush-e Jan!*

Note: Choose either batter #1 or batter #2 at your preference.

Honey Almonds

Makes 25 pieces
Preparation time: 15 minutes
Cooking time: 10 minutes

Sohan asal

Batter #1
1 cup sugar
3 tablespoons pure honey
4 tablespoons corn oil
1½ cups unsalted slivered almonds
½ teaspoon ground saffron
   dissolved in 2 tablespoons of rose
   water

4 tablespoons unsalted chopped
   pistachios for decoration

Batter #2
½ cup unsalted melted butter
½ teaspoon saffron dissolved in
   ½ cup rose water
⅔ cup unsalted slivered almonds
8 tablespoons sugar
3 tablespoons pure honey

4 tablespoons unsalted slivered
   pistachios for decoration

Batter #1

1. In a heavy saucepan over high heat, melt the sugar, honey, and oil for 5 minutes, stirring occasionally.

2. Add the slivered almonds to the mixture. Stir from time to time, for about 3 to 5 minutes, until the mixture is firm and golden.

3. Add the saffron-rose water mixture and cook for another 2 to 4 minutes, stirring occasionally, until the mixture is a golden brown color. Be careful: it should not be dark brown.

4. Place a bowl of ice water next to the stove. Drop a spoonful of the hot almond mixture in the water: If it hardens quickly, the mixture is ready. Reduce the heat to very low.

5. Spread a piece of wax paper on a cookie sheet. Place teaspoonfuls of the mixture on wax paper, leaving a 1-inch space between each. Immediately garnish with the chopped pistachios.

6. Allow the almonds to cool, then remove them from the paper.

7. Arrange on a serving platter. Cover with a sheet of aluminum foil to keep the honey almonds crisp or keep in an airtight container or cookie jar. *Nush-e Jan!*

Batter #2

In a heavy saucepan, place ½ cup of butter, ½ teaspoon saffron dissolved in ½ cup rose water, ⅔ cup slivered almonds, 8 tablespoons sugar, and 3 tablespoons honey. Boil over high heat for about 7 to 10 minutes. Stir occasionally with a wooden spoon until the mixture is golden brown. Proceed with step 4 in batter #1 instructions.

White Mulberries

1½ to 2½ cups ground almonds
1 teaspoon ground cardamom
1 cup confectioners' sugar
2 tablespoons rose water
1 tablespoon orange-flower water
1 cup sugar
2 tablespoons slivered pistachios

Makes 25 pieces
Preparation time: 30 minutes

Tut

1. Mix 1½ cups ground almonds, cardamom, and confectioners' sugar in a mixing bowl. Slowly blend in the rose water and orange-flower water, stirring constantly to make a soft dough. Add more ground almonds if necessary so that the dough does not stick to your hands.

2. Take small spoonfuls of dough and shape into 1-inch white mulberries. Roll each in sugar and insert a sliver of a pistachio as a stem.

3. Arrange on a serving platter and cover tightly with plastic wrap to keep them from drying out. Store in an airtight container or cookie jar. *Nush-e Jan!*

Note: Orange-flower water and rose water are available at Iranian specialty stores.

Toasted Almonds in Caramel

½ cup natural whole almonds
1 cup sugar

Makes 12 servings
Preparation time: 5 minutes
Cooking time: 40 minutes

1. Toast the almonds in a non-stick heavy frying pan over high heat for about 10 minutes. Reduce heat and add the sugar.

2. Allow the sugar to melt over low heat, about 30 minutes, or until it turns to a caramel color. Stir occasionally with a wooden spoon.

3. Remove from heat. Immediately pour the hot almond mixture through a wide strainer set over a bowl.

4. Allow the toasted almonds to cool until hardened. Remove them from the strainer and separate into individual almonds.

5. Arrange the toasted almonds on a platter and serve immediately, or keep in an airtight container. *Nush-e Jan!*

Badam-sukhteh

Barbari Bread

Makes 6 loaves
Preparation time: 40 minutes
plus 6 hours' rising time
Cooking time: 12 minutes

نان بربری

Nan-e barbari

1 package or 1 tablespoon dry yeast
3 cups warm water
1 teaspoon sugar (optional)
2 teaspoons salt
7 to 8½ cups sifted all-purpose flour
    or more
4 tablespoons oil or butter
½ cup yellow cornmeal

1 tablespoon sesame seeds
Baking stone
Baker's peel

Glaze
½ teaspoon baking soda
½ teaspoon flour

1. In a mixing bowl, dissolve the yeast in 1 cup warm water. Add the sugar and set aside for 10 minutes.

2. Add 2 cups of warm water and salt to the yeast mixture and mix well. Gradually add the flour and stir constantly. When 6 cups of flour have been added and you have a dough, add 1 tablespoon oil and knead for 15 minutes, adding the rest of the flour if necessary, until the dough is no longer sticky.

3. Pour the oil or butter into another large bowl and place the dough over it. Cover the bowl entirely with a clean damp towel and allow the dough to rise for 4 hours, without moving it, in a warm, dark place (oven or pantry).

4. Punch the air out of the dough while it is still in the bowl and flip it over. Cover with a new damp towel and allow to rise 2 more hours.

5. Place a baking stone in the lower level of the oven and preheat the oven to 500°F for at least 20 minutes.

6. To make the glaze, mix ½ teaspoon baking soda with ½ teaspoon flour. Blend in 1 tablespoon warm water, and mix well until smooth.

7. With oily hands, divide the dough into 6 balls. Place each ball on a lightly oiled surface. Use a thin oiled rolling pin to roll each ball out to about 10 inches in diameter. Place loaves on an oiled surface, cover with a towel, and leave at room temperature for 20 minutes. Dust the baker's peel with the cornmeal and transfer loaves to the baker's peel. With damp fingers, make dents on the top of each loaf, brush the glaze down the length of the dough, and sprinkle the tops with sesame seeds.

8. Immediately slide the dough onto the hot baking stone in the oven, cornmeal side down, and bake the sesame side up for 8 to 10 minutes in the oven.

9. Using a baker's peel, remove bread from oven by sliding the loaves onto a clean cutting board. Cover with a clean towel; serve hot. Otherwise, wrap in aluminum foil and save in freezer. If you are not serving the bread fresh, toast or warm it before serving. *Nush-e Jan!*

Note: Barbari bread is a flat oval or round 1 to 1½-inch thick loaf. It is at its best eaten fresh, like French bread.

Variation: For Shirmal Bread, you may replace the water with milk and add 1 tablespoon sugar to the glaze mixture.

Lavash Bread

Makes 12 small loaves
Preparation time: 40 minutes
plus 3 hours' rising time
Cooking time: 3 to 4 minutes
per loaf

نان لواش

Nan-e lavash

Dough #1
1 package or 1 tablespoon dry yeast
½ cup warm water
6 to 7 cups sifted all-purpose flour
1 teaspoon salt
½ cup unsalted butter or
   margarine, melted
2 cups milk
2 tablespoons poppy or sesame
   seeds for garnish

Dough #2*
1 package or 1 tablespoon dry yeast
2½ cups warm water
1½ teaspoons salt
1 teaspoon sugar (optional)
4 to 5 cups sifted all-purpose flour

Oil for handling the dough
Baking stone
Baker's peel

Choose either dough #1 or dough #2 according to preference.

1. In a mixing bowl, dissolve the yeast in a ½ cup warm water; add 1 tablespoon flour and 1 teaspoon salt. Allow to ferment for 10 minutes at room temperature.

2. For dough #1, add the butter and milk. Gradually add 4 cups of sifted flour, stirring constantly for 15–20 minutes to make a soft dough. Cover with a clean towel and allow to rise for 2 hours in a warm place.

3. Turn the dough onto a floured surface and knead for 15 minutes. If using dough #1, add another 2 cups of sifted flour. Cover again and leave to rise for 1 hour.

4. Place a baking stone on the lower shelf of your oven; preheat oven to 500°F.

5. Working on a floured surface, knead the dough for a few minutes by hand. Divide it into 12 balls the size of apples. Place a ball on a lightly floured surface or wooden board and use a thin rolling pin to roll it out as thin as possible, to about 10 inches in diameter. Flip the dough across the back of your hand to stretch it a little. Repeat this process for each ball of dough.

6. Lightly flour the baker's peel. Transfer the dough to the far end of the peel and sprinkle poppy or sesame seeds onto the dough. Press topping into the dough as necessary, open oven door and quickly slide dough onto the hot baking stone. Close oven door and bake the dough in the lower level for 3 to 4 minutes. Remove from the oven. Cook each loaf individually and continue until all 12 loaves have been baked. Wrap the *lavash* bread loaf in a clean towel and set aside for 10 minutes while the towel absorbs excess moisture; remove the towel and serve the bread hot. Otherwise, wrap the bread in aluminum foil or a clean cloth, or place it in a plastic bag. *Nush-e Jan!*

Note: Light and crusty *lavash* is the oldest known bread in the Middle East. It comes in various shapes—round or oval—and is about 2 feet wide. Since it keeps well for long periods of time, it is baked only once every few months, in a *tanour* or bread oven. Then it is wrapped in clean cloths and eaten as needed.

*Note: If using dough #2, proceed as with dough #1. Dissolve the yeast in the warm water, add salt and sugar and then add flour. As there is no need to prove this dough, turn it out of the bowl onto an oiled board and with oily hands, divide the dough into 6 even-sized pieces.

Stone-Baked Bread

1 package or 1 tablespoon dry yeast
2½ cups warm water
1½ teaspoons salt
3 cups sifted whole-wheat flour
1 cup sifted all-purpose white flour
4 tablespoons sesame seeds, poppy
    seeds, or nigella seeds to garnish

Oil for handling dough
Baking stone
Baker's peel

Makes 6 loaves
Preparation time: 30 minutes
plus 3 hours' rising time
Cooking time: 7 to 10 minutes for
each loaf

Nan-e sangak

1. In a mixing bowl, dissolve the yeast in ¼ cup of warm water.

2. Let stand for a few minutes. Add salt, 1½ cups warm water, and let stand for 10 minutes.

3. Gradually add all the flour and the rest of the water to the yeast mixture; mix for 20 minutes to create a dough that is smooth and elastic.

4. In another bowl pour 2 tablespoons of oil and place the dough in it. Cover the bowl with a damp towel and let the dough rise in a warm, dark place overnight.

5. Place the baking stone in the lower level of the oven.

6. Preheat the oven to 500°F for 15 minutes. Remove the dough from the bowl and knead with oiled hands for another 10 to 15 minutes.

7. On an oiled surface, divide the dough into 6 portions and, using an oiled rolling pin, flatten each piece to ½-inch thick. Lightly flour the baker's peel and transfer the dough to the far end of the peel. Perforate the top of each loaf with wet fingers and sprinkle with sesame, poppy, or nigella seeds.

8. Pull out the oven rack with the stone. Brush it with peanut oil. Place 1 loaf on the hot stone and quickly return the rack to the oven. Bake for 1 minute, then press down on the dough with the baker's peel. Cook for 3 minutes more, and then turn over and cook for 2 minutes.

9. Remove the bread from the stone with the aid of a baker's peel. Cover it with a clean towel. Continue until all the loaves have been baked. Serve hot. Otherwise, wrap in aluminum foil and save it in the freezer; toast it before serving. *Nush-e Jan!*

Note: *Nan-e sangak* is a flat, dark, oval bread that is usually baked directly on hot gravel stones in a bakery. You can also bake this bread without using any stones if you wish.

Armenian Sweet Bread or Easter Choreg

1 package or 1 tablespoon dry yeast
¼ cup warm water
5 eggs
1 cup sugar
1 teaspoon ground *mahleb**
2 cups low-fat milk
1 cup unsalted butter or margarine, melted

7 to 8 cups sifted all-purpose flour

Glaze
2 egg yolks
1 tablespoon hot water

Makes 8 loaves
Preparation time: 20 minutes
plus 4 hours' rising time
Cooking time: 35 to 40 minutes

Nan-e gisu

This bread is associated with Easter.

1. In a mixing bowl or food processor, dissolve the yeast in ¼ cup warm water. Set aside for 10 minutes.

2. Beat the eggs, add the sugar, the *mahleb*, milk, and butter. Gradually add 1 cup of flour at a time and stir for about 20 minutes or until the dough pulls away from the bowl and does not stick to your fingers.

3. On a floured surface, divide the dough into 8 balls, cover and let rise for 3 hours.

4. Working with 1 ball of dough at a time, divide it into 3 equal portions. Roll each portion into a rope about 12 inches long. First secure them at one end, then braid the 3 equal ropes together. Place this braid on an ungreased baking sheet.

5. Follow the same procedure to braid the remaining dough balls. Cover and let the braids rise again for another hour.

6. Preheat oven to 350°F. Brush the tops with the mixture of egg yolks diluted with 1 tablespoon hot water.

7. Bake in the oven for 35 to 40 minutes, until golden brown. Serve either warm or at room temperature. *Nush-e Jan!*

Note: You could prepare the dough the night before or early in the morning: it won't hurt the dough to rise overnight. If you prepare it in the morning, then plan to bake in the afternoon. This sweet bread freezes well and comes in handy when you have unexpected guests. It goes well with butter or preserves or by itself.

**Mahleb* powder is used for aromatic flavor and can be found in Iranian specialty stores.

Rice-Noodle Sweet

Makes 8 servings
Preparation time: 15 minutes
Cooking time: 30 minutes

رشته برشته

Reshteh bereshteh

¼ **pound rice sticks (thin rice noodles)**
4 cups oil for frying

1 cup confectioners' sugar
1 tablespoon cardamom powder

When Herodotus visited Persia in about 500 B.C.E., he mentioned the delicacy of the sweet dishes served after meals.

1. Divide the rice sticks into ½-ounce portions and set aside.

2. Heat 4 cups of oil in a deep-fat fryer to 375°F.

3. Drop each rice-stick portion into the hot oil and fry it for 2 seconds until it rises to the surface and turns a white color. With a skimmer, remove the rice noodles from the oil.

4. Place the rice noodles on paper towels on a large tray. Repeat the process until all the rice noodles are fried.

5. While the rice noodles are hot, sprinkle them on both sides with a mixture of confectioners' sugar and cardamom powder. *Nush-e Jan!*

Variation: Place a drop of food coloring on different portions before frying to turn the noodles into different colors, which is very pleasing to the eye.

Note: Rice sticks are available in Iranian specialty stores. The best brand is Trade Ocean from China.

Sugar-Coated Almonds

Noghls

2 cups sugar
1 cup water
1 cup rose water
½ **cup blanched almonds**

1. In a saucepan, bring the sugar and water to a boil and add the rose water. Reduce heat. Simmer over medium heat for 30–35 minutes. Remove from heat.

2. Spread the almonds on a non-stick cookie sheet. Very gradually add half of the syrup, shaking and tossing the almonds constantly until they are thickly coated. Allow to cool for a few minutes and then repeat for a second layer. When completely cool separate from each other.

Variation: You may also coat the almonds individually by hand with the warm sugar syrup.

Date Cakes

1 cup coarsely chopped walnuts
3 cups pitted dates

Dough
1½ cups sifted all-purpose flour
1 cup unsalted butter
1 teaspoon ground cinnamon
½ cup confectioners' sugar
½ teaspoon ground cardamom
1 cup ground unsalted pistachios or
    shredded coconut for decoration

Makes 15 pieces
Preparation time: 30 minutes
Cooking time: 20 minutes

Ranginak

1. In a skillet, toast the walnuts over medium heat for 5 minutes. Set aside and allow to cool.

2. Place a few walnut pieces inside each date.

3. Arrange the dates, packed next to each other, in a flat 9-inch serving dish.

4. In a large deep skillet, fry the flour in butter over medium heat, stirring constantly for about 15 to 20 minutes, until the mixture is a golden caramel color.

5. Spread the hot dough over the dates and pack and smooth it well with the back of a spoon to create an even surface.

6. Meanwhile, combine the cinnamon, confectioners' sugar, and cardamom and sprinkle evenly over the cake.

7. Sprinkle with 1 cup ground pistachios or shredded coconut evenly over the surface. Allow to cool.

8. Cut in small square-shaped pieces. Carefully arrange these on a serving platter, or serve on the same plate. *Nush-e Jan!*

Raisin Cookies

1 cup unsalted butter, melted
4 eggs
1 cup oil
1¾ cups sugar

2 cups raisins
2⅓ cups all-purpose flour

Makes 90 cookies
Preparation time: 15 minutes
Cooking time: 10 to 15 minutes

نان کشمش

Nan-e keshmeshy

1. Preheat oven to 350°F. Spread out wax paper on a cookie sheet.

2. In a mixing bowl, combine melted butter, eggs, oil, and sugar. Mix well until creamy.

3. Add raisins and mix well.

4. Gradually add flour and mix with a wooden spoon until a soft dough forms.

5. Drop teaspoonfuls of batter on the wax paper, leaving about 2 inches between each spoonful.

6. Place the cookie sheet in the center of the oven and bake 10 to 15 minutes, or until slightly golden.

7. Remove the cookies from the oven and allow them to cool. Gently lift the cookies off the wax paper.

8. Arrange the cookies on a plate in the shape of a pyramid. Serve with tea. *Nush-e Jan!*

Saffron Almond Brittle

½ cup butter
1 teaspoon flour
1 tablespoon dark corn syrup
1 tablespoon honey
1 cup sugar

1 cup slivered almonds
½ teaspoon ground saffron, dissolved
   in 2 tablespoons hot water
¼ cup chopped pistachios (for garnish)

Makes 90 cookies
Preparation time: 15 minutes
Cooking time: 10 to 15 minutes

سوهان قم

Sohan-e qom

This recipe comes from Faezeh.

1. In a heavy saucepan, melt the butter over medium heat. Add flour, corn syrup, honey, and sugar, stirring occasionally. Add the slivered almonds.

2. Stir constantly with a wooden spoon for 4–5 minutes, then add the saffron water. Continue stirring for 2–3 minutes until it is caramel in color.

3. Spread the mixture onto a cookie sheet immediately. Sprinkle the top with pistachios.

4. Allow to cool for 10–15 minutes, then remove from cookie sheet. *Nush-e Jan!*

Armenian Christmas Pastry

Makes 24 pieces
Preparation time 30 minutes
plus overnight refrigeration
Cooking time: 20 to 30 minutes

Nazuk or *Gata*

1 package or 1 tablespoon dry yeast
1 cup sour cream
1 cup unsalted butter or margarine*
1 egg
1 tablespoon vegetable oil
1 tablespoon vinegar
3 cups sifted all-purpose flour plus
   ½ cup flour for kneading

Filling
1 cup butter or margarine, melted*
2 cups sifted all-purpose flour
1¼ cups sugar
½ teaspoon vanilla

Glaze
2 egg yolks, beaten
1 teaspoon yogurt

1. In a mixing bowl, combine the yeast with 1 cup sour cream; set aside for 10 minutes.

2. Add butter and mix well.

3. Add the egg, oil, and vinegar and mix well.

4. Add the sifted flour gradually and continue mixing.

5. Knead dough for about 15 minutes until smooth and firm so that it does not stick to your hands.

6. Gather dough into a ball and cover with plastic wrap. Refrigerate the dough overnight

7. To make the filling, mix together 1 cup of the melted butter and 2 cups flour. Add 1¼ cups sugar and ½ teaspoon vanilla; stir constantly for 1 minute, so that the mixture does not stick to your hands and becomes smooth and even. Set aside.

8. Preheat oven to 350°F.

9. Remove dough from the refrigerator; divide it into 8 equal balls. Place each ball on a lightly floured board.

10. Roll each ball out to a rectangle measuring 10-by-6 inches, or as thin as possible with the aid of rolling pin. Paint each rectangle with melted butter.

11. Spread ¼ cup filling into the center of each rectangle and roll out the filling over it with the aid of a rolling pin.

12. Fold in about ½ inch of the rectangle on each side.

13. Roll up dough into a cylinder.

14. Place rolling pin on pastry roll and flatten slightly lengthwise. Cut the roll

__Note:__ Chiffon sweet margarine works quite well for this recipe.

diagonally with a sharp knife or serrated knife into 2-inch equal slices.

15. Place pastry about 2 inches apart on a lightly floured baking pan. (Be careful not to spill out any filling.)

16. Paint the surface of each pastry with the glaze (mixture of beaten egg and yogurt) with a paint brush.

17. Place baking pan in the oven and bake for 15 to 30 minutes, or until golden brown.

18. Remove the baking pan from oven and allow the pastries to cool. *Nush-e Jan!*

This is an excellent pastry, to be served during a morning coffee break or for afternoon tea. This pastry can also be made in different shapes and without the filling. In this case, roll out the dough to its maximum size and as thin as possible. Brush the surface with melted butter. Fold the dough in half and brush the surface with butter; fold in half again. Fold it into your desired shape, round or rectangular, then brush the top with egg-yolk glaze. It is also sometimes called *gata* or *ketah*.

My friend Seda gave me this recipe.

Bas relief from 600 B.C.E. showing soldiers preparing meals in tents while the king sits on his throne.

King Khusraw and His Knight, 4th C. Middle Persian Coming-of-Age Manual

A boy stood before the king with his hands under his shoulder and said, "My father died during my childhood and I am the only son. I received from my parents my hereditary share, stately riches in cash and food of all kinds and beautiful fine clothes. I have learned by heart all great works of literature and history and have become well versed in learned speech. My skill in riding, archery, and sword fighting is such that others must be fortunate to escape my arrow. I am also skillful in the tar and dotar. In the game of chess I am superior to my comrades. Now my family is ruined, and my mother has departed this life. If it pleases you put me to the test in anything whatsoever.

The gourmet king of kings despite all the boy's other talents, asks: Which fowl is the finest and the most savory? The boy replies: May you be immortal! The pheasant, and the hen, and the gray partridge with the white tail and the red wings, and the lark, and the male crane.

But with the male domestic fowl, that has been fed on hemp-seeds and the butter of olives, no fowl can contest. First, on the day it is killed one must chase and frighten it, and then must hang it up by its trunk, and on the second day must hang it by the neck, and roast it on a spit.

The king of kings agreed with him and when he had heard his narrative and his superior knowledge of food, he gave the boy a high position with dignity.

"Joseph Enthroned," circa 1550

Seville oranges with orange blossom petals

Zuleykha has the ladies peel oranges as Yusuf walks into the room—they all cut their fingers.

Fruit Chutney
Torshi-e miveh
Recipe page 255

Lavash, Sangak, Taftun, Shirmal, and Barbari Bread

Almond Delight
Qottab
Recipe page 290

"Feast in a Garden," from a copy of the Shahnameh, *1560*

*1. Dough texture prepared
in food processor
2. Texture of dough*

*3. Prepare pistachio filling
in food processor
4. Using fingers prior to
rolling dough*

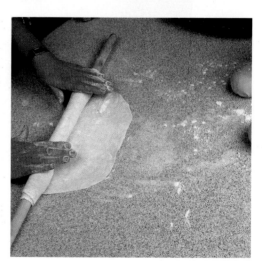

*5. Rolling dough
6. Rolling further*

7. Pinching edge of dough
8. Second layer of dough

9. Cutting diamond shapes
10. Pinching edges

11. Oil prior to placing in oven
12. Syrup after cooking

Baklava
Baqlava
Recipe page 284

314

Painting from Haft Awrang, (*Seven Thrones*), *circa 1500*

Rice Cookies
Nan-e berenji
Recipe page 282

Chick-pea Cookies
Nan-e nokhodchi
Recipe page 283

317

From top: Saffron Pudding, Paradise Custard, Saffron Brownie

Date Cakes
Ranginak
Recipe page 300

319

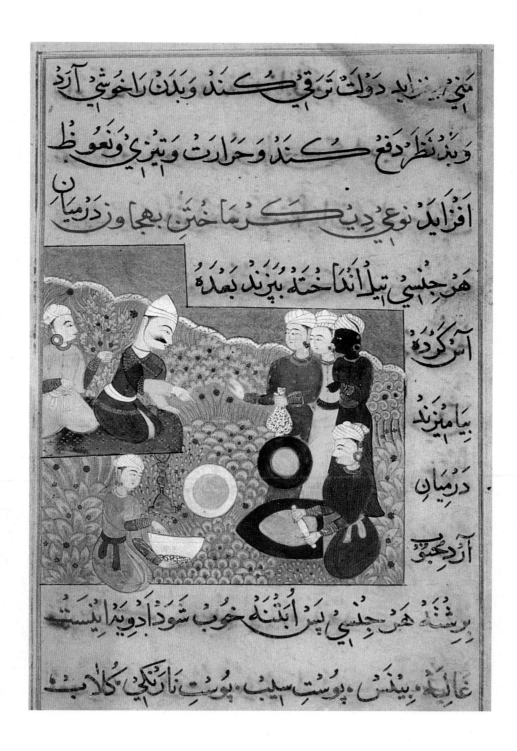

From the Ni'matnameh, *circa 1500*

Quince blossoms
Quince blossom paste recipe (Loz-e gol-e beh), page 346

Sour Cherry Jello
Jeleh-ye albalu
Recipe page 344 (variation)

322

Pomegranate Jello
Jeleh-ye anar
Recipe page 344

Armenian Pastry with Tea
Nazuk *or* Gata
Recipe page 302

Drinks, from left: Dugh, Behlimu, Narenj, Albalu, Sekanjebin, Ablimu, *and* Gol-e Sorkh

White Mulberries
Tut
Recipe page 294

Detail from Majnun Eavesdrops on Layla's Camp, from the Haft Awrang of Jami, attributed to Shaykh Mohammad, circa 1550

High tea at the Shah Mosque, Isfahan

DESSERTS

Rice Stick Sorbet with Sour Cherries and Saffron Ice Cream
Paludeh va bastani-e gol-o bolbol
Recipes pages 347 and 350

دسرها و غذ اکای شیرین

D e s s e r t s

The rice desserts of Iran are served at any time of the day, not just at the end of a meal. Some are associated with special events.

Katchi, a saffron cream, for example, is eaten by new mothers on the first and fifth days after giving birth as part of a ceremony in which a holy person whispers the newborn child's name in his or her ear. It is also very good for nursing mothers.

Halva, a saffron brownie, is prepared during the first three days after a death and after the eve of the seventh and fortieth days of mourning. It is offered to family, friends, and the poor.

Sholeh zard, a saffron pudding, is reserved for the holiday in remembrance of the dead. It serves as an offering to the poor or as thanksgiving for a wish come true.

All of these dishes may be eaten hot or cold. I prefer to serve them well-chilled. They may be presented in individual dishes or in a large serving bowl.

Saffron Pudding

1 cup rice
10 cups water or more
3½ cups sugar
¼ cup unsalted butter
½ cup unsalted slivered almonds
½ teaspoon ground saffron dissolved in 2 tablespoons hot water
1 teaspoon ground cardamom
½ cup rose water

Garnish
2 teaspoons ground cinnamon
2 teaspoons slivered almonds
2 teaspoons slivered pistachios

Makes 8 servings
Preparation time: 5 minutes
Cooking time: 1 hour 40 minutes

شُله زرد

Sholeh zard

This dish is associated with the giving of alms during religious ceremonies.

1. Clean and wash the rice, changing the water several times. Drain.

2. Combine the rice with 8 cups of water in a large pot and bring to a boil, skimming the foam as it rises. Cover and simmer for 35 minutes over medium heat until the rice is quite soft.

3. Add 2 more cups of warm water if necessary and sugar, cook for 25 minutes longer, stirring occasionally (do not stir too much). Add the butter, almonds, saffron water, cardamom, and rose water. Mix well. Cover and simmer over low heat for 20 minutes; remove the cover and cook over low heat uncovered for another 20 minutes or until the mixture is cooked and has thickened to a pudding.

4. Spoon the pudding into individual serving dishes or a large bowl. Decorate with cinnamon, almonds, and pistachios. Chill in refrigerator.

5. Serve the pudding cold. *Nush-e Jan!*

Saffron Pudding
Sholeh zard
Recipe page 332

Saffron Brownie

Syrup
1 cup water
1 cup sugar
1 teaspoon ground saffron dissolved
   in ¼ cup hot water
¼ cup rose water
½ teaspoon ground cardamom

Dough
2 cups sifted all-purpose flour
1½ cups unsalted butter, melted

Garnish
2 tablespoons ground pistachios

Makes 6 servings
Preparation time: 10 minutes
Cooking time: 30 minutes

حلوا

Halva

This dish is associated with the giving of alms during religious ceremonies or funerals.

1. Bring the water and sugar to a boil in a saucepan. Remove from heat and add the saffron water, rose water, and ground cardamom. Mix well and set aside.

2. In a large, deep skillet, toast the flour for about 10 minutes over high heat, stirring constantly with a wooden spoon. Add melted butter and fry, mixing constantly with a wooden spoon for 7 to 15 minutes longer, or until golden brown. (This stage is very important: be careful that the flour is not over- or undercooked). Remove the skillet from the heat.

3. Gradually stir the syrup into the hot flour-and-butter mixture, stirring quickly and constantly with a wooden spoon for about 5 minutes. To make a thick, smooth paste, transfer to a food processor and mix well for 5 minutes (if the paste does not set, then place it over high heat again and stir constantly to achieve a thick, smooth paste).

4. Spoon onto a flat plate and pack firmly with a spoon. Decorate by making geometric patterns with a spoon and garnish with ground pistachios.

5. Cover and chill the saffron brownie in the refrigerator. Cut it into small pieces and serve them cold as a main dish with *lavash* bread or alone as a dessert. *Nush-e Jan!*

Note: You can use oil instead of butter or whole-wheat flour instead of white flour. In the case of wheat flour, add ¼ cup more water and ¼ cup more sugar to the syrup.

Saffron Brownie
Halva
Recipe page 334

335

Paradise Custard
Yakh dar behesht
Recipe page 337

Paradise Custard

Makes 6 servings
Preparation time: 10 minutes
plus 2 hours' setting time
Cooking time: 15 minutes

Yakh dar behesht

¾ cup corn starch or rice starch (rice
    flour)
4 cups milk
1 cup sugar
10 cardamom pods, peeled
¼ **cup rose water**

Garnish
⅓ **cup slivered almonds, toasted, or**
    1 teaspoon ground pistachios

1. In a saucepan, dissolve the corn starch in milk and add the sugar.

2. Cook over medium heat for about 5–10 minutes, stirring constantly until the mixture has thickened.

3. Add the cardamom pods and rose water. Cook for a few minutes or longer until the mixture reaches the consistency of a pudding, stirring constantly to prevent sticking and lumping. Remove the saucepan from the heat.

4. Transfer the custard to a serving dish. Decorate with toasted almonds or pistachios.

5. Chill the custard in the refrigerator for 2 hours and serve it cold. *Nush-e Jan!*

پدرم پشت زمان ها مرده است .

پدرم وقتی مرد ، آسمان آبی بود ،

پدرم وقتی مرد ، پاسبان ها همه شاعر بودند .

مرد بقال از من پرسید : چند من خربزه می خواهی ؟

من از او پرسیدم : دل خوش سیری چند ؟

My father has died beyond the ages.
When my father died the sky was blue . . .
When my father died, the police were all poets.
The grocer asked me, "How many pounds of melons do you want?"
I asked him, "How much an ounce for a happy heart?"

Sohrab Sepehri

Carrot Brownie

Makes 12 servings
Preparation time: 15 minutes
Cooking time: 40 minutes

حلوای هویج

Halva-ye havij

2 pounds carrots
3 cups water
2 cups sugar
2 cups sifted rice flour
⅔ cup unsalted butter or oil
1 teaspoon ground saffron dissolved
    in ¼ cup rose water
½ teaspoon ground cardamom
2 tablespoons ground pistachios for
    garnish

This dish is associated with the winter festival, Shab-e Yalda.

1. Wash, scrape, and grate the carrots. Cover with 1 cup of water and bring to a boil. Reduce heat, cover, and simmer over medium heat for about 15 minutes or until tender.

2. Place 2 cups water and the sugar in a saucepan. Bring to a boil until the sugar completely dissolves. Remove the pan from heat, add the syrup to the carrots and mix well.

3. In a skillet, fry the rice flour and butter or oil over high heat for 10 to 15 minutes until the mixture turns golden brown. Add mixture of carrot and syrup.

4. Add the saffron-rose water and cardamom and cook over medium heat for another 10 minutes, stirring quickly and constantly with a wooden spoon to make a thick, smooth paste. Transfer the carrot brownie to a food processor and mix well for 5 minutes.

5. Spoon onto a flat serving platter; pack firmly with a spoon. Decorate by making geometric patterns with the spoon and garnish with ground pistachios. Chill the brownie in the refrigerator. Cut into small pieces and serve either as a main dish with *lavash* bread, or alone as a dessert. *Nush-e Jan!*

Variation: Grape brownie—You may substitute the carrot with 2 cups grape paste.

Note: Grape paste is available at Iranian specialty stores.

Rice Pudding

½ cup rice, cleaned and washed
2 cups water
¼ teaspoon salt
3 cups milk
½ cup half-and-half or cream
 (optional)
¼ cup rose water
1 teaspoon ground cardamom

Makes 6 servings
Preparation time: 5 minutes
Cooking time: 1 hour 30 minutes

Shir berenj

This pudding is associated with Ramazan, the month of fasting.

1. Place the rice in a saucepan with 2 cups of water and ¼ teaspoon salt. Bring to a boil and reduce the heat. Cover and cook over medium heat for 20 minutes, or until the rice is tender.

2. Add the milk and half-and-half or cream. Bring to a boil and reduce the heat. Cover and cook over low heat for about 55 minutes, or until the mixture has thickened to a pudding consistency. Add rose water and cardamom and cook over low heat for 10 minutes longer.

3. Remove the pudding from the heat. Spoon it into a serving bowl or individual bowls and chill in the refrigerator. Serve with grape essence or syrup, sugar, jam, or honey. *Nush-e Jan!*

Note: Grape essence or paste is available at Iranian specialty stores.

Saffron Cream

Makes 6 servings
Preparation time: 10 minutes
Cooking time: 45 minutes

Katchi

1 cup unsalted butter
2 cups sifted all-purpose flour or rice
    flour
5½ cups water
2½ cups sugar
1 teaspoon ground saffron dissolved
    in ¼ cup hot water
¼ cup rose water
½ teaspoon ground cardamom

Garnish
2 tablespoons slivered almonds
2 tablespoons slivered pistachios

Katchi is especially made for the woman who has recently given birth in order for her to regain her strength.

1. In a large, deep skillet, melt the butter and stir in the flour gradually, stirring constantly with a wooden spoon. Cook over medium heat for about 20 to 25 minutes or until it is golden brown.

2. Bring the water and sugar to a boil in a saucepan. Add the saffron water, rose water, and ground cardamom and gradually stir in the flour-and-butter mixture, stirring quickly and constantly with a wooden spoon. Simmer until the mixture reaches a creamy consistency. You may add more water if the mixture becomes too thick.

3. Transfer the saffron cream to a serving bowl. Garnish it with almonds and pistachios immediately and serve hot. *Nush-e Jan!*

Note: *Katchi* is a liquid form of *halva*, with three times the amount of water. *Katchi* should be served hot.

Rice Cream

¼ cup rice flour (ground rice)
4 cups milk
2 tablespoons rose water
½ cup sugar

Makes 6 servings
Preparation time: 5 minutes
Cooking time: 45 minutes

Fereni

This dish is recommended for infants.

1. In a saucepan, combine the rice flour, milk, rose water, and sugar. Cook for about 15 to 20 minutes over medium heat, stirring frequently with a wooden spoon, until the mixture has thickened and has reached a creamy consistency.

2. Remove the cream from the heat. Ladle it into a serving bowl or individual bowls, and chill in the refrigerator. *Nush-e Jan!*

دوش دیدم که ملائک در میخانه زدند   گل آدم بسرشتند و به پیمانه زدند

ساکنان حرم ستر و عفاف ملکوت   با من راه نشین باده مستانه زدند

حافظ

Last night I saw the angels knocking at the tavern door
Modeling the clay of man, becoming drunk with the original wine;
The inhabitants of the sacred enclosure and of the divine Malakut
Drank from one cup with me, the Pilgrim.

Hafez

Pomegranate Jello

3 envelopes unflavored gelatin
5 cups freshly squeezed
   pomegranate juice
2 tablespoons sugar
   (if pomegranates are too sour)
Seeds of 4 fresh pomegranates
2 tablespoons slivered pistachios

Makes 6 servings
Preparation time: 15 minutes
Setting time: 8 hours

ژله لنار

Jeleh-ye anar

1. In a large bowl, sprinkle the unflavored gelatin over 1 cup of cold pomegranate juice. Let stand for 1 minute.

2. In a saucepan, warm 4 cups of pomegranate juice.

3. Add the softened gelatin to the saucepan. Stir constantly for 5 minutes, until gelatin is completely dissolved.

4. Taste it. If too sour, add the sugar to your taste. Pour the pomegranate-juice mixture into a mold or a bowl. Let it cool.

5. Scatter the pomegranate seeds on top of the mixture. Chill it in the refrigerator until firm.

6. Serve pomegranate jello with whipped cream or ice cream sprinkled with pomegranate seeds or slivered pistachios. *Nush-e Jan!*

Notes: You can also make individual servings of this jello.

Prepared pomegranate juice is available at Iranian specialty stores.

Variation #1: Sour-cherry jello—You may substitute the pomegranate juice with sour cherry juice plus more sugar to your taste.

Variation #2: Rhubarb jello—You may substitute the pomegranate juice with rhubarb juice.

Quince Custard

6 pounds quince or 6 quinces
3 cups water
2 cups sugar
**A few quince seeds placed in cheese-
cloth, tied in a knot**
1 tablespoon cardamom pods, peeled
1 cup ground pistachios for garnish

Makes 6 servings
Preparation time: 15 minutes
Cooking time: 2 hours

لوزِبه

Loz-e beh

This dish is often associated with the Winter Festival, Shab-e Yalda.

1. Wash and core the quinces, cut into wedges, and place in a pot. Cover with the 3 cups of water, add ¼ cup sugar and the quince seeds and bring to a boil. Reduce heat, cover and simmer over low heat for about 1½ hours or until tender. Stir occasionally. Remove the quince seeds from the pot.

2. Remove the quince from the pot, puree in a food processor, and return to the pot. Add remaining sugar and cardamom, stirring occasionally with a wooden spoon. Cover and simmer over medium heat for 25 minutes, or until all the water has evaporated. Reduce heat, uncover, and continue stirring for another 15 minutes over low heat.

3. Remove the pot from heat and transfer the quince custard to a flat serving platter. Pack it firmly with a spoon and garnish with ground pistachios. Cover firmly, chill the custard in the refrigerator, then cut it into small pieces and serve as a dessert. *Nush-e Jan!*

Quince-Blossom Paste

**2 cups fresh quince blossoms
    or ½ cup dried blossoms**
½ cup water
1 cup confectioners' sugar
½ cup chopped pistachios

Makes 2 servings
Preparation time: 35 minutes
Cooking time: 25 minutes

Loz-e gol-e beh

This is a spring dish prepared during the quince blossom season. It is very nutritious as well as delicious.

1. Carefully wash the quince blossoms, separate the petals, and place them in a steamer. Steam for 10 minutes, then place petals in a food processor. Grind petals, then add confectioners' sugar and water, blending well.

2. Transfer to a pot. Cook over low heat for about 20 minutes, or until the sugar dissolves completely. Stir constantly to obtain the consistency of a paste. Remove pan from heat. Add the pistachios and mix well.

3. Transfer the quince-blossom paste to a greased flat plate and pack it down firmly with a spoon. Chill in refrigerator, then serve as a dessert. *Nush-e Jan!*

Variation: Rose Petal Paste—You may replace the quince blossoms with rose petals. Add 1 pound of flour for each pound of confectioners' sugar.

Saffron Ice Cream

4 cups milk
¾ cup sugar
4 teaspoons powdered *sahlab**
¼ teaspoon ground saffron dis-
    solved in 3 tablespoons rose
    water
½ cup whipping cream
2 tablespoons slivered pistachios
    for decoration

Makes 4 servings
Preparation time: 20 minutes
Cooking time: 3 hours

Bastani-e gol-o bolbol

1. In a large saucepan, stir the milk and sugar together and bring to a boil over medium heat.

2. Put the *sahlab* in a bowl and add 1 cup of the warm milk-and-sugar mixture. Mix very well until the mixture is quite smooth.

3. Add this mixture to the warm milk in the saucepan. Simmer over low heat, stirring constantly, until the mixture thickens. At this stage, the mixture should be slightly elastic. Remove the pan from the heat.

4. Add saffron-rose water. Mix well. Allow to cool for 2 hours. Pour the entire mixture into an ice-cream machine.

5. Follow your ice-cream machine's directions for making ice cream.

6. Pour a thin layer of whipping cream into a *flat plate* and place it in the freezer until a ¼-inch frozen creamy crust forms. Remove the crust from the freezer, let it stand for 2 minutes, then break off ½-inch pieces of the crust and mix them with the finished ice cream.

7. Serve saffron ice cream in small crystal bowls; sprinkle the top with ground pistachios. *Nush-e Jan!*

Variation: You may simply use 1 pint vanilla ice cream. Simply add frozen cream pieces, saffron-rose water, and slivered pistachios. Mix well.

*Note: *Sahlab* is a starch made from a powdered root. It is available in Iranian specialty stores.

Cantaloupe and Peach Cocktail

2 peaches
1 cantaloupe or honeydew melon
2 tablespoons sugar
1 tablespoon fresh lime juice
2 tablespoons rose water or orange
   blossom water
5 leaves fresh mint

Makes 2 servings
Preparation time: 15 minutes
plus 30 minutes to chill

کمپوت هلو و طالبی

Compot-e hulu va talebi

1. Peel and slice the peaches.

2. Peel and slice the cantaloupe or melon into small 1-inch pieces. Use a melon baller if you have one.

3. In a crystal bowl, combine sugar, lime juice, and rose or orange blossom water; add the sliced melon and peaches. Stir gently. Cover and let chill in the refrigerator.

4. Adjust the taste by adding more sugar if necessary. Decorate with mint leaves and serve immediately. *Nush-e Jan!*

Variation #1: You may puree and combine all the ingredients in a food processor and chill in the refrigerator. Or pour the mixture into a sorbet maker. Follow your machine's directions for making sorbet.

Variation #2: *Paloodeh-e Garmak*—Puree the cantaloupe with sugar and 3 ice cubes in a food processor. Add a few drops of rose water, and decorate with mint leaves and rose petals.

Dried Fruit Cocktail

1 cup dried apricots
1 cup pitted prunes
1 cup warm water
2 tablespoons slivered pistachios
2 tablespoons slivered almonds
Fresh mint leaves for garnish

Makes 2 servings
Preparation time: 10 minutes
Soaking time: 24 hours

Khoshab-e miveh-ye khoshk

This is an excellent winter dessert.

1. Wash and drain the dried fruit.

2. Place the fruit in a bowl and add 1 cup warm water. Refrigerate overnight, turning the fruit in the water.

3. Add pistachios and almonds, mix well, and serve in individual serving dishes. Decorate with mint leaves. *Nush-e Jan!*

Variation: You may cook the fruits for 15 minutes over medium heat; chill in the refrigerator. Or you may puree the cooked or soaked fruit in a food processor.

Rice Stick Sorbet with Sour Cherries

Sorbet
2 ounces thin rice noodles or
    Chinese rice sticks, broken into
    2-inch pieces
2½ cups sugar
1 cup water
3 tablespoons rose water

Garnish
2 tablespoons slivered pistachios
2 tablespoons sour cherries or black
    mulberries
¼ cup light sour cherry syrup
2 tablespoons fresh squeezed lime
    juice (optional)

Preparation time: 15 minutes
Cooking time: 1 minute
Setting time: 24 hours

فالوده شیرازی

Paludeh-ye shirazi

1. Cover the noodles in cold water and soak for 30 minutes. Drain.

2. In a saucepan, boil the rice noodles in water for 20 seconds. Drain, run cold water over them, and set aside.

3. Put sugar and 1 cup water in a saucepan and bring to a boil. Remove the pan from the heat immediately. Add rose water and allow to cool.

4. Pour the mixture into an ice cream maker. Add the rice noodles. Follow your machine's instructions for making sherbet.

5. Spoon the sorbet into individual crystal bowls. Garnish with pistachios, sour cherries or black mulberries, and some sour-cherry syrup over the top. *Nush-e Jan!*

Note: To prepare your own noodles, slowly blend ½ cup corn starch with 3 cups water in a saucepan. Mix well until smooth, then bring to a boil over medium heat, stirring constantly until the mixture reaches the consistency of rich, smooth, white cream. Gently strain the mixture through a cheesecloth over a bowl of ice water, then proceed with the rest.

PERSIAN SNACKS

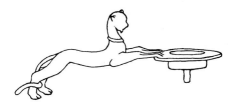

Dried Fruits and Nuts

Ajil, the Persian mixture of dried fruits with roasted nuts and seeds, is a wonderful snack for nibbling that appeals to children as well as adults and fits in at any time of day. Exactly what goes into this snack and what proportions to use depend as much on what is at hand as on the whim of the person who is preparing it. Because it has an infinite number of combinations, there can be no conventional recipe for *ajil*; you have to invent your own. Among the dried fruits to choose from are figs, apricots, peaches, raisins, and mulberries. Dried pears, prunes, and currants can also be used. Nuts and seeds can include roasted hazelnuts, almonds, walnuts, pistachios, cashews, chick-peas, watermelon seeds, and pumpkin seeds. Mix the fruits, nuts, and seeds together and serve in a bowl. People help themselves to what they want, using their fingers.

There are three major *ajil*:

1. *Ajil-e shab-e chahar shanbeh sury* (always served on the eve of the last Wednesday of the year) literally means "Red Wednesday Night."

2. *Ajil-e shab-e chelleh* or *shab chareh* (night grazing) is associated with winter festivals and always contains watermelon seeds).

3. *Ajil-e moshgel gosha* (unraveling problems): you make a wish and if your wish comes true, you must hand out *ajil*.

Ajil

Sweet Chick-pea Powder

2 cups roasted chick-pea powder
1 cup confectioners' sugar

Makes 3 cups
Preparation time: 5 minutes

قاهوت

Ghahut

1. Mix together the chick-pea powder and sugar.

2. Pour into a bowl. *Nush-e Jan!*

As children we loved *ghahut*. Today, as adults, we make it for our children and help them eat it, sometimes with our hands and sometimes with spoons. The best way to eat this snack is to take a handful, tilt your head back, and then pour it into your mouth.

Note: Roasted chick-pea powder is available in Iranian specialty stores.

Peeled Walnuts

**1 pound fresh walnuts, salted
    to taste**

*Preparation time: 10 to 15
minutes plus overnight
refrigeration*

Gerdu

1. Shell the walnuts. If they are dried, wash them and soak them in very hot water with 1 teaspoon salt. Cover and refrigerate overnight.

2. Remove the outer membrane from the walnuts and drop them in a large bowl of cold water until ready to use.

3. Drain the nuts and sprinkle them with salt to taste.

4. Serve these nuts as a snack or as a side dish with feta cheese and pita bread. *Nush-e Jan!*

Variation: You may also use dried almonds instead of walnuts.

Note: Peeled walnuts are usually prepared with fresh walnuts in season but you can substitute dried walnuts that are available almost year-round by soaking them in hot water for several hours. Like *balal*, *gerdu* is sold by street vendors in Iran.

Charcoal-Roasted Corn on the Cob

2 tablespoons salt
2 quarts warm water
8 ears of corn, shucked

Makes 4 servings
Preparation time: 20 minutes
Cooking time: 10 minutes

Balal

1. Prepare a charcoal fire and dissolve the salt in the warm water.

2. When the coals are ready, roast the corn on all sides on the grill, turning the ears frequently.

3. Plunge the roasted corn into the salted water; serve immediately. *Nush-e Jan!*

Note: *Balal* is a popular snack and *balal* vendors are a familiar sight on the streets of Persian towns and cities, like pretzel vendors in the United States or chestnut vendors in Paris.

Baked Potatoes

سینی منبخت

Sibzamini pokhteh

Baked potatoes, or *sibzamini pokhteh*, are a popular snack, and vendors are a familiar sight in Iranian towns and cities, similar to pretzel vendors in the United States or chestnut vendors in Paris.

Sibzamini pokhteh is usually prepared with new potatoes. Traditionally, potatoes are roasted by burying them in the hot ashes of a brazier or in a *tanur* (bread oven), then served with salt, angelica powder (*gol-par*), and Persian pickles (*torshi*), sometimes even with bread. Potatoes can also be wrapped individually in aluminum foil, pierced in a few places with a fork, and baked in a 350°F oven for about 1 hour, or until thoroughly baked. You can also try to cook them in the fireplace. *Nush-e Jan!*

During the winter after school, as evening approached, we sat around the *korsi* (a low square table covered with a thick cloth overhanging on all sides). A brazier with hot coals was placed under the table. With our legs underneath the table and the cloth over our laps, one by one we unearthed our potatoes buried in the hot ashes of the brazier, peeled them, sprinkled salt and angelica powder (*gol-par*) over them, and savored every bite with Persian pickles (*torshi*). What a memory!

Baked Beetroots

لبو تنوری

Labu-ye tanuri

Hot beetroot, or *labu*, is a popular snack and its vendors are a familiar sight in Iranian cities. *Labu* is usually prepared with sweet fresh beets in season. Traditionally, the beetroots are roasted in a *tanur*, or bread oven, and then peeled and sliced before serving. Alternatively, they can be cooked in an oven. Place the beetroots, unpeeled, in an ovenproof baking dish. Cover them with water and bake for 2 to 3 hours at 350°F, depending on their size. Turn them over occasionally; add more warm water, if necessary, until tender. Peel and slice the beetroots. Or, if you prefer, you may steam the beetroots in a steamer for 1 hour. *Nush-e Jan!*

Hot Fava Beans in the Pod

بافلی پخته

Baqala pokhteh

Hot fava beans, *baqala pokhteh*, are a popular snack, and *baqala pokhteh* vendors are a familiar sight in Persian towns and cities. *Baqala pokhteh* is usually prepared with fresh fava beans in the pod. Traditionally, the fava beans are boiled with salt, water, and vinegar, then sprinkled with angelica powder (*gol-par*) before serving. For making this snack at home use 2 pounds of fresh fava beans in the pod or 1 pound of frozen fava beans. Wash them and place them in a large pot, add 8 cups of water and 2 tablespoons of salt. Cover and cook for 1 hour over medium heat (if using frozen fava beans without pods, cook for 35 minutes, or until tender). Drain and transfer to a platter, sprinkle with vinegar and then with angelica powder (*gol-par*). These fava beans make a wonderful winter afternoon snack. *Nush-e-Jan!*

Unripe Fresh Almonds and Sour Green Plums

چغاله با دالم

Chaghaleh badum va gojeh-sabz

Wash the almonds and plums and then sprinkle with salt. Serve as a snack.

As children we loved *chaghaleh* and *gojeh*. They were a popular after-school snack. Vendors appeared near the school in the spring and sold small bags of fresh *chaghaleh* and *gojeh* sprinkled with salt. What heavenly memories. Walking home, we would finish a whole bag. *Nush-e-Jan!*

Unripe almonds and sour green plums are available at Iranian specialty food stores during the spring.

Popped Rice

2 cups rice
1teaspoon salt
4 cups water
4 cups oil for deep-frying

1 teaspoon salt or confectioners'
    sugar for garnish

Makes 4 cups
Preparation time: 20 minutes,
plus overnight soaking
Cooking time: 11 to 12 minutes

Berenjak

1. Clean and wash rice and soak in 4 cups water overnight.

2. Drain the rice and pat **completely** dry using paper towels.

3. In a deep frying pan, heat the oil over high heat (375°F). Drop in 1 grain of rice. If it rises immediately, the oil is ready. Add 1 teaspoon salt. Reduce heat to medium.

4. Place rice in the frying pan for 20–30 seconds (count up to 30) until individual grains of rice swell and rise up. Immediately remove using a slotted spoon, and set aside to cool. Sprinkle with the rest of the salt or 1 teaspoon confectioners' sugar. *Nush-e jan!*

Popped Lentils

2 cups lentils
4 cups water
2 teaspoons salt
4 cups oil for deep frying

Makes 3 cups
Preparation time: 10 minutes
plus 3 hours' soaking time
Cooking time: 2 to 3 minutes

Adasak

1. Clean and wash the lentils and soak in 4 cups water and 1 teaspoon salt for 3 hours.

2. Drain the lentils and dry **completely** with paper towels.

3. In a deep frying pan, heat the oil over high heat (375°F). Add 1 teaspoon salt.

4. Place the lentils in the frying pan and cook for few minutes until individual lentils swell and rise (1–2 minutes).

5. Remove the lentils from the oil, drain, and leave to cool. *Nush-e-Jan!*

Variation: Wheat grains can also be prepared using this method.

میوهٔ کال صدرا را آن روز، می جویدم در خواب .

آبی بی فلسفه می خوردم .

توتی بی دانشی می چیدم .

تا اناری ترکی برمی داشت، دست فواره خواهش می شد .

In dreams that day I chewed on God's unripe fruit.
I drank a water without philosophy;
I picked a berry without knowledge.
No sooner did a pomegrante crack than it became the
    hand of the fount of yearning.

Sohrab Sepehri

HOT AND COLD DRINKS

بایساقی آن می که حال آورد   کرامت فـــزایدکمال آورد

به من ده که بس بیدل افتاده ام   وز این هردو بحاصل افتاده ام

بیساقی آن می کز او جام جم   زند لاف بینائی اندر عدم

به من ده که گردم به تأیید جام   چو جم اگه از سرّ عالم تمام

Saghi! Come, that wine that rapture bringeth,
Give me. For I, much heart-bereft, have fallen;
Saghi come. That wine, wherefrom the cup of Jamshid,
Boasteth of seeing into non-existence.

Give me, so that by the aid of the cup,
I may be like Jamshid,
Ever acquainted with the world's mystery.

Hafez - Saghi Nameh

The Story of Jamshid Shah

One day, as King Jamshid sat under his tent watching his archers practice, a large bird appeared in the sky. It seemed to be struggling to stay aloft. Jamshid saw that a snake was wrapped around the bird's neck and was threatening the bird with its fearsome fangs.

For Jamshid, this was a hateful sight. He could not stand by and allow the bird, a symbol of good, to be devoured by a snake, the foulest symbol of evil.

Without hesitation, the king ordered his best archer to kill the snake without harming the bird. A few moments later, the serpent fell to the ground, an arrow through its head.

The great bird soared toward the sun in homage to the triumph of good over evil, then swooped down and landed next to Jamshid. It opened its beak and dropped a few bright green seeds at the king's feet. Jamshid had never seen seeds like these. He looked up to question the bird, but it had already flown away.

When the king returned to his palace, he summoned his best gardeners and consulted the wisest men in his kingdom, but not one was able to identify the strange seeds. Finally, he ordered that the seeds be planted in the most fertile soil of the royal gardens.

Some time later, a strange plant rose from the ground. During the warm season it proliferated, sending out long branches covered with many large leaves. But once winter arrived, it began to dry up and shrivel to the ground, as if to protect itself from the cold.

Finally, one spring the first of its fruit ripened. A gardener brought some of it to Jamshid, who examined them in wonder. The fruit was as strange as the plant that bore it. On each stem, there grew not one but twenty to forty dark blue, round berries. The skins burst easily, releasing the juice within. So that not a drop would be lost, the king ordered his servants to gather all the fruit and place it in large receptacles.

One evening the king returned to the palace very thirsty after a long day's hunt in the hot sun. He decided to try a glass of the mysterious juice, believing it would be a refreshing fermented drink. No sooner had he taken the first bitter sip than he spat it out.

"This must be a dreadful poison," he said. "I must make certain it does not fall into the hands of the wrong people."

He turned his attention to more pressing royal concerns and thought no more about the matter. Months passed.

Now as it happened, Jamshid had a beautiful slave girl who had become his favorite. One day while he was away, she fell violently ill, suffering from terrible headaches that none of the palace doctors could cure. The pain was so intense she decided to kill herself. Remembering the strange juice and the king's remark that it was poison, she drank one glass and was quite surprised to find that it did not have the bitter taste the king had complained of. To ensure that she would die, she drank a second, then a third glass, and finally fell into a deep sleep.

When she awoke, her terrible headache was gone. Although her mouth felt dry, she believed that she was healed.

When the king returned to the palace, she confessed what she had done and described the miraculous cure the drink had brought about. Because Jamshid loved the beautiful slave girl, he did not punish her. Instead, he asked to try the juice himself. He tasted it, cautiously at first, then with more and more pleasure. Unable to disguise his delight, he decreed the drink would be used as a remedy for all the people. The effect was so beneficial, especially among the elderly, that the liquid came to be called *daru-shah*, the king's medicine.

That, according to legend, is the origin of the grapevine and the discovery of wine.

Cynics will probably question the truth of this tale. It is certain, however, that the grapevine originated in the Middle East, and it was there that, one long-forgotten day, the juice of the grapes turned into wine.

The Moslem religion forbids believers to seek paradise on Earth through artificial intoxication. The Koran promises its followers a far more precious nectar—but in another world.

Seville Orange Syrup

Makes 2 pints
Preparation time: 5 minutes
Cooking time: 35 minutes

شربت نارنج

Sharbat-e narenj

5–6 pounds Seville oranges (2 cups Seville orange juice)
4 cups sugar
2 cups water

Garnish
Fresh orange leaves
Orange blossoms

Narenge (wild orange) is known as the Seville orange in English, and orange amere *in French. The* narenje *tree and fruit existed in the Caspian region 2000 years ago. The orange graft was brought to Persia by the Portuguese from China; hence the name for orange in Persian,* porteghal.

1. To make juice use 5 to 6 pounds of Seville oranges. First wash and remove a ring of orange peel from around the middle of the Seville oranges. Cut in half. Remove the seeds and press the oranges in a juicer.

2. In a saucepan, bring the sugar and water to a boil over high heat. Pour in the Seville orange juice and simmer over medium heat for 20 minutes, stirring occasionally. Remove from the heat, cool, pour into a clean, dry bottle, and cork it tightly.

3. In a pitcher, mix 1 part syrup, 3 parts water, and 2 ice cubes per person. Stir with a spoon and serve well chilled. Decorate with orange leaves or orange blossoms. *Nush-e-Jan!*

Lime Syrup

Makes 2 pints
Preparation time: 5 minutes
Cooking time: 25 minutes

شربت آبلیمو

Sharbat-e ablimu

6 cups sugar
2 cups water
1½ cups fresh lime juice

Garnish
Sprigs of fresh mint
Lime slices

1. In a saucepan, bring the sugar and water to a boil. Pour in the lime juice and simmer over medium heat, stirring occasionally, for 15 minutes. Cool, pour into a clean, dry bottle, and cork tightly.

2. In a pitcher, mix 1 part syrup, 3 parts water, and 2 ice cubes per person. Stir with a spoon and serve well chilled, garnished with sprigs of fresh mint and slices of lime. *Nush-e Jan!*

Variation: In a saucepan, bring the sugar and water to a boil and let simmer for 15 minutes. Store in a clean, dry bottle. To use, add fresh lime juice to your taste and ice cubes to a pitcher and fill ⅔ of way with cold water. Pour into glasses and garnish with sprigs of fresh mint and slices of lime.

Sour-Cherry Syrup

3 pounds fresh or frozen pitted sour cherries (about 3 cups of sour-cherry juice)
8 cups sugar
4 tablespoons lime juice
5 cups water

Makes 1 pint
Preparation time: 20 minutes
Cooking time: 35 minutes

Sharbat-e albalu

1. Squeeze the cherries or process them in a juicer.

2. Bring the sugar, lime juice, and water to a boil in a laminated pan. Add the cherry juice and boil for 10–15 minutes over medium heat, stirring occasionally, until the syrup thickens.

3. Remove the pan from the heat and allow to cool.

4. Pour syrup into a clean, dry bottle, and cork tightly.

5. In a pitcher, mix 1 part syrup, 3 parts water, and 2 ice cubes per person. Stir with a spoon and serve well chilled. *Nush-e-Jan!*

Variation: Another way to make this syrup is to bring the sugar and water to a boil, tie the sour cherries with the pits in cheesecloth, and add the cloth to the sugar and water. Boil for 25 minutes. Squeeze and remove the cheesecloth and add ¼ teaspoon vanilla extract to the syrup. Allow to cool, pour the syrup into a clean, dry bottle, and cork tightly. Serve as in Step 5 above.

Quince-Lime Syrup

2 pounds quinces (about 2 cups juice)
4 cups sugar
2 cups water
½ cup fresh lime juice

Makes 1 pint
Preparation time: 10 minutes
Cooking time: 55 minutes

شربت به لیمو

Sharbat-e beh limu

1. Quarter the quinces and remove cores with a knife. Do not peel. Wash and pat dry, and process in a juicer.

2. Bring the sugar and water to a boil in a saucepan. Add the quince juice and boil for 30 minutes over medium heat, stirring occasionally; add the lime juice and cook for another 15 minutes or until the syrup thickens.

3. Remove the saucepan from heat. Allow to cool. Pour the syrup into a clean, dry bottle and cork tightly.

4. In a pitcher, mix 1 part syrup, 3 parts water, and 2 ice cubes per person. Stir with a spoon. *Nush-e-Jan!*

Variation: Another way to make this syrup is to tie up the cleaned, sliced, and washed quince in doubled muslin or two layers of cheesecloth. Cover and cook in a pot with 4 cups water for 1 hour and 30 minutes over medium heat, until the quince is tender. Squeeze and remove the cheesecloth, add 2 cups of sugar, 2 cups of water, and ½ cup of fresh lime juice to the pot; cover and cook over medium heat for another 30 minutes. Continue with Step 3 above.

Rhubarb Syrup

**2 pounds rhubarb (about 2 cups
    rhubarb juice)**
2 cups water
4 cups sugar
2 tablespoons lime juice

Makes 1 pint
Preparation time: 35 minutes
Cooking time: 30 minutes

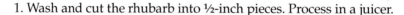

Sharbat-e rivas

1. Wash and cut the rhubarb into ½-inch pieces. Process in a juicer.

2. Bring the water and sugar to a boil in a saucepan. Add the rhubarb juice and lime juice and boil for 20 minutes over medium heat, stirring occasionally.

3. Allow to cool. Pour the syrup into a clean, dry bottle; cork tightly.

4. In a pitcher, mix 1 part syrup, 3 parts water, and 2 ice cubes per person. Stir with a spoon and serve well chilled. *Nush-e-Jan!*

Variation: In a saucepan, bring the sugar and 4 cups water to a boil. Tie up the rhubarb pieces in cheesecloth. Place the cheesecloth in the sugar and water and simmer over medium heat for 30 minutes, or until the syrup thickens. Remove the cheesecloth, pour the syrup into a clean, dry bottle, and cork tightly. Serve as in step 4 above.

Rose Water Syrup

2½ cups water
4 cups sugar
¼ cup fresh lime juice
½ cup rose water

Makes 1 pint
Preparation time: 5 minutes
Cooking time: 20 minutes

Sharbat-e gol-e Mohammadi

1. Bring water and sugar to a boil in a saucepan. Simmer for 10 minutes. Add the lime juice and rose water and cook 10 minutes longer, stirring occasionally.

2. Remove the pan from heat and allow to cool. Pour the syrup into a clean, dry bottle; cork tightly.

3. In a pitcher, mix 1 part syrup, 3 parts water, and 2 ice cubes per person. Stir with a spoon and serve well chilled. *Nush-e-Jan!*

Note: Rose water may be purchased in Iranian specialty stores.

Variation: This syrup can also be used to prepare basil-seed syrup *(Sharbat-e Tokhm-e Sharbaty)*. Soak 1 cup of basil seeds in 2 cups of water for a few hours, then add soaking seeds to the syrup in Step 2. An excellent syrup, this *sharbat* is especially associated with the mother of a newborn baby.

Vinegar Syrup

Makes 1 pint
Preparation time: 10 minutes
Cooking time: 35 minutes

Sharbat-e sekanjebin

6 cups sugar
2 cups water
1½ cups wine vinegar
4 sprigs fresh mint
1 cucumber, peeled and grated

Garnish
Lime slices
Sprigs of mint

1. Bring the sugar and water to a boil in a saucepan. Simmer for 10 minutes over medium heat, stirring occasionally, until sugar has thoroughly dissolved.

2. Add the vinegar and boil 15 to 20 minutes longer over medium heat, until a thick syrup forms. Remove the saucepan from heat.

3. Wash the mint sprigs and pat dry. Add them to the syrup. Allow to cool. Remove the mint and pour the syrup into a clean, dry bottle. Cork tightly.

4. In a pitcher, mix 1 part syrup, 3 parts water, and 2 ice cubes per person. Add the cucumber and stir well. Pour into individual glasses and decorate each with a slice of lime and a sprig of fresh mint. Serve well chilled. *Nush-e-Jan!*

Yogurt Drink

Makes 2 servings
Preparation time: 10 minutes

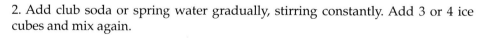

Dugh

1 cup whole-milk yogurt
1 teaspoon chopped fresh mint or
   a dash of dried mint flakes,
   crushed
¼ teaspoon salt
¼ teaspoon freshly ground
   black pepper
1½ cups club soda or spring water,
   chilled

1. Pour yogurt, mint, salt, and pepper into a pitcher. Stir well.

2. Add club soda or spring water gradually, stirring constantly. Add 3 or 4 ice cubes and mix again.

3. Serve chilled. *Nush-e-Jan!*

Note: This drink is associated with Rice with Kabab (*Chelow Kabab*).

MADE AND STORED KITCHEN INGREDIENTS

Yogurt

Makes 6 servings
Preparation time: 20 minutes
plus 12 hours setting time

Mast

2 quarts whole milk (8 cups)
1–2 cups plain yogurt
1 cup half-and-half (optional)

1. Bring the milk to a boil over medium heat in a very clean, nonreactive pot. Dirty or greasy utensils will not produce the desired results.

2. Remove the milk from heat; let stand until cool but not completely cold. The temperature of the milk is very important at this stage. It should not be too cold or too hot: If the milk is too cool, the culture will not grow; if it is too warm the heat will kill the bacteria in the culture. If using a thermometer, the temperature should be 106°F to 109°F, or with some experience you can test by hand. Put your little finger in the milk and count to 20. The temperature is correct if you can just tolerate the heat.

3. Pour the milk into a Pyrex dish, reserving 1 cup for step 4. Pull out the rack in the center shelf of the oven and place the dish on it.

4. Dilute the yogurt in 1 cup cooled milk and the half-and-half (if used). Gradually add the mixture to a different corner of the Pyrex dish. Cover the dish with its lid and gently push the rack back inside the oven. Close the oven door and turn on the inside light. **Do not heat the oven.** Allow to rest undisturbed at least overnight. (Yogurt must be stored in a draft-free, protected spot and not moved or touched during this period, and your oven is the ideal place for this. You may want to wrap the dish with a large towel or blanket and let it rest undisturbed in a corner of your kitchen for at least 24 hours.)

5. Yogurt can be stored in a refrigerator for 3 to 4 days. *Nush-e Jan!*

Note: For low-fat yogurt, use low-fat milk and eliminate the half-and-half.

To make sour yogurt, store the yogurt at room temperature for a few hours, and then refrigerate.

The correct temperature is essential in making yogurt. Also, it is important that the pot not be moved during the process.

Variation: Thick yogurt (*mast-e kisei*)—Pour the yogurt into 3 layers of cheesecloth or a cotton bag, pull the ends together and then hang the bag for 15 to 20 minutes over a large pot to catch the yogurt drips. All the liquid will slowly drain out, leaving behind thick and creamy yogurt. Or you may use a yogurt funnel; see the specialty stores list in the back of this book for a mail order source.

Persian-American Method: Place 3 or 4 layers of paper towels over the top of the bowl of yogurt for a few hours to absorb the excess liquid. Place the bowl of yogurt into a larger container to catch the drips from the paper towels and store the yogurt in the refrigerator. After a few hours remove the paper towel.

Persian Cheese

½ gallon whole milk
1 cup plain yogurt
2 tablespoons salt
¼ cup fresh lime juice
Cheesecloth for straining
   the mixture
½ teaspoon salt for Step 5

Makes 6 servings
Preparation and cooking time: 20
minutes plus 6 hours to settle
before setting

Panir

1. Pour the milk into a large pot. Bring to a boil over low heat.

2. Add the yogurt, 2 tablespoons salt, and lime juice to the pot of milk. Mix well and simmer over low heat for 3 to 5 minutes, or until its color turns yellowish.

3. Line a strainer with three layers of cheesecloth and place the strainer in a large container. Remove the pot from the heat and immediately pour the milk-yogurt mixture over the cheesecloth. Let drain for several minutes. Save the liquid in the large container for Step 5.

4. To remove excess water from the milk-yogurt mixture, bundle the free ends of cheesecloth together over the mixture to enclose it. Place the cheesecloth in the center of the strainer and place a heavy weight on top of the cheesecloth. Allow to stand for about 3 hours, then remove the weight and open up the cheesecloth. Remove the cheese and place it in a container. Refrigerate for 3 hours to set thoroughly.

5. Cut the cheese into pieces and place the pieces in a sterilized jar. Fill the jar with the strained liquid from Step 3 and add ½ teaspoon salt. Refrigerate until ready to serve.

6. Serve the cheese with bread and fresh vegetables and herbs. *Nush-e Jan!*

Liquid Whey

8 cups yogurt
½ tablespoon salt

Makes one-half pint
Preparation time: 2 days
Cooking time: 4 days in a warm oven

Kashk

This recipe was given to me by Mr. Parsa.

Kashk is a drained, salted and sun-dried yogurt. It can also be obtained by drying yogurt.

1. Make sour yogurt as for the yogurt recipe (page 372) or use commercial sour plain yogurt. Store yogurt for 2 days at room temperature for it to become sour. Place the soured yogurt in a blender and mix for 5 minutes, until it reaches a smooth consistency.

2. Transfer the yogurt to a Pyrex dish. Cover it with another glass and place it in a warm oven (140°F to 150°F). After few hours check the amount of condensation on the lid. No condensation indicates that the temperature is too high. Slight condensation means the temperature is correct. Adjust the heat.

3. Leave the glass dish covered in the warm oven for 3 to 4 days; do not disturb it.

4. Remove the dish from the oven and uncover it. Observe the color and scent: The contents should be yellowish and have a distinctive smell.

5. Line a strainer with 2 layers of cheesecloth and place it over a large pot. Pour the contents of the container over the cheesecloth. Tie the end shut and allow to drain for several hours so that the excess water drains away. Catch drips in the pot.

6. Remove the contents from the cheesecloth and place in a food processor. Add ½ tablespoon salt and mix in food processor for another 3 minutes to obtain *kashk*.

7. Place *kashk* in an airtight jar and keep in the refrigerator for 2 weeks, or store in separate small plastic bags in the freezer and use as needed

Note: Low-fat yogurt can be used to produce a low-fat *kashk*. Pass through a blender, drain, and pour in a fruit dehydrator. The drying process is reduced to a few hours.

Persian-American Method: In a food processor, combine 2 cups drained yogurt with ½ cup grated mature cheddar cheese (which provides the tang associated with *khask*). Add 1 cup sour cream, 1 teaspoon salt, and mix well. Use as needed.

Variation: Black whey (*Qaraqorut*)—Cook the whey over high heat for 20 minutes. Add ½ teaspoon flour, mix well, and continue cooking until it reaches a consistency of thick, black paste, which is extremely sour and has a lot of nutritional properties. It is used for soup, fish, and sometimes sauces.

Dried Tamarind Liquid

1 pound dried tamarind pods
8 cups water

Makes one-half pint
Preparation time: 10 minutes
Cooking time: 40 minutes

آب تمرهندی

Ab-e tamr

1. Place the tamarind pods in a large saucepan and cover with the water.

2. Bring to a boil, reduce the heat, and simmer for 30 minutes over medium heat, until soft. Add more water if necessary.

3. Place a colander over a bowl, drain the softened tamarind through the colander, and with a masher push through and crush the pods to extract as much liquid as possible.

4. Pour more boiling water over the pods if necessary to extract more liquid.

5. Transfer the liquid into a clean, dry jar, seal, and store it in a cool, dark place.

Note: Dried tamarind and liquid tamarind are available at Iranian specialty stores.

Pomegranate Paste

8 cups fresh pomegranate juice (if
the pomegranate juice is sweet
rather than sour, add the juice of
2 limes to make it sour)
1 tablespoon salt

Makes one-half pint
Preparation time: 20 minutes
Cooking time: 1 hour

رب انار

Rob-e anar

1. In a large and heavy laminated pan, pour in the pomegranate juice.

2. Bring to a boil over high heat. Reduce the heat, add 1 tablespoon salt, and let simmer uncovered for about 1 hour or more over medium heat.

3. Gently stir occasionally until the syrup has thickened, then remove the pan from the heat.

4. Sterilize jars in boiling water; drain and dry thoroughly. Fill the jars with pomegranate paste. Seal them and keep in a cool, dark place.

A 16th-century cookery book from the Safavid Court describes rob, *which are fruit and vegetable juices cooked down to a paste. Juices mentioned included quince, barberry, sour grape, apple, Seville orange, and pomegranate.*

Tomato Paste

12 pounds large red tomatoes
2 tablespoons salt

Makes 2 pints
Preparation time: 45 minutes
Cooking time: 1 hour 30 minutes

1. Wash the tomatoes and peel them.

2. Using a food processor or juicer, extract the tomato juice.

3. Pour the tomato juice into a large laminated pot, add 1 tablespoon salt and bring to a boil. Reduce the heat and cook for about 1 hour, stirring occasionally with a wooden spoon.

4. Add another tablespoon salt and continue cooking over medium heat until the water evaporates, leaving the paste behind.

5. Fill sterilized jars with the paste, seal them tightly, and store them in a cool, dark place.

رب گوجه فرنگی

Rob-e gojehfarangi

Persian Allspice for Rice

Makes about one-half cup

2 tablespoons ground dried rose
** petals**
2 tablespoons ground cinnamon
2 tablespoons ground cardamom
1 tablespoon ground cumin

1. Mix all the ground spices together in a bowl. Store in an airtight container to preserve freshness.

ادویه پلو

Advieh-ye polow

Persian Allspice for Pickle

Makes about 1 cup

Advieh-ye torshi

2 tablespoons ground green
cumin seed
2 tablespoons ground black
cumin seed
3 tablespoons ground angelica
(*gol-par*)
½ teaspoon freshly ground
black pepper

1 tablespoon ground saffron
½ teaspoon ground turmeric
3 tablespoons ground coriander
2 tablespoons ground cinnamon
3 tablespoons ground ginger
1 tablespoon ground cardamom

Mix all the ground spices together. Store in an airtight container to preserve their aroma.

Persian Allspice for Khoresh

Makes about one-third cup

Advieh-ye khoresh

2 tablespoons ground dried
rose petals
2 tablespoons cinnamon
1 teaspoon ground cardamom
½ teaspoon freshly ground
black pepper
1 teaspoon ground angelica
(*gol-par*)

1 teaspoon ground nutmeg
1 teaspoon ground cumin
½ teaspoon ground coriander seeds
1 teaspoon dried Persian lime powder (*limu-omani*)

Grind all the spices and mix. Store in an airtight container to preserve freshness.

Dried Persian Lime Powder

With the help of a knife, crack open each dried lime into halves and remove any seeds. Then place the dried limes in a food processor and grind. Transfer to an airtight jar and use as needed.

Note: Commercial Persian lime powder is bitter because the seeds are ground with the limes.

Gard-e limu-omani

Removing Bitterness from Orange Peel

10 oranges

Makes about 3 cups

چگونه تلخی پوست پرتقال را بگیرید

Talkhi gereftan-e pust-e porteqal

1. Wash the oranges. Peel thin layers with a peeler and leave the pith on the orange; save the oranges for a fruit salad.

2. Cut the orange peel into slivers of desired length.

3. Place the slivers in a large saucepan and cover with water. Bring to a boil, reduce heat, and cook for 10 minutes over medium heat. Drain in a colander. Store the orange peel slivers in a plastic bag in the freezer and use as needed.

Removing Bitterness from Eggplants

Method #1

Peel and cut the eggplants into slices of desired thickness and length. Place the eggplant slices in a colander, and place the colander in the sink. Sprinkle the eggplant with water and then with 2 tablespoons salt. Let stand for 20 minutes. The salt will draw out bitter, black juices from the eggplant. Rinse the eggplant with cold water and pat dry.

چگونه تلخی بادمجان را بگیرید

Talkhi gereftan-e bademjan

Method #2

Soak the sliced eggplant in a large container full of cold water with 2 tablespoons salt for 20 minutes. Drain, rinse with cold water, and pat dry.

Cleaning Dried Barberries

چگونه زرشک را پاک کنید و بشویید

Tamiz kardan-e zereshk

Fruit of the barberry bush has been popular since ancient times in Iran. Small, red, sour and tiny, barberries are too sour to eat raw and are a valuable source of malic acid.

In Iran, barberries (*zereshk*) are dried and stored. Be sure to use red-colored dried barberries and not dark ones, which may be old and from a previous season. The color and taste of the barberries depends on the quality of the berry.

Dried barberries contain a lot of sand. When washed properly, they have a beautiful red color.

Clean barberries by removing their stems and placing them in a colander. Place the colander in a large container full of cold water and allow the barberries to soak for 15 minutes. The sand will settle to the bottom of the container. Take the colander out of the container and run cold water over the barberries; drain and set aside. Pat dry and store in a freezer to retain their fresh color.

Seville Orange Paste

20 oranges

Preparation time: 45 minutes
Cooking time: 1 hour 30 minutes

رب نارنج

Rob-e narenj

1. Wash and remove a ring of orange peel from around the middle of each orange. Cut each orange in half and remove the seeds. Process the juice in a juicer to make 5 to 6 cups of juice, or use commercial Seville orange juice.

2. Pour the juice into a laminated container. Bring to a boil, reduce the heat, and simmer over medium heat for about 1 hour 30 minutes or until the juice has thickened. Be sure not to overcook. Remove from the heat.

3. Put the Seville orange paste in a sterilized jar, seal it tightly, and store in a cool, dark place.

Grape Essence

10 pounds seedless grapes
2 cups grape juice
¼ cup charcoal powder or 4 charcoal
    tablets
½ teaspoon ground cardamom

(شیره) دوشاب انگور

Dushab-e angur

1. Wash and separate the grapes from the stems and seeds. Puree in a food processor, then place them in a laminated pot.

2. Process 1 pound of the grapes in a juicer to obtain 2 cups of juice, or use commercial grape juice. Add 4 charcoal tablets to the juice. Mix well until the tablets are completely dissolved. Let stand for 20–40 minutes, then gently pour the juice into the laminated pot, leaving the sediment behind.

3. Bring the pureed grapes to a boil. Reduce heat and simmer over low heat for a few hours, stirring frequently with a wooden spoon, until all the juice has evaporated and the paste has thickened.

4. Add cardamom and remove from heat. Place in sterilized jars, seal tightly and store in a cool dark place.

Note: Charcoal tablets are available at pharmacies.

Candied Orange Peel

3 large oranges
4 cups sugar
3 cups water
4 tablespoons lime juice

Makes 3 cups
Preparation time: 20 minutes
Cooking time: 30 minutes

خلال پوست پرتقال شیرین

Pust-e porteqal-e shirin

1. Scrub and wash the oranges. Peel the oranges, leaving the pith on them. Save the fruit for a fruit salad.

2. Cut the orange peel into thin slivers.

3. To remove the bitterness from the orange-peel slivers, place them in a large saucepan and cover with water. Bring to a boil, reduce heat, and cook for 10 minutes over medium heat, then drain in a colander.

4. Place the orange peel back in the saucepan and add 4 cups of sugar and 3 cups of water. Bring to a boil, reduce heat, and gently simmer uncovered for 1–1½ hours, or until all the water has evaporated. Add lime juice and continue cooking for 5 minutes longer.

5. Drain orange peel and spread on wax paper. Allow to dry for a few hours. Store in a plastic bag in the refrigerator. Use as needed.

Variation: Grapefruit can be substituted for the orange peel. To remove the bitterness from the grapefruit, boil the grapefruit peel for 20 minutes, drain, and pass through cool water.

Essence of Wheat Germ for *Sofreh-ye Haft-Sinn*

**1 pound whole-wheat grain with
    skin or ready-made sprouts
2 to 4 cups cold water
4 pounds whole-wheat flour
¼ cup pistachios
¼ cup almonds
¼ cup hazelnuts**

*Preparation time: 20 minutes
plus 7 days for making sprouts
Cooking time: 1 day*

Samanu

*Halva is the Arabic derivative of
sweet, referring to Sen pudding
cream made from wheat sprouts.
Originally made in Zoroastrian
times as a celebratory dish, it was
prepared on the last day of the
new year to sustain the ancestors
on their heavenward journey
following their annual visit to
the east.*

1. Place the grain in a bowl; cover with cold water. Let it soak for 2 days; change the water twice.

2. Drain and spread the whole-wheat grain over a cotton napkin. Bundle the free ends of the napkin together.

3. Place the napkin with the soaked wheat grain in the bowl for 2 more days. Sprinkle with water several times.

4. Remove the cloth bundle from the bowl and spread the grains over a flat plat-ter. Cover with the damp cloth. Place the platter in a warm place for about 3 days. Sprinkle the cloth with cold water twice a day.

5. Check to see if the wheat grain has sprouted. Cut the early, silvery sprouts for use, or use ready-made sprouts.

6. Place the sprouts in a food processor, add 2 to 3 cups cold water, and puree them until creamy.

7. Gradually add the flour to the food processor. Mix well so no lumps remain. Add more water if necessary. Transfer into a large pot and cook over low heat for several hours, stirring occasionally, until the color changes and the mixture forms a caramel paste the color of peanut butter. Add more warm water until the paste turns into a sweet cream; mix well so that no lumps remain. Add pistachios, almonds, and hazelnuts. Cover and simmer over low heat for 20 minutes.

Note: Do not add any sugar. The wheat and flour combination will create its own sugar.

زندگی خالی نیست

مهربانی هست ، سیب هست ، ایمان هست

آری

تا شقایقی هست ، زندگی باید کرد .

Life isn't empty:
There's kindess, there are apples, there's faith.
Yes,
While there's still an anemone one must live.

Sohrab Sepehri

CEREMONIES

'Tis spring, flowers full and happiness in the green-
    grass vine
All the blossoms are blooming except mine
Lose not heart free spirit on New Year's day
I heard from the lips of a lily today
Do not sing the seven shams this New Year's eve I
    beg thee
Complaint, curse, corruption, cacophony,
    clumsiness, chaos, and cruelty
The seven symbols, serene greenery, scented hyacinth
    and sweet apple
Senged, samanu, salway and song spell.
Send the seven symbols to the table of a lover
Throw the seven shams to the door of an ill wisher.
'Tis New Year's eve, rid the heart of darkness
Eventually this black night will turn to light
Carry out the New Year tradition and God willing
Bring back the feeling to that of the excellent
    beginning.

Bahar

SPRING FESTIVAL OR NEW YEAR'S CELEBRATION

NOWRUZ

In harmony with the rebirth of nature, the Iranian New Year celebration, or *Nowruz*, always begins on the first day of spring. The year changes on the vernal equinox, or *Tahvil*,
which may occur on March 20, 21, or 22. It makes its arrival at the precise moment that the
sun crosses the equator. Although Ferdowsi, the great Persian poet of the tenth century,
describes in his *Shahnameh* (The Book of Kings) how for the first time the legendary King
Jamshid celebrated *Nowruz*, many of its rituals go back at least three thousand years.

   Nowruz ceremonies are symbolic representations of two ancient concepts—the End and
the Rebirth, and Good and Evil. To this day, a few weeks before the new year, Iranians

New Year's Haft Sinn Setting

thoroughly clean and rearrange their homes. They make new clothes, bake pastries and germinate seeds as signs of renewal. The ceremonial cloth (*sofreh-ye haft-sinn*) is set up in each household. Troubadours, referred to as *Hadji Firuz*, disguise themselves with make-up and wear brightly colored outfits of satin. These *Hadji Firuz*, singing and dancing, pa-rade as a carnival through the streets with tambourines, kettle drums, and trumpets to spread good cheer and the news of the coming new year.

On the eve of the last Wednesday of the year (*Shab-e chahar shanbeh sury*, literally the eve of Red Wednesday or the eve of celebration), bonfires are lit in public places and people leap over the flames, shouting, "*Sorkhi-e to az man o zardi-e man az to!*" (literally, "Give me your beautiful red color and take back my sickly pallor!"). With the help of fire and light, symbols of good, we hope to see our way through this unlucky night—the End of the Year—to the arrival of spring's longer days.

Traditionally, it is believed that the living were visited by the spirits of their ancestors on the last days of the year. Many people, especially children, wrap themselves in shrouds symbolically reenacting the visits. By the light of the bonfire, they run through the streets, banging on pots and pans with spoons called *qashogh-zany*, to beat out the last, unlucky Wednesday of the year, while they knock on doors to ask for treats. Indeed, Halloween is a Celtic variation of *Shab-e chahar shanbeh sury*. In order to make wishes come true, it is cus-tomary to prepare special foods and distribute them on this night: *Ash-e reshteh-ye nazri* (Noodle Soup), a filled Persian delight (*Baslogh*), and special snacks called *ajil-e chahar shanbeh soury* and *ajil-e moshkel gosha*. The last, literally meaning unraveler of difficulties, is made by mixing seven dried nuts and fruits—pistachios, roasted chick-peas, almonds, ha-zelnuts, peaches, apricots, and raisins. Another ritual is *fal-gush*, in which someone makes a wish and then stands at the corner of an intersection, or on a terrace or behind a wall. That person will know his fortune when he overhears conversations of passersby.

A few days prior to the New Year, a special cover is spread onto the Persian carpet or on a table in every Persian household. This ceremonial table is called *sofreh-ye haft-sinn* (lit-erally cloth of seven dishes, each one beginning with the Persian letter *sinn*). The number seven has been sacred in Iran since ancient times, and the seven dishes stand for the seven angelic heralds of life—rebirth, health, happiness, prosperity, joy, patience, and beauty. The symbolic dishes consist of *sabzeh*, or sprouts, usually wheat or lentil, representing re-birth. *Samanu* is a pudding in which common wheat sprouts are transformed and given new life as a sweet, creamy pudding, and represents the ultimate sophistication of Persian cooking. *Sib* means apple and represents health and beauty. *Senjed*, the sweet, dry fruit of

New Year's Haft Sinn setting painted by a student of Kamal-ol Molk, Hosein Sheikh

the lotus tree, represents love. It has been said that when the lotus tree is in full bloom, its fragrance and its fruit make people fall in love and become oblivious to all else. *Seer*, which is garlic in Persian, represents medicine. *Somaq,* sumac berries, represent the color of sunrise; with the appearance of the sun Good conquers Evil. *Serkeh,* or vinegar, represents age and patience.

To reconfirm the hopes and wishes expressed by the traditional foods, other elements and symbols are also on the *sofreh.* Two books of tradition and wisdom are laid out: a copy of the Koran; and a volume of the poems of Hafez, one of the great lyric Persian poets of the fourteenth century. A few coins placed on the *sofreh* represent prosperity and wealth; a basket of painted eggs represents fertility. A Seville orange floating in a bowl of water represents the earth floating in space, and a goldfish in a bowl of water represents life and the end of the astral year—Pisces. A flask of rose water, known for its magical cleansing power, is also included on the tablecloth. Nearby is a brazier for burning wild rue, a sacred herb whose smoldering fumes ward off evil spirits. A pot of flowering hyacinth or narcissus is also set on the *sofreh*: these are the two Persian flowers that bloom in spring, and their sweet odor acknowledges the fifth sense. On either side of a mirror are two candelabra holding a flickering candle for each child in the family. The candles represent enlightenment and happiness. The mirror represents the images and reflections of Creation as we celebrate anew the ancient Persian traditions and beliefs that creation took place on the first day of spring, or *Nowruz.* With the help of fire and light, we hope for enlightenment and happiness throughout the coming year.

On the same table many people place seven special sweets because, according to a three-thousand-year-old legend, King Jamshid discovered sugar on *Nowruz* (the word candy comes from the Persian word for sugar, *qand*). These seven sweets are *noghls* (sugar-coated almonds); *Persian baklava,* a sweet, flaky pastry filled with chopped almonds and pistachios soaked in honey-flavored rose water; *nan-e berenji* (rice cookies), made of rice flour flavored with cardamom and garnished with poppy seeds; *nan-e badami* (almond cookies), made of almond flour flavored with cardamom and rose water; *nan-e nokhodchi* (chick-pea cookies), made of chick-pea flour flavored with cardamom and garnished with pistachios; *sohan asali* (honey almonds), cooked with honey and saffron and garnished with pistachios; and *nan-e gerdui* (walnut cookies), made of walnut flour flavored with cardamom and garnished with pistachio slivers.

A few hours prior to the transition to the New Year, *Tahvil-e sal,* family and friends sit around the *sofreh-haft sinn.* Everyone sings traditional songs, and the poems of Hafez and verses from the Koran are recited. I remember an amusing story about my aunt. She would always carry a tattered divan of the poems of Hafez and, just prior to the *Tahvil* (equinox), while we were all sitting around the *sofreh*, she would ask each of us to make a wish so that she could ask Hafez about our fortune. Then she would lay the closed book, spine down, on the palm of her left hand while she passed her right index finger several times up and down the page edges. With her eyes closed she would ask out loud:

Ay Hafez-e Shirazi to ke mahram-e har razy! To ra be Shakh-e Nabatat qassam...

Oh Hafez of Shiraz, knower of all secrets, by the love of your sweetheart, *Shakh-e Nabat...* She would continue with the rest of her questions in silence and finally she would open the book by placing her fingernail randomly into the pages. With the first glance at the verses on the page, she would cry out, *bah- bah!* wonderful, wonderful, how beautiful! She would go on like this for a good minute or two while we sat round-eyed and impatient, waiting to know our fortunes. At last she would begin the first verse of the poem:

Nafas-e bad sabah...   نفس باد صبا مشک فشان خواهد شد

The gentle breeze will blow anew / Vitality to the barren earth / The old will become young...

For the new year, some families float a Seville orange in a bowl of water, while other families place an egg on top of a mirror. They believe there is a small movement at the moment of equinox, and the Seville orange will move in the water or the egg on the mirror, indicating the precise moment of the transition of the year.

As the sun enters the constellation Aries from Pisces on the stroke of the equinox, *Tahvil*, the passage, is announced by firing cannons and on radio and television. The oldest person present begins the well-wishing by standing up and giving everyone a sweet pastry, some gold or silver coins, and lots of hugs. Calm, happiness, sweetness, and perfumed odors are very important on this day of rebirth, since the mood on this day is said to continue throughout the year. An old saying goes, "Good thought, good word, good deed— to the year end, happy indeed."

The New Year celebration continues for twelve days after the equinox occurs. Traditionally, during the first few days, it is the younger members of the family who visit their older relatives and friends in order to show their respect. Sweet pastries and delicious frosty drinks are served to visitors, and there is a general air of festivity all around. The children receive gifts, usually crisp new notes of money; in America, dollar bills. In the remaining days, the elders return the visits of the younger members of the family.

On the thirteenth day of *Nowruz*, called *Sizdeh-bedar*, literally outdoor thirteen, entire families leave their homes to carry trays of sprouted seeds in a procession to go picnic in a cool, grassy place. Far from home, they throw the sprouts into the water and complete the process of the end of one year and the rebirth of another. Wishing to get married by the next year, unmarried girls tie blades of grass together. There is much singing, dancing, eating, and drinking on this joyful day that marks the end of the *Nowruz* celebration.

Fish and noodles are usually served on New Year's Day. It is believed they bring good luck in the year that lies ahead. The traditional menu usually includes:

Noodle Soup—*Ash-e reshteh*, noodles representing the Gordian knots of life. Eating them symbolically helps toward unraveling life's knotty problems.

Rice with Fresh Herbs and Fish—*Sabzi polow ba mahi*, fresh herb rice representing rebirth, fish representing life.

Herb Kuku—*Kuku-ye sabzi*, eggs representing fertility.

Bread, Cheese, and Fresh Herbs—*Nan-o panir-o sabzi khordan*, representing prosperity.

Man carrying sprouts

Have I enough? Am I secure or not?
Will blessings and my joys endure or not?
Ah, fill my cup with wine—who knows, the breath
Inhaled, I may exhale for sure or not?

Omar Khayyam

WEDDING CEREMONY
JASHN-E ARUSI

Facing Kaaba, or the Sacred House of God, (*ru be Qebleh*) and dressed in white satin or silk with gold embroidery, the bride sits facing a mirror, *ayeneh-ye bakht*, or the mirror of fate. It is framed in silver, gold, or crystal and lit by two candelabra, one on either side, one representing the bride and the other, the groom. According to tradition, the mirror and candlesticks, symbolizing purity and love, should be gifts from the groom. Just before sunset, when he enters the room in the bride's home where the ceremony will be held, what he sees first should be the face of his wife-to-be, reflected in the mirror.

The *sofreh-ye aqd*, the wedding cloth, a fine hand-sewn *termeh* glittering with gold and silver threads, is spread out before the mirror. Food and objects traditionally associated with marriage are arranged on the *sofreh*. These are:

A tray of *atel-o-batel* (spices to guard against witchcraft and to drive the evil spirits away). This tray consists of seven elements in seven colors: poppy seeds (to break spells and witchcraft), wild rice, angelica, salt and green leaves (to remove the evil eye), nigella seed, gunpowder and frankincense (*kondor*), to burn the evil spirits;

An assortment of sweets and pastries prepared in the bride's home but paid for by the groom. Among them are *noghls*, sugar-coated almonds; *nabat*, sugar crystals; *baqlava*, a sweet, flaky pastry; *tut*, mulberry-almond paste; *nan-e berenji*, rice cookies; *nan-e nokhodchi*, chick-pea cookies; *nan-e badami*, almond cookies; and *sohan asali*, honey almonds;

A large flat *sangak* bread with a blessing (*mobarak-bad*) written in calligraphy with saffron or cinnamon or nigella seeds;

A platter of feta cheese and fresh herbs to be shared with the guests immediately after the ceremony to bring the new couple happiness and prosperity;

A basket of colored eggs and a basket of almonds and walnuts in the shell to symbolize fertility;

A bowl of honey to make the future sweet;

Two large loaves of sugar, *kallehqand*, to be used in the ceremony;

Fresh flowers, such as tuberose, gardenia, jasmine and baby's breath, in abundance, to express the hope that beauty will adorn the couple's life together;

An open flask of rose water to perfume and purify the air;

A needle and seven strands of seven colored threads to sew up the mother-in-law's mouth—only figuratively, of course;

A small brazier burning wild rue, *espand*, the fumes of which are said to drive away evil spirits; and

An open Koran or other holy books.

As the ceremony begins, the women who are happily married, friends, or relatives of the bride are invited by the bride's mother to gather in the ceremony room. Two of them hold a square of white silk or cotton over the bride's head while another sews a piece of tissue using the seven colored threads; yet another rubs two sugar loaves together to symbolize the raining of sweet joy and happiness down upon the bride and groom. With each stitch, the seamstress chants, "I am sewing the mother-in-law's tongue, now I am sewing the sister-in-law's tongue, now I am sewing up all the other family members' tongues." Others chant, "Endear her, endear her."

A holy man chosen by the couple reads the marriage contract and recites the traditional prayers. (During the reading of the marriage contract, all the unmarried women are asked to leave the room, the belief being that their own marriages would be jinxed.)

The holy man then asks the bride, "Young and noble woman, do you realize you are marrying an honorable man for this *mahr?*"

But the bride is silent and those in attendance pretend the bride is absent, saying such things as, "She is not here. She went out to gather rosebuds." Again he asks the question. This time the guests might answer, "The bride went to the library."

The holy man repeats the question three times and the bride finally answers with a shy, barely audible, "Yes." He then declares the couple husband and wife. The groom kisses the bride, although the groom cannot join the bride until after the *Arusi*, the reception celebration. (Traditionally, *arusi* follows the *aqd* on the same night or may be held on a later day.)

The bride and groom moisten their little fingers with some honey and place it in each other's mouths, then they each place a *noghl*, a sugar-coated almond, in the other's mouth. Friends and relatives shower them with more *noghls* and gold or silver coins before offering them their wedding gifts.

At this moment the mother of the bride takes off the bride's right shoe and puts out the candles with it. The shoe symbolizes *bakht* (fate).

To bring sweetness and energy for the wedding night, sometimes an egg omelet is cooked and sprinkled with the same sugar that the bride and groom were showered with; this is then served to the bride and groom.

The wedding is a splendid affair, held in the home of the groom. A lavish meal is offered, sometimes with a whole roast lamb as the centerpiece. *Shirin polow*, or sweet rice, is always served, along with many other dishes and an elaborate wedding cake. The celebration, with so much feasting, singing, and dancing, is a day for all to remember.

After the guests have gone home, it is customary to give the remaining pastries to those who were unable to come and to those who helped make the day a success. The *kallehqand*, or sugarloaf, is kept by the bride.

Before they enter their home, the bride kicks over a bowl of water placed in the doorway. The water spilled on the threshold represents enlightenment, happiness, and purification for her new house. A friendly competition starts with the bride and groom as the bride tries to enter her house while stepping on her husband's feet. This act makes the bride the boss in the household.

During the past many years, the Persian communities abroad have changed and adopted the life-styles of their host countries. Our ceremonies can also be modified according to these changes to create a simple yet meaningful and joyful experience.

For all the guests to be able to participate, you may choose to have your wedding ceremony setting over a table rather than on the floor. Meet with your holy man and mention the length of the ceremony and perhaps go through a rehearsal (five to ten minutes should be the maximum length of this speech). The bride and groom may wish to recite a favorite poem that applies to the occasion. Remember, every symbol and superstition in the ceremony is intended to create a positive air and energy to bless the marriage with sweetness, fertility, and tranquility. Preparing for the way you will conduct the ceremony is as important as the beauty of the setting.

I invite you to make a photocopy of the wedding ceremony section of this book and make it available to your non-Persian friends who may be attending the wedding (you can roll up the pages, tie them with a ribbon, and give one to each of the guests). In this way they may better understand our culture and the various elements in the ceremony.

Note: The section read from the Koran during the ceremony is frequently the sura *Al-Room* XXX, verses 20–21.

THE PROCEDURE FOR A PERSIAN MARRIAGE

Step #1. The suitor, or *khastegar*, with his parents or close elder relatives, pays a visit to the parents and close relatives of his future wife, and asks for her hand in marriage.

Step #2. Engagement Ceremony, *shirni-khory* and exchanging of rings and eating of sweets: Both sets of parents give formal permission for the future bride and groom to get better acquainted.

Step #3. *Ba'leh borun*: A ceremony that is attended by the close elder families of both the bride and the groom to discuss financial matters, rules and conditions of marriage, such as *mahr* and *jahaz*, and items of the dowry listed in the marriage contract. The *mahr* is a sum of money, an object of value, or a piece of property that the groom agrees to give to the bride. It is her financial security in case of marital discord. The bride brings her dowry, or *jahaz*, to her new home. The details of the *mahr* and *jahaz* are spelled out in the *qabaleh*, or marriage contract. The dowry can be silver, gold, carpets, household equipment, sometimes even land and real estate. Nowadays, the best dowry for any woman is a billion dollars, but lacking that, it is her education and career, which stay with her forever.

Step #4. *Aqd*, or marriage-contract ceremony: The betrothal ceremony where the legal contract, *aqdnameh* or *qabaleh* is read, agreed upon, and signed. *Aqd* is the legal and religious union of the marriage, while the true ceremony establishes the spiritual union of the bride and groom.

Step #5. *Arusi*: A lavish reception and celebration held after the *aqd*. Through this reception, the social recognition and union of the bride and groom are established, and this marks the beginning of their married life.

Step #6. *Pa-takhty* (Literally, by the bed!): The last phase of the wedding. Friends and family who were invited for the *aqd* and the *arusi* pay a visit to the newlywed couple the day after the wedding to offer their blessings and more gifts. At the close of *Pa-takhty* the couple is considered truly married.

Some important points for the mothers of the bride and groom to keep in mind before the ceremony. Remember, this is meant to be a joyful event and a spiritual ceremony, and not a performance or competition with another family.

1. Set the wedding date together with both families.

2. Set a budget.

3. Get in touch with the holy man who will perform the ceremony.

4. Get information about the state's marriage laws.

5. Get medical examinations.

6. Make a guest list including addresses. Usually older people are invited for *Aqd* (marriage-contract ceremony), and younger people are invited to the reception (*Arusi*).

7. Reserve a place for the reception. (Keep in mind that *Aqd* is always in the home of the bride's parents, or that of her close relatives. *Arusi* is hosted by the parents or relatives of the groom.

8. Print and mail invitation cards.

9. Arrange food catering.

10. Arrange pastry and flower catering and photography or video.

11. Get in touch with musicians.

12. Make an appointment with your hairdresser and your makeup artist.

13. Make arrangements for the transportation of gifts.

14. Choose and buy a gift for the bride/groom. If you are member of the groom's close family, you must buy a gift for the bride (traditionally jewelry or family jewelry) and vice versa.

15. Arrange a wedding shower (usually arranged by close family or friends of the bride).

A wedding shower is an old Persian custom still practiced in the villages of Iran. A few days before the marriage, an old wise woman of the community goes around with a large bag and collects gifts and household items for the newlywed couple-to-be to alleviate financial difficulties they will face starting their new life. However, it is quite all right to arrange a wedding shower by close friends or relatives.

16. Prepare a bridal registry. Check with major department stores and specialty shops. Good luck, and *mobarak-bad*.

Sweet Fritters
Zulbia
Recipe page 291

398

ماه شعبان منه از دست قدح کاین خورشید   از نظر تا شب عید رمضان خواهد شد

In the month Sha'ban, put not the goblet from thy hand. For this sun,
Only till the night of the 'id of Ramazan out of sight—shall be.

Hafez

RAMADAN, THE MONTH OF FASTING
RAMAZAN

Ramazan, the Muslim equivalent of Lent, is the ninth month of the lunar calendar, and fasting during Ramazan is one of the basic creeds of Islam. For thirty days Muslims must fast from dawn to dusk. Besides total abstinence from food and water, they must also refrain from such things as cigarettes, sex, evil thoughts, and lying. Fasting is a cleansing process for the body and the soul. By fasting, one concentrates less on food and materialism and gives the body a month's rest to detoxify. This cleansing has recently become fashionable in the West by going to health spas.

During this period, fasting is observed from dawn to dusk, so that it is permissible to eat at two times of the day, *sahari* (before dawn) and *eftari* (after sunset). These times are announced by a cannon shot across the town or by radio and television.

In our house, a few hours before dawn, my father Aqajan was the first to wake up. It was the sound of my Aqajan's *monajat*, a combination of poetry and improvisational prayers, that pulled us out of bed. I still remember his lyrical voice pouring out devotional prayers before dawn. These magical supplications addressed to God were very soothing and gave me strength and a sense of security, and they sometimes even made me cry.

Soon after Aqajan's prayers, a large embroidered cloth (*sofreh*) was spread on our colorful Persian carpet and covered with an array of warm aromatic and appetizing foods such as rice, stew, breads, cheese, fresh herbs, *mast-o-khiar* (yogurt and cucumber), and *tah-chin-e morgh* (baked rice with chicken). The *sahari* was a substantial meal since it had to sustain us throughout the day. I remember the radio announcers who reminded us that there was little time left before the last sip of water, the last bite of food, the last cigarette before dawn. After the *sahari*, everyone prayed and then most of us eagerly returned to bed.

The hardest part of the day was the last couple of hours before sunset. I remember Aqajan sitting in a corner over a *sajadeh* (prayer rug) where he meditated, murmuring prayers and waiting for the *Azan-e eftar*, or call for prayer, from the minaret. The kitchen was buzzing with activity at this point. Our housekeeper, my mother, and other members of our family were busily preparing the meals of *eftar* and *sahari*. The smells of the fried onion, garlic and mint, the cutlets, eggplants, and the *kuku* and the *kababs* were floating throughout the house, driving us all crazy.

Finally, the cry of the muezzin from the radio announced the *eftar*. We would all gather around the *sofreh* and samovar. Aqajan would always break his fast with a glass of sweet warm water, a soft-boiled egg, and a date. Nonetheless, a sumptuous feast was set on the *sofreh,* including different breads (*sangak, lavash, roghani,* and *shirmal*), cheeses, fresh herbs, butter, marmalade, cutlets, *kuku, mast-o-khiar,* sometimes *sholeh zard,* and especially *ash* and soup and different kinds of rice and stews. Most important were the sweet fritters (*zulbia va bamieh*), a dessert always associated with Ramazan.

In our house, we celebrated practically every night of the month of Ramazan except the night of *Ahyaz* (Ali, the cousin of the Prophet, was stabbed by an assassin's dagger on the nineteenth and died on the twenty-first); we spent this night in observance of that tragedy. On other evenings we had parties or gatherings of friends and family, as well as open houses. Many would join us for *eftar,* and others would arrive afterwards. There was always plenty of food, along with poetry recitation, interesting discussions, raconteurs, music, and games (particularly backgammon and chess). In my mind, I always thought of Ramazan as a time of festivity, which reminds me of Hafez's *ghazal* quoted above.

After thirty days, the sighting of the new moon marks the end of Ramazan, which was announced on the radio. This occasion, *Eyd-e Fetr,* is a popular festival on the Islamic calender. On this day, every good Muslim must break his fast by eating at least a date, and he must give alms both for his own sake and for the sake of all those for whom he is responsible, including the guest who may have spent the previous night under his roof. This type of legal alms consists of a sum of money (*fetriyeh*) corresponding to the price of a maund of wheat, about six pounds. There is also another donation usually passed on to the poorer sections of the community called *kafareh.* This sum is the cash equivalent of an individual's daily food expenses, to cover those who, for some reason or another, were not able to fast during Ramazan.

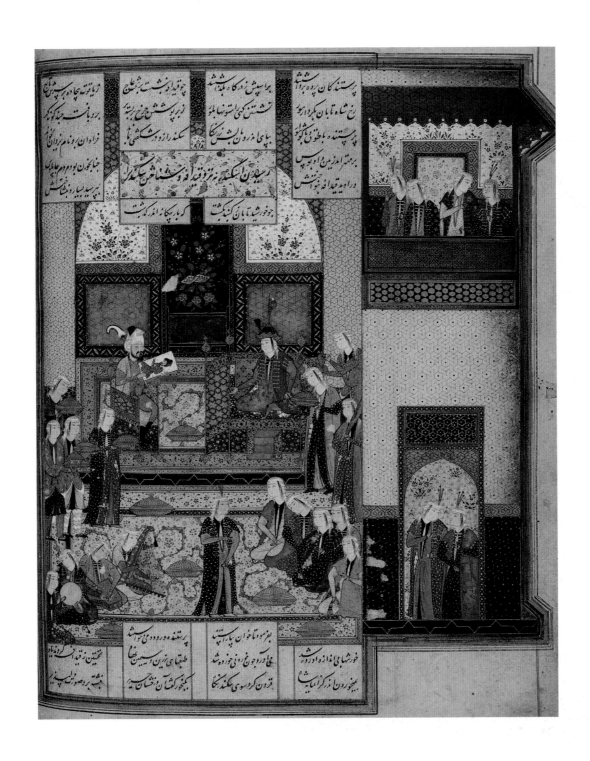

Iskandar is recognized by Queen Nushaba, 1560

Meeting of Khizr and Ilyas at the Fountain of Life

HAJJ AND THE DAY OF SACRIFICE
AYD-E QORBAN

The Hajj, or annual pilgrimage, is one of the pillars of Islam. Every year from the seventh to tenth day of *Ze-l'hajja*, the last month of the Islamic calendar, pilgrims don the *Ihram* (seamless white garments) and visit the Kaaba sanctuary, or the sacred House of God. They kiss the black stone, *Hajar al-Aswad*; perform seven circumambulations of the Ka'bah; and ascend, descend, and run between Mt. Safa and Mt. Marwah seven times. For the second stage of the ritual, the pilgrim proceeds from Mecca to Mina, a few miles away; from there he goes to Arafat, where it is essential to hear a sermon and to spend the afternoon. The last rite consists of spending the night at Muzdalifah, between Arafat and Mina, the following day proceeding to Mina, collecting pebbles on the way with which to stone the devil, represented by pillars, and offering animal sacrifice on the last day of the *Ihram*, which is the *Ayd-e Qorban*, or Festival of Sacrifice. Symbolically reliving the time Abraham was asked to sacrifice his son as proof of his devotion to him (Sura XXXVII (Saffat): 100–111), each pilgrim offers a lamb in sacrifice to God. The sheep must be purchased the day before the holiday. In some parts of Iran, on the day of the festival, henna is applied to the lamb's head and back. The edges of its eyelids must be rubbed with *kohl*, and sugar is put into its mouth before it is sacrificed. When the sheep is slaughtered, it must be facing Mecca, the Sacred House of God, and it must be killed with a single gash in the neck (*zebh*), but without severing the head. The meat is divided into three parts: one portion goes to the family, the second portion goes to friends, the third portion goes to the poor. The skin is usually kept as a rug and sometimes the intestines and the right eye are dried and preserved since they have the power to ward off evil.

During this festival, like any other, friends and family get together and cook a variety of foods associated with this celebration: big pots of meat soup (*ab-gusht*), sheep's head and feet soup (*kalleh-pacheh*), and tripe soup (*sirab-shirdan*). They make many kinds of kababs from the sheep's body parts, including the liver, heart, and kidneys.

Teahouse

We drank tea on the meadow of the table.

I opened the door: a piece of sky fell into my glass.
I drank the sky down with the water.

Sohrab Sepehri

چای را خوردیم روی سبزه زار میز .

در کشودم : قسمتی از آسمان افتاد در لیوان آب من .

آب را با آسمان خوردم

TEA

CHA'I

Tea was discovered about five thousand years ago in China.

In the early seventeenth century, tea was introduced to England and its Chinese name, *tay*, changed to the English name, tea. In England tea was brewed in china teapots. The English believed that a drop of milk in the teapot would prevent it from breaking and thus the tradition of drinking tea with milk started.

Around 1868, an Iranian merchant, later nicknamed *Chaikar*, or tea planter, brought tea from India to Iran. Tea became very popular in Iran and nowadays every Persian family has at least one samovar.

In most Iranian households, a samovar, a large metal container with three compartments—the top for keeping the teapot warm, the middle for water, and the bottom for hot coals (although today most samovars are electric)—sits on a large tray with a bowl called the *jaam* under the spout to catch the drips. The teapot, a jar of tea, and a covered bowl of sugar are set beside the samovar, which is kept steaming all day long. As soon as visitors step over the threshold, a small glass of tea with three lumps of sugar and a teaspoon is offered to them.

In Iran the color and appearance of tea is as important as its aroma and taste; therefore, tea is usually served in small glasses on saucers or in *engareh*, silver or gold holders that hold the glass.

However, it is interesting that Iranian teahouses are still called *qahveh khaneh*, which literally means coffeehouse. This name is left over from the time when coffee was served. Today the main drink served in these coffeehouses is tea! The *qahveh khaneh* are centers of social interaction.

In Iran tea is never drunk with milk. We take tea with sugar or with half a lime, honey, dates, raisins, or dried sweet white mulberries. A spoonful of sour-cherry jam dropped into a glass of tea gives it an excellent taste. Tea should always be served hot. I still remember our afternoon teas in the summer of my golden childhood years in Iran. We would all sit on the colorful Persian carpets over wooden benches around a stone pool full of goldfish, with the fountain gently spraying, the pomegranate tree in full bloom, and the smell of the watered brick-yard combined with the aroma of jasmines and gardenias floating through the air. Bronze samovars were lit, and a few tables were arranged with fruits and sweets. People would come and go, sitting near the pool and sometimes smoking the hookahs *(qalyan)*. We drank tea, talked, talked and drank tea. Sometimes even here at home, when I am alone and miss those childhood days, my eight-year-old son, Rostam, says, "Maman, don't be sad, lets have a chat over a glass of tea."

Here is how to make a good cup of tea:

Boil the water in a samovar or a kettle.

Warm a teapot by swirling some boiling water in it, then pour it out or into the *jaam*. Place 2 teaspoons of tea leaves to the pot. A 50/50 blend of Earl Grey and Darjeeling teas closely resembles Persian tea.

Fill the teapot half full with boiling water and steep the tea for 5 to 10 minutes on the top of the samovar or kettle, or by using a tea cozy. Do not let the tea steep for more than 10 minutes—the quality of it will deteriorate and you will have to start all over.

Before serving, pour a glassful of tea and return it to the pot to make sure the tea is evenly mixed.

Fill each glass halfway with tea, then add boiling water from the samovar or kettle. In this way the tea can be diluted to a fine color and to taste: some prefer their tea strong, others weak. Put the teapot back on top of the samovar or kettle or place the tea cozy on top of it to keep it hot. *Nush-e Jan!*

COFFEE
QAHVEH

The Persian word for coffee is *qahveh* and comes from the Arabic meaning something undesirable; in the case of coffee, it removes the appetite for food and sleep. Its first recorded use in the Middle East was in fifteenth-century Yemen, but its origin can be traced to Ethiopia. It is said that a shepherd first discovered coffee when his sheep were eating beans under a coffee tree. Coffee was drunk in mystical Sufi orders, especially *zikrs*. Thus, it was initially seen as an aid to staying awake for pious purposes. Coffeehouses flourished in the sixteenth century because of the need at the time for social gathering places. With the competition among the various coffeehouses came the provision of entertainment such as story-telling, *naqali* (recitations from the *Shahnameh*, the Book of Kings), puppet shows, jugglers, tumblers, and music. They also provided a forum for poets and writers (the precursors of the French cafe society). Later in nineteenth-century Iran tea replaced coffee as the favorite drink and most coffeehouses were replaced by teahouses, yet the name in Persian continues to remain coffeehouse, *qahveh khaneh*.

Iranian coffee is like Turkish coffee, thick and very strong. In fact, in Iran it is called Turkish coffee. It is made from coffee beans ground to a very fine powder and then simmered with sugar. It is usually made in a long-handled copper ewer called *ibriq*, and then poured into very small cups. It is easy to make:

1. For each small cup, put 1 teaspoon coffee, 1 teaspoon sugar, and 1 Turkish cup (small cup) water in an *ibriq*. Stir with a spoon.

2. Simmer over low heat until foam rises to the surface. If desired, add a dash of ground cardamom. Remove from the heat. To make sure that every cup of coffee has the same correct consistency, it is important fill each cup a little at a time until each is full. You have to sip the coffee carefully so as not to swallow any grounds. *Nush-e Jan!*

After drinking the coffee, remove the saucer and place it on top of the cup. Invert the cup and saucer away from yourself with your left hand (the hand of the heart) and let stand for 5 minutes without disturbing it. Then turn the cup over. A fortune-teller—or just a clever friend—can read your fate in the patterns of the grounds left behind in the cup.

Serve the coffee with pastries or fruit. Interestingly, for Armenian Iranians coffee is a social drink associated with festivals, while for Muslim Iranians coffee is associated with

WATER FESTIVAL
JASHN-E TIRGAN

Jashn-e Tirgan is a summer water festival celebrated in July (on the thirteenth day of the fourth month of the year on the Iranian calendar, called *Tir*). The month *Tir* refers to the archangel *Tir*, or *Tishtar*, lightning bolt, who appeared in the sky to create thunder and lightning, which announced the much-needed rain.

According to Iranian mythology, in legendary times, by mutual consent between Turan and Iran, Arash-e Kamangir shot his arrow over disputed land on the thirteenth day of the month of *Tir* to delineate their mutual border. The path of the arrow's flight thus established peace between the two countries. Commemoration of rain falling over peaceful lands may be one of the most ancient origins of summer water festivals. In these festivals, people shower each other with water to symbolize rain and its purity and magical cleansing powers.

This festival is still celebrated in some parts of Iran, and there is dancing, singing, eating, drinking, playing the tambourine, and reciting poetry. Spinach soup and beetroot *shuly* are associated with this day.

FIRE FESTIVAL
JASHN-E SADEH

زهوشنگ ماند این سده یادگار   بسی باد چنین او دگر شهریار

Jashn-e sadeh is the ancient festival of fire. The word *Sadeh* comes from the Persian word *sad*, which means one hundred. Sadeh is celebrated on the 31st of January, one hundred days after the beginning of the "great winter," which started on the first of *Aban* (October 21–23) in the old Iranian calendar. *Sadeh* has also been attributed to Kumarz, who celebrated it when the number of his children reached one hundred.

Others say that *Sadeh* comes from a legend related to Hushang Shah, an ancient Persian king who was out riding when a long black snake appeared in front of him. Scared and surprised, Hushang Shah threw a stone at the snake. He missed the snake but the stone hit some rocks and sparks flew up. The fire ignited by the sparks engulfed the snake and destroyed it.

This event is marked as the festival of *Sadeh*. Throughout the preceding day, the people gather firewood and kindling to build a huge bonfire. After sunset, seven magi clad in white robes arrive with torches to light the fire. The celebration begins. Holding hands and wearing colorful masks, people dance and sing around the fire. There are offerings of sandalwood, frankincense, *kondor*, and aromatic leaves to the fire. Jugglers and dancers perform by firelight, much to the delight of the excited children.

Potatoes and chestnuts, roasted in the ashes of the fire, are associated with this festival, as is barberry soup. Traditional sweets and drinks are the specialty of this day.

AUTUMN FESTIVAL
JASHN-E MEHREGAN

Jashn-e Mehregan is an autumn festival celebrated on the ninth or tenth day of October. Its origins lie in an ancient ritual dedicated to Mehr or Mitra, God of Light. *Mehregan* may also be one of the most ancient origins of the thanksgiving harvest ceremonies celebrated in the West.

In Iran, family and friends gather on *Mehregan* to reaffirm friendships and to make bread and food to share with the needy; a popular snack to prepare is a roasted nut mixture, *ajil*, to present to the less fortunate encountered on the streets. This celebration ends with bonfires, and fireworks light the way to the promise of a new dawn.

Ajil

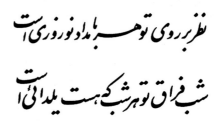

Sight of you each morning is a new year
Any night of your departure is the night of yalda.

Sa'di

WINTER FEAST
SHAB-E YALDA

In the East more than in the West, life-styles have often remained more in tune with nature. Therefore, natural rhythms change from morning to evening, from month to month, and finally from season to season. This integration of nature into life cycles is especially true in Iran. The winter solstice, December 21 or 22, is the longest night of the year. In Iran this night is called *Shab-e yalda*, which refers to the birthday or rebirth of the sun. The ceremony is traced to the primal concept of Light and Good against Darkness and Evil in the ancient Iranian religion. This night with Evil at its zenith is considered unlucky. From this day forward, Light triumphs as the days grow longer and give more light. This celebration comes in the Persian month of *Day*, which was also the name of the pre-Zoroastrian creator god (deity). Later he became known as the God of creation and Light, from which we have the English word day (the period of light in 24 hours).

In the evening of *Shab-e Yalda* bonfires are lit outside, while inside family and friends gather in a night-long vigil around the *korsi*, a low, square table covered with a thick cloth overhanging on all sides. A brazier with hot coals is placed under the table. All night the family and friends sit on large cushions (futons) around the *korsi* with the cloth over their laps. Formerly fruit and vegetables were only available in season and the host, usually the oldest in the family, would carefully save grapes, honeydew melons, watermelons, pears, oranges, tangerines, apples, and cucumbers. These were then enjoyed by everyone gathered around the *korsi,* or a fireplace.

On this winter night, the oldest member of the family says prayers, thanks God for the previous year's crops, and prays for the prosperity of next year's harvest. Then with a sharp knife, he cuts the thick yogurt, the melon, and the watermelon and gives everyone a share. The cutting symbolizes the removal of sickness and pain from the family. Snacks are passed around throughout the night: pomegranates with angelica powder (*gol-par*) and *Ajil-e shabchareh* or *Ajil-e shab-e yalda*, a combination of nuts and dried fruits, particu-

night-grazing; eating nuts is said to lead to prosperity in days to come. More substantial fare for the night's feast include eggplant stew with plain saffron-flavored rice; and rice with chicken; thick yogurt; saffron, and carrot brownies. The foods themselves symbolize the balance of the seasons: watermelons and yogurt are eaten as a remedy for the heat of the summer, since these fruits are considered cold or *sardi*, and *halva*, the saffron and carrot brownies, is eaten to overcome the cold temperatures of winter (since they are considered hot or *garmi*). On into the night of festivities, the family keeps the fires burning and the lights glowing to help the sun in its battle against darkness.

They recite poetry and play music, tell jokes and stories, talk and eat and eat and talk until the sun, triumphantly, reappears in the morning.

Early Christians took this very ancient Persian celebration to Mitra, Goddess of Light, and linked it to Christ's birthday. Today the dates for Christmas are slightly changed but there are many similarities: lighting candles, decorating trees with lights, staying up all night, singing and dancing, eating special foods, paying visits, and, finally, celebrating this longest night of the year with family and friends.

Why Is That Sufi in the Bath? from Haft Awrang of Jami, *attributed to Qadimi, circa 1550*

*I saw a woman pounding light with a mortar
    and pestle;
There was bread on their spread at noon,
There were greens, a plate of dew and a piping hot
    bowl of affection*

Sohrab Sepehri

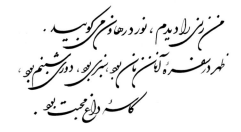

PERSIAN PUBLIC BATHS

HAMMAM-E UMUMY

Persian public baths are usually dome-shaped, skylit, and built next to a mosque. The public bath was one of the centers of community life and a source of information, particularly about suitors and marriage possibilities, and a place for discussions, singing, dancing, tambourine playing, jokes, gossip, hair coloring, and even doing laundry. From a sociological point of view, therefore, the public bath was of special importance. Women spent the whole day there, socializing and taking steam baths. Before going to the public bath they often prepared snacks and lunch, such as fruits, meatballs, chick-pea patties, meat paste, Persian pickles, flat *sangak* bread, romaine lettuce to be eaten with vinegar syrup (*sekanjebin*), pomegranate seeds with angelica powder and salt, white cheese and fresh herbs, and sometimes even noodle soup.

Generally the public bath has two sections: the *sarbineh*, or dressing room, and the indoor bath, or steam room. In the steam room one can stretch out, have a massage, be scrubbed with a wool bath mitt, or *kiseh*, and *sefidab*, a white abrasive cream which helps the peeling and scrubbing process. The scrubbing and massage are given by a masseur, or *dallak*. All the washing with soap, scrubbing of feet with pumice stone (*sang-e pa*), dyeing of hair with henna and conditioning takes place in the steam room. The final step is a rinse in the large pool (*khazineh*), which is now frequently replaced by showers.

After dressing, one is offered tea, cigarettes, or the *hookah*. Even today, going to the public bath is an enjoyable ritual for many women, whether they have baths in their own house or not.

For a mother, going to the bath ten days after her baby's birth is an important ritual and has a special ceremony. The night before this ceremony, women friends and close family wrap the mother's waist with an egg yolk and chick-pea powder paste. In the bath they rub this mixture and a special oil (*roghan-e momyai*) all over her body for hours, and celebrate the joy of a healthy birth by passing around drinks made with rose water and basil (*tokhm-e sharbaty*), and pastries and fruits.

چوں گل رفت و گلستان درگذشت   نشنوی زان پس ز بلبل سرگذشت
چوں گل رفت و گلستان شد خراب   بوی گل را از که جوئیم از گلاب

When the rose is gone and the garden fades, the nightingale's story will be heard no more
When the rose is gone and the garden laid, where should we seek the rose's scent? From the rosewater

Masnavi of Rumi

ROSE WATER
GOLAB

Rose water has been made in Iran from ancient times. Rose water and rose petals are used to make drinks and add scent to food and pastries. It is also used in mosques and public places to freshen the air. Rose water was also a part of every woman's makeup, and men use it as a cleanser for their moustaches and beards. In Iran, rose water comes mostly from Qamsar and Naissar, two small towns near Kashan in central Iran.

Roses are picked in the early morning when their scent is at its peak. The pickers place the flowers in a bag that hangs from their neck. After all the flowers are picked, they are transferred to bigger bags and transported to the rose-water factory for distillation.

The flowers are spread out on the floor in a cool room and sorted. The petals are then placed in a large iron pot with some water and covered with a pottery dish. The pot is heated and the rose petals and water form steam. The rose vapors rise up into a bamboo pipe, which runs into another pot that has been set in cold running water. As the warm vapors flow down into the cold pot, they condense and become liquid rose water. After the rose water has cooled, it is transferred into glass bottles. The rose water at the bottom of the iron pot is very concentrated and has a stronger aroma. This portion, which we know as oil of rose water, is poured into separate bottles and used as perfume. The residual rose petals are used as animal food.

If rose water is kept cool, its aroma will last for years.

MY MOTHER'S CLASSIFICATION ON "HOT" AND "COLD" FOODS

People are considered to have "hot" and "cold" natures, as does each type of food. This concept has nothing to do with the temperature or the spice and pepper content of the food; it is a system particular unto itself. For Persians, it is essential for persons with "hot" natures to eat "cold" foods and vice versa, in order to create a balanced diet.

Recipes in this book present a balanced diet by combining the opposing elements of "hot" and "cold." It should be noted that spices also play an important role in their pharmacological qualities rather than their culinary ones.

Meat

Beef, veal	cold
Duck	hot
Hen	hot
Lamb	hot
Red snapper	hot
All other fish	cold
Rooster	cold
Turkey	cold

Vegetables

Beets	cold
Cabbage	cold
Cardoons	cold
Carrots	hot
Cauliflower	cold
Celery	cold
Corn	hot
Cucumber	cold
Eggplants	cold
Garlic	hot
Grape leaves	cold
Green beans	cold
Green peas	cold
Green peppers	hot
Lettuce	cold
Mushrooms	hot
Okra	hot
Onions	hot
Potatoes	cold
Pumpkins	cold
Rhubarb	cold
Shallots	hot
Spinach	cold
Tomatoes	cold
Turnips	cold

Cereals and Beans

Barley	cold
Barley flour	cold
Chick-peas	hot
Corn starch	hot
Kidney beans	cold
Lentils	cold
Mung beans	hot
Pinto beans	cold
Rice	cold
Wheat flour	hot
Yellow fava beans	cold
Yellow split peas	hot

Fruits and Nuts

Almonds	hot
Apples	hot
Apricots	cold
Barberries	cold
Dates	hot
Figs	hot
Grapefruit	cold
Mangoes	hot
Nectarines	cold
Oranges	cold
Peaches	cold
Pears	neutral
Pistachios	hot
Prunes	cold
Quinces	hot
Raisins and grapes	hot
Sour cherries	cold
Sweet melon	hot
Walnuts	hot
Watermelon	cold

Herbs

Bay leaf	hot
Chives	hot
Coffee	cold
Coriander	cold
Dill weed	hot
Fenugreek	hot
Garden angelica	hot
Marjoram	hot
Mint	hot
Parsley	hot
Tarragon	hot
Tea	neutral
Whole Persian limes	cold

Spices

Cardamom	hot
Cinnamon	hot
Cloves	hot
Cumin seed	hot
Curry powder	hot
Ginger	hot
Nigella seed	hot
Nutmeg	hot
Pepper	hot
Saffron	hot
Salt	hot
Sumac	cold
Turmeric	hot

Other

Vanilla	hot
Eggs	hot
Feta cheese	neutral
Honey	hot
Lemon juice	cold
Milk	cold
Persian pickles	hot
Pomegranate paste	cold
Rose water	hot
Sugar	cold
Tamarind	cold
Tomato paste	cold
Sour grape juice	cold
Vinegar	hot
Whey	hot
Yogurt	cold

K I T C H E N   E Q U I P M E N T

Persian cooking does not require any special kitchen tools or equipment, although a heavy stew pot is essential and an electric rice cooker and food processor are helpful. An electric juice extractor is also helpful for preparing fruit syrups. The well-equipped kitchen should also have the following:

Cutting boards for vegetables, meat, and fish
Knives for cutting, slicing, filleting, boring, and chopping
Fish scaler
Rolling pin
Saucepans and frying or sauteing pans
Cast-iron pot with a cover for *khoresh*
Teflon-lined pot with lid for making golden-crust rice
Soup tureens
Ovenproof casserole dish with cover
Cookie sheets
Wax paper
Ladles/skimmers/spatulas
Kitchen tongs
Wooden spatula/spoon
Spice mill
Large stainless steel bowl for washing vegetables
Garlic crusher
Salad basket or spinner
Electric rice cooker
Food processor
Electric juice extractor
Cookie cutters
Rosette iron or window-cookie mold
Baking stone
Baker's peel

EQUIVALENT MEASURES

U.S.	Equivalents	Metric
Liquid		
1 teaspoon	60 drops	5 ml
1 tablespoon	3 teaspoons	15 ml
2 tablespoons	1 fluid ounce	30 ml
4 tablespoons	¼ cup	60 ml
5½ tablespoons	⅓ cup	80 ml
8 tablespoons	½ cup	120 ml
10⅔ tablespoons	⅔ cup	160 ml
12 tablespoons	¾ cup	180 ml
16 tablespoons	1 cup or 8 ounces	240 ml
1 cup	½ pint or 8 fluid ounces	240 ml
2 cups	1 pint	480 ml
1 pint	16 ounces	480 ml
2 pints	1 quart	960 ml (approx. 1 liter)
2 quarts	½ gallon	
4 quarts	1 gallon	3.8 liters
Weight		
1 ounce	16 drams	28 grams
1 pound	16 ounces	454 grams
1 pound	2 cups liquid	454 grams
1 kilo	2.20 pounds	1,000 grams

Temperature

Fahrenheit	200	225	250	275	300	325	350	375	400	425	450	475
Gas Mark			1	2	3	4	5	6	7	8	9	
Centigrade	93	110	130	140	150	170	180	190	200	220	230	240

ESSENTIAL INGREDIENTS

Whenever possible, use fresh herbs, beans, fruit, and nuts, which are more and more commonly available in most supermarkets. Below is a list of some essential ingredients that should be kept in your pantry in dried form. Make the syrups, jams, and pickles from time to time, store them in jars, and use as needed.

DRIED HERBS

Barg-e bu—bay leaf
Gard-e-limu-omani—dried Persian lime powder
Gishniz—coriander leaves; also called cilantro or Chinese parsley
Gol-par—garden angelica
Limu-omani—whole dried Persian limes
Marzeh—summer savory
Na'na—mint
Reyhan—basil
Shanbalileh—fenugreek
Shivid—dill weed
Tareh—chives
Tarkhun—tarragon

DRIED BEANS

Adas—lentils
Baqali—green fava beans or lima beans
Baqali-e zard—yellow fava beans
Jow—barley
Lapeh—yellow split peas
Lubia chiti—pinto beans
Lubia qermez—kidney beans
Nokhod—chick-peas

SPICES

Advieh—a mixture of 4–8 ground spices
Darchin—cinnamon
Hel—cardamom
Jowz-e hendi—nutmeg
Kari—curry powder
Mikhak—cloves
Siah daneh—nigella seeds (black caraway seeds)
Somaq—sumac
Vanil—vanilla
Za'feran—saffron
Zanjebil—ginger
Zardchubeh—turmeric
Zireh—cumin seed

OTHER

Ab ghureh—sour grape juice
Ablimu—lemon juice
Basmati—brand long-grain rice
Beh—quince
Golab—rose water
Kashk—whey
Nurenj—Seville orange
Piaz—onions
Roghan zeytun—olive oil
Sir—garlic
Serkeh—vinegar
Torshi—Persian pickles

PASTES

Shireh-e angur—essence of grape
Rob-e gojeh farangi—tomato paste
Rob-e-anar—pomegranate paste
Rob-e narenj—Seville-orange paste

SYRUPS AND JAMS

Moraba-ye albalu—sour-cherry preserve
Pust-e porteqal—orange peel
Sekanjebine—vinegar syrup

DRIED FRUITS, FLOWERS AND NUTS

Alu—prunes
Gole-e sorkh—rose petals
Gerdu—walnuts
Gheisi—dried apricots
Keshmesh—raisins
Khalal-e-badam—almond slivers
Khalal-e-pesteh—pistachio slivers
Khorma—dates
Zereshk—barberries
Tamr—tamarind
Bahar narenj—orange blossom
Gol-e Beh—quince blossom
Pesteh—pistachios
Narenj—Seville orange

PERSIAN–ENGLISH GLOSSARY

A

Ab ghureh— sour grape juice

Ab-limu—lime or lemon juice

Advieh—a mixture of ground seasonings, including rose petals, cinnamon, cardamom, black pepper angelica, nutmeg, and cumin seed

Afshoreh—a nonalcoholic beverage made from the juice of fresh fruits such as watermelon, pomegranates, or oranges, and squeezed or processed in a blender and served over ice

Ajil—a mixture of nuts, dried fruits, and seeds

Albalu—sour cherries

Alu zard—golden plums

Ash—soup

B

Balal—corn

Bamieh—okra

Baqali or *Baqala*—fava beans

Barg-e bu—bay leaf

Beh—quince

C

Cha'i—tea

Chelow—cooked plain rice

D

Daneh-ye khashkhash—poppy seeds

Dolmeh—cooked vegetables or vine leaves stuffed with any mixture of meat, rice, and herbs

Donbalan—lamb fries

Dugh—a yogurt drink with mint

F

Farvardin—the first month of the Persian year

G

Garmi—hot (nature or metabolism)

Gerdu—walnuts

Gishniz—coriander; also called cilantro or Chinese parsley

Gojeh sabz—unripe plums

Golab—rose water

Gol-par—garden angelica

Ghureh—sour grapes

Gusht-e kubideh—a paste of cooked meat and vegetables

H

Haji firuz—town clowns who appear before and during the New Year

Haft sinn—the seven items beginning with the letter "s" in Persian that are set out for the New Year's Celebration

Halva—saffron brownie

Hel—cardamom

J

Ja'fary—parsley

Jahaz—the bride's dowry

Jow—barley

Jowz-e hendi—nutmeg

K

Kabab—lamb brochettes

Kangar—cardoons

Kashk—whey

Khiar—cucumber

Khoresh—a refined stew of meat or poultry with vegetables and/or fruit and nuts

Khoshab—syrup

Korsi—traditionally placed in the family living

room, a low, square table covered with a thick cloth overhanging on all sides. A brazier with hot coals is then placed under the table. In cold winter weather family and friends spend the day and sometimes all night sitting on large cushions (futons) around the korsi with their legs underneath the table and the cloth over their laps; hours pass eating, drinking, and chatting; reading, reciting poetry, and sometimes playing footsie—enjoying the cozy warmth. Today a small electric space heater can be effectively used instead of the brazier and a television often replaces the poetry.

Kuku—a vegetable or meat dish with beaten eggs that is oven-baked in a casserole dish

L

Labu—steamed red beets
Lapeh—yellow split peas
Lavash—flat Persian bread
Lavashak—fruit paste rolls
Limu-omani—dried Persian limes
Lubia chiti—pinto beans
Lubia qermez—kidney beans

M

Mahr—a sum of money, piece of property, or object of value a groom agrees to give to his bride as financial security in case of marital discord
Marzeh—summer savory
Mash—mung beans
Mey—wine
Meygu—shrimp
Mikhak—cloves
Miveh—fruit
Mokhalafat—appetizers and condiments
Moraba—jams or preserves
Mosama—a rich, unctuous stew
Musir—shallots

N

Nabat—sugar crystals
Nan—bread
Na'na—mint

Noghl—sugar-coated almonds
Nokhod—chick-peas
Nowruz—New Year's Day; the Iranian year begins on March 20 or 21, the first day of spring

P

Panir—Persian cheese, like feta
Pesteh—pistachios
Piazcheh—scallions or spring onions
Polow—cooked rice
Pust-e porteqal—orange peel

Q

Qabaleh—marriage contract
Qahut—sweetened roasted chick-pea powder
Qeymeh—small cubes of meat sauteed and seasoned in oil
Qormeh—meat chunks sauteed in oil with seasoning, to keep on hand in the refrigerator

R

Reyhan—basil
Reshteh—noodles
Rivas—rhubarb
Rub-e anar—pomegranate paste

S

Sabzeh—sprouts
Sabzi-khordan—fresh herbs
Samovar—metal urn with a device for heating water for tea. A teapot kept on top brews tea throughout the day.
Sardi—cold (nature or metabolism)
Sekanjebin—vinegar
Shab-chareh—or *ajil*, a mixture of nuts, dried fruits and seeds, which literally means night-grazing
Shab-e Yalda—the longest night of the year; the winter solstice
Shahnameh—The Book of Kings, by the poet Ferdowsi
Shanbalileh—fenugreek
Sharbat—syrup made of fruit juice cooked with sugar and then stored in bottles

Shivid—dill
Siah-daneh—nigella seeds
Sirab shirdun—tripe
Sobhaneh—breakfast
Sofreh—a cotton cloth embroidered with prayers and poems that serves as a tablecloth on a table or is spread on a Persian carpet
Sofreh-ye haft sinn—the necessary elements laid out on a handmade cloth for the Persian New Year
Somaq—sumac

T

Tah chin—lamb or chicken, marinated in egg, yogurt, and saffron, mixed and arranged in the bottom of a pot or baking dish and cooked for a long time, until a golden crust forms (*tah dig*)
Tah dig—a layer of golden rice that sticks to the bottom of the pan when rice is cooked

Tanur—bread oven
Tareh—chives
Tarkhun—tarragon
Tut—mulberries
Torobcheh—radishes
Torshi—Persian pickles

V

Vanil—vanilla

Z

Zaban—tongue
Za'feran—saffron
Zanjebil—ginger
Zard-chubeh—turmeric
Zereshk—barberries
Zireh—cumin seed

Basil	ریحان	**Dill Weed**	شیوید
Chives	تره	**Summer Savory**	مرزه
Cilantro (Chinese parsley)	گشنیز	**Tarragon**	ترخان

424

MENU SUGGESTIONS

Suggestions for Breakfast
1. Hot bread, usually *barbari*
   Hot sweet tea
   Feta cheese
   Butter
   Fig or quince preserve

2. Fried eggs
   Hot *barbari* bread
   Hot sweet tea or hot milk
     with honey
   Butter
   Preserves

3. For a very active day:
   Halim or porridge
   Hot tea
   Hot bread

4. Head and feet soup
   Tripe soup
   Hot bread
   Hot sweet tea

Suggestions for Lunch
1. Ground meat or chicken
     kabab with grilled tomato
     and sumac
   Lavash bread
   Fresh herbs
   Yogurt drink

2. Eggplant kuku
   Sour cherry rice
   Shirazi salad
   Fresh herbs and bread
   Sour cherry drink
   Sharbat-e albalu

3. **For Spring**
   Rice meat balls
   Yogurt
   Bread
   Fresh herbs
   Melon
   Hot tea

4. Stuffed vegetables
   Yogurt
   Baked rice with chicken
   Fresh herbs, bread and
     feta cheese
   Melon
   Hot tea

5. Fresh herb kuku
   Drained thick yogurt
   Fresh herbs and feta cheese
   Hot bread

6. Potato stew
   Fava bean and fresh
     dill rice
   Chicken kabab
   Fresh herbs
   Bread
   Yogurt and cucumber
   Melon or grapes
   Hot tea

7. **For Summer**
   Yogurt and cucumber
   Eggplant kuku
   Fresh herbs, feta cheese,
     and *lavash* bread

8. Romaine lettuce with
     vinegar syrup
   Chick-pea patties with
     lavash bread
   Fresh herbs and feta cheese

9. Cold yogurt and
     cucumber soup
   Fresh herbs, feta cheese,
     and *lavash* bread
   Meat kuku

10. **For Winter**
    Any of the *ashes*
    Heart, liver kabab
    Fresh herbs, feta cheese,
      and *lavash* bread
    Paradise custard
    Hot tea

11. Any of the *ashes*
    Meat patties with
      lavash bread
    Fresh herbs, pickles
    Vinegar syrup

12. Baked leg of lamb
    Rice with lentils
    Pickles
    Shirazi salad
    Fresh herbs, feta cheese,
      and *lavash* bread
    Hot tea

13. Pomegranate khoresh
      jeweled rice
    Roasted duck
    Drained yogurt (*Kise'i*)
    Shirazi salad
    Melon
    Hot tea

14. Cream of barley soup
    Stuffed chicken
    Saffron-flavored steamed
      plain rice
    Fresh herbs, feta cheese
      and bread
    Melon, grapes
    Hot tea

Sunday Brunch
    Rice with meat kabab
    Grilled tomato
    Yogurt
    Shirazi salad
    Fresh herbs and feta cheese
    Yogurt drink

Dinner
1. Stuffed chicken
    Oven-baked rice with
      barberries
    Orange khoresh
    Salad
    Nuts
    Hot tea

2. Quince or apple khoresh
    Baked saffron yogurt rice
    Salad
    Yogurt and cucumber dip
    Quince-lime syrup drink

For New Year's Dinner
    Noodle soup
    Fresh herb kuku
    Fresh herb rice
    Smoked white fish
    Shirazi salad
    Bread, fresh herbs, and
      feta cheese
    Pickles
    Melon
    Hot tea

For a Persian/American Thanksgiving
    Sweet and sour stuffed
      turkey
    Sour cherry rice
    Butternut squash or
      pumpkin khoresh
    Saffron-flavored rice
    Shirazi salad
    Fruit pickles
    Fresh herbs, cheese, bread
    Saffron brownie
    Hot tea

For a Wedding
    Sweet rice
    Stuffed whole lamb
    Saffron-steamed plain rice
    Meat or chicken kabab
    Fresh herbs
    Potato kuku
    Pomegranate khoresh
    Fresh herb khoresh

For a Funeral Wake
    Rice with lentils
    Rice with potato khoresh
    Saffron brownie
    Dates
    Turkish coffee

Fruit
To most Iranians, dessert is fruit. Certain kinds of fruit are also used as appetizers, such as watermelons, pomegranates, grapes, and white mulberries. Fruit is also frequently used as a morning and late evening snack.

SPECIALTY STORES & RESTAURANTS

Arizona

Apadana Restaurant
Tempe
(602) 945-5900

Haji Baba Middle Eastern
    Food & Restaurant
Tempe
(602) 894-1905

International Foods
    Wholesale
Tempe
(602) 894-2442

California

Ahwaz International
    Groceries
Anaheim
(714) 772-4492

Alvand Market
Costa Mesa
(714) 545-7177

Amamchyan Market
Hollywood
(213) 462-8675

Anoush Deli & Grocery
Hollywood
(213) 465-4062

Anoush Family Restaurant
Hollywood
(213) 662-5234

Apadana Market & Deli
Westlake Village
(818) 991-1268

Arian Del Mart
Sacramento
(916) 363-6982

Basmati Rice Imports, Inc.
Irvine
(714) 474-4220

Beverly Hills Kabab
Beverly Hills
(213) 657-6257
(Firouz)

Bazjian's Grocery, Inc.
Hollywood
(213) 663-1503

Caspian Persian Cuisine
Sunnyvale
(408) 248-6332

Caspian Restaurant
Irvine
(714) 651-8454

Charlie Kabob
Santa Monica
(213) 393-5535

Chatanoga Restaurant
Santa Clara
(408) 241-1200

Chelokababi
Sunnyvale
(408) 737-1222

Colbeh Iran
Reseda
(818) 344-2300

Danaian's Bakery
Hollywood
(213) 664-8842

Darband Restaurant
Beverly Hills
(213) 859-8585

Darya Restaurant
Orange
(714) 921-2773

Daryoush Restaurant
Lawndale
(213) 644-8672

Downtown Kabab
Los Angeles
(213) 612-0222

Family Market
Northridge
(818) 349-2222

Farid Restaurant
Los Angeles
(213) 622-0808

Golestan Restaurant
Los Angeles
(213) 470-3867

Hassan's Restaurant
Newport Beach
(714) 675-4668

Hatam Restaurant
San Rafael
(415) 454-8888

Iran Markets, Inc., #1
Reseda
(818) 342-9753

Iransara
San Jose
(408) 241-3912

Jamai Products Co.
Glendale
(818) 241-8156

Javan Restaurant
Los Angeles
(213) 207-5555

Jilla's Gourmet Catering
Berkeley
(510) 938-6537

Hafez Restaurant
San Francisco
(415) 563-7456

Kabab House
(Kabab Khouneh)
Glendale
(818) 243-7001

Kabob House Restaurant
Anaheim
(714) 991-6262

Kaboby Restaurant
Sherman Oaks
(818) 501-9830

Karoun Market
Hollywood
(213) 665-7237

Kashmiri Grocery
Hawthorne
(213) 978-1927

Kasra Restaurant
San Francisco
(415) 752-1101

Khatoon
San Diego
(619) 459-4016

Lavash Corporation
    of America
Los Angeles
(213) 663-5249

Mahtab Market
Rancho Palos Verdes
(213) 833-6026

Massoud Restaurant
Los Angeles
(213) 748-1768

Maykadeh Restaurant
San Francisco
(415) 362-8286

Norooz Bazar
San Jose
(408) 295-2323

Paradise Restaurant
Mt. View
(415) 968-5949

Paradise Salar
    Restaurant
Sherman Oaks
(818) 789-7788

Pars Cellars
Napa
(707) 257-6664

Pars Market
Los Angeles
(213) 859-8125

Pars Market
San Diego
(619) 566-7277

Pars Restaurant
San Bruno
(415) 871-5151

Persian Center Bazar
San Jose
(408) 241-3700

Pouri Bakery
Glendale
(818) 244-4064

Raffi's Place #1
Glendale
(818) 241-9960
Raffi's Place #2
Glendale
(818) 247-0575

Ramsar Market
Los Angeles
(213) 651-1601

Rose's Restaurant
Canoga Park
(818) 716-5222

Saam Middle East
    Restaurant
Pasadena
(818) 793-8496

Sabrina Middle East
    Restaurant
Culver City
(213) 398-2308

Salar Restaurant
Glendale
(818) 500-8661

Samirami's Market
San Francisco
(415) 824-6555

Saray Ghalandar
Reseda
(818) 343-5115

Sepah Market
Irvine
(714) 559-4510

Sepahan Market
Van Nuys
(818) 988-6278

Shahrzad International
    Market
Santa Ana
(714) 850-0808

Shahrzad Restaurant
Encino
(818) 906-1616

Shahrzad Restaurant
Los Angeles
(213) 470-3242

Shamshiri Restaurant
Glendale
(818) 246-9541

Shamshiri Restaurant
Hollywood
(213) 469-8434

Shamshiri Restaurant
Los Angeles
(213) 474-1410

Shamshiri Restaurant
Northridge
(818) 885-7846

Shamshiri Restaurant
San Jose
(408) 998-0122

Sheik Cafe
San Diego
(619) 234-5888

Shekarchi Kabab
Los Angeles
(213) 746-4600

Shekarchi Kabab
Los Angeles
(213) 474-6911

Shemshad Food Inc.
La Crescenta
(818) 249-9066

Shish Kabob Cafe
San Diego
(619) 265-7800

Sholeh Restaurant
Los Angeles
(213) 470-9131

Shoosh International
San Francisco
(415) 626-1847

Sorento Garden
San Francisco
(415) 882-4400

Sultani Restaurant
Hollywood
(213) 876-3389

Tea Sara
San Jose
(408) 241-5115

Tehran Market
Santa Monica
(213) 393-6719

Ureni Persian
    Restaurant
Orange
(714) 282-1010

Your Place Restaurant
Beverly Hills
(213) 858-1977

Zand Market
Albany
(510) 528-7027

Connecticut

Sharzad Grocery
Stamford
(203) 323-5363

District of Columbia

International Market
    & Deli
Washington
(202) 293-0499

Kolbeh Restaurant
Washington
(202) 342-2000

Nakeysa Restaurant
Washington
(202) 337-6500

Taverna Market
Washington
(202) 333-1972

428

University Market Place
Washington
(202) 667-2206

Florida

Shiraz Food Market
Miami
(305) 264-8282

Georgia

1001 Nights Restaurant
Atlanta
(404) 851-9566

Shahrzad International
Atlanta
(404) 843-0549

Illinois

Arya Food Imports
Chicago
(312) 878-2092

International Foods
Chicago
(312) 478-8643

International Golden
Foods, Inc.
Niles
(312) 764-3333

Middle East Trading
Chicago
(312) 262-2848

Middle Eastern Bakery
& Grocery
Chicago
(312) 561-2224

Pita Inn
Skokie
(708) 677-0211

Saba Meat & Market
Chicago

(312) 539-0080
Sahar Meat & Grocery
Chicago
(312) 583-7772

Maryland

Bismillah Halal
Meat Market
Langley Park
(301) 434-0051

Caravan Market
Gaithersburg
(301) 258-8380

E. & I. International
Rockville
(301) 984-8287

Epicurean International,
Inc.
Rockville
(301) 231-0700

International House
Rockville
(301) 279-2121

Moby Dick Cafe
Bethesda
(301) 654-1838

Persepolis Restaurant
Bethesda
(301) 656-9339

Villa Market
Chevy Chase
(301) 951-0062

World Market
Bethesda
(301) 654-4881

Yas Bakery
& Confectionery
Rockville
(301) 762-5416

Yekta Middle Eastern
Grocery
Rockville
(301) 984-1190

Massachusetts

Ararat Restaurant
Watertown
(617) 924-4100

Michigan

International Market
Livonia
(313) 522-2220

Virginia's Mid-East Cafe
Sylvana Lake
(313) 681-7170

Minnesota
Caspian Bistro
Minneapolis
(612) 623-1113

Nevada

Middle Eastern Bazar
Las Vegas
(702) 731-6030

New Jersey

Alex & Maria's Restaurant
Cliffside Park
(201) 945-4121

Amir Bakery
Paterson
(201) 345-5030

New York

Bahar Market
Great Neck
(516) 466-2222

Caravan Restaurant
New York
(212) 262-2021

Choopan Kabab House
Flushing
(718) 886-0786

Colbeh Restaurant
Great Neck
(516) 466-8181

International Food
Market
Roslyn Heights
(516) 625-5800

International Grocery Store
New York
(212) 279-5514

Kababi-e-Nader
New York
(212) 683-4833

Kabul Kabab House
Flushing
(718) 461-1919

Persepolis Restaurant
New York
(212) 535-1100

Shish Kabob Palace
Great Neck
(516) 487-2228

Shish Kabab Restaurant
Port Washington
(516) 883-9309

Taverna
Roslyn
(516) 484-8860

North Carolina

University Pantry Deli
Charlotte
(704) 549-9156

Ohio

Aladdin's Middle
  East Bakery
Cleveland
(216) 861-0317

Oregon

International Food Bazar
Portland
(503) 228-1960

Rose International Foods
Beaverton
(503) 646-7673

Texas

Super Vanak
  International Food
Houston
(713) 952-7676

Virginia

Assal Market
Vienna
(703) 281-2248

Bahar Restaurant
Vienna
(703) 242-2427

Bread & Kabab
Falls Church
(703) 845-2900

Cafe Rose
Falls Church
(703) 532-1700

Cafe Vienna
Vienna
(703) 255-3000

Culmore Restaurant
Falls Church
(703) 820-7171

Moustache Cafe #1
Alexandria
(703) 765-0933

Moustache Cafe #2
Tysons Corner
(703) 893-1100

Washington

Pars Market
Bellevue
(206) 641-5265

Rooz Super Market
  & Deli
Seattle
(206) 363-8639

**PERSIAN GOURMET
CATERING**

California

Miss Ketayoune Esfendiari
San Francisco
(415) 579-1835

Mrs. Esfendiari
San Francisco
(415) 343-5833

Mrs. Afsar Panahi
San Francisco
(415) 457-3333

Mrs. Mahin Afghani
San Francisco
(415) 967-3442

Mrs. Meher Shahin Pirooz
San Francisco
(415) 386-4179

Maryland

Mrs. Ma'sumi
Rockville
(301) 948-4643

Virginia

Mr. & Mrs. Abbas Mahmud
Virginia
(703) 768-4255

Canada

Bijan Specialty Food
Ambleside, Vancouver
(604) 925-1055

Darvish Restaurants
Toronto
(416) 535-5530

Nasr Mini Market
Scarborough
(416) 757-1611

Pars International Market
N. Vancouver
(604) 988-3515

Restaurant Georges
Chomedy
(514) 681-8189

Ayoub's Fruit &
  Vegetables Market
Ottawa
(613) 233-6417

Sayfy's Groceteria
Montreal
(514) 277-1257

Main Importing
  Grocery, Inc.
Montreal
(514) 861-5681

England

Yas Restaurant
London
(071) 603-9148

Yas Restaurant
London
(071) 603-3980

Hafez #1
London
(071) 794-4179

Hafez #2
London
(071) 431-4546

Super Bahar
London
(071) 603-5083

Yas Super
London
(071) 371-4119

Reza Super Market
London
(071) 603-0924

4 Ways Super Market
London
(081) 202-0588

Leyla Food
London
(071) 435-2370

Sheikh Grocery
London
(081) 458-5544

روزه داری و قناعت هوسِم بود ولی

چشمکی میزند آن مُرغ و فنجان که مپُرس

To fast and lead a frugal life
Was all I ever wished.
But the Food of Life's temptation
Is too much—do not ask!

Bos'haq Ata'meh

INDEX

BIBLIOGRAPHY

Afshar, Iraj. *Ashpazi-e dore-ye Safavi* (Cooking in the Safavid Period). Tehran: Seda va sima Publishing, 1981.

Amir Ebrahimi, Mansureh. *Nush-e jan konid* (Enjoy it). Tehran: Elmi, 1967.

Amir Hoseyni, Fakhri. *As ashpazkhaneh ta sofreh* (From the kitchen to the table). Tehran: 1968.

Ashpaz-Bashi, Mirza Ali Akbar Khan. *Sofreh-ye ata'meh* (Gourmet table). Tehran: Elmi, 1974.

Chacourzadeh, Ebrahim. *'Aqayed va rusum-e mardom-e Khorasan* (Beliefs and customs of the province of Khorassan). Tehran: Sorouch, 1985.

Emami, Goli. *Ashpazy-e beduneh gusht* (Cooking without meat). Tehran: Zamineh Publishers, 1982.

Endjavi, S. Abolghhasem. *Jashnha va adab va mo'taqedat-e zemestan* (Festival and customs and beliefs of winter). Tehran: Amirkabir, 1975.

Ghanoonparvar, M. R. *Persian Cuisine, Book One: Traditional Foods.* Lexington, KY: Mazda Publishers, 1982.

—— *Persian Cuisine, Book Two: Regional and Modern Foods.* Lexington, KY: Mazda Publishers, 1984.

Khavar, Zari. *Honar-e ashpazi dar Gilan* (The art of cooking in Gilan). Tehran: Ashyaneh, 1987.

Mazda, Maideh. *In a Persian Kitchen, Favorite Recipes from the Near East.* Rutland, VT: Charles E. Tuttle Company, 1968.

Montazami, R. *Honar-e ashpazi* (The art of cooking). Tehran, 1968.

Pirouzian, A. S. *The Armenian Kitchen.* Armenia: Haybed-Hrad, 1963.

Ramazan, Nesta. *Persian Cooking: A Table of Exotic Delights.* Charlottesville, VA: University Press of Virginia, 1974.

Reid, Montamen Mehri. *Gourmet Cooking: Persian Style.* Cekesville, MD, 1989.

Richard, Josephine. *Tabakhi-e Neshat* (Pleasure of cooking). Tehran: Mozafari.

Shirazi, Hallaj Maulana Boshaq. *Divan Molana Bos'haq Hallaj Shirazi mashhur be Sheykh Ata'meh* (Divan of molana bos'haq hallaj shirazi, known as sheykh ata'meh). Shiraz: Ma'refat Shiraz, 1980.

Simmons, Shirin. *Entertaining the Persian Way.* Luton, England: Lennard Publishing, 1988.

ACKNOWLEDGMENTS

During my research for this book I have been fortunate in finding many scholars who have given me suggestions and ideas for trying to achieve my aim of bringing together Persian food, art, and literature.

For his many good suggestions and for guiding me through both the Freer and the Sackler Galleries' archives, I would like to especially thank Milo Beach. At the Fogg Art Museum at Harvard, I would like to thank Carey Welch, who not only loves Persian art but Persian food as well, which in itself proves my point that "all is one." Thanks are also due to Mohammad Isa Waley at the British Library, Barbara Epstein at the Metropolitan Museum, Judith Gardner-Flint at Johns Hopkins University, and Massoud Nader in New York.

For their help and suggestions in finding food-related pieces from classical Persian literature I wish to thank Jalal Matini, a good friend and a great resource for all Iranians here in Washington. I am also indebted to two great professors of Persian literature now living in Germany: Djalal Khaleghi Motlagh who, despite the enormous task of editing the *Shahnameh*, found time to send me texts and translations in middle Persian from the Sasanian period; and everyone's teacher in Persian literature during the past fifty years, the wonderful Zabihollah Safa. Thanks are also due to Heshmat Moayyad at the University of Chicago, Hossein Zia'i at UCLA, and Abbas Amanat at Yale for their help and suggestions. For their ideas and inspiration I would like to thank Florence Lloyd and Ruth Landman. Thanks are also due to Habib Bahar, who has inherited his family's good taste in Persian poetry; Hasan Javadi, whose collection of books and suggestions have been invaluable; Dariush Ashuri, a wordsmith, philosopher and friend; the special representative for all Iranian publications at the Library of Congress, Ibrahim Pourhadi, who was always helpful; and Abolghasem Parto, who was a great help with ancient Persian symbols.

My traditional Persian food advisers have been Mrs. Nowshiravani in London and Mrs. Ma'sumi here in Washington; I am indebted to them for parting with many of their secrets and techniques.

During the photography I was helped by many friends in the Washington area who generously brought their family heirlooms and other treasures, from beautiful embroidered cloths and textiles to antique samovars and dishes decorated according to their families' traditions. Special thanks go to Chapo, Mina, Nazi, Nilufar, Roya, Sheila, Suzy, and Raz.

I wish to specially thank everyone at Neam's market in Georgetown; whenever we needed anything, from unripe almonds to pomegranates in June, they would find them. Mr. Satery at Kolbeh, Mr. Alborz at Nakeysa, Mr. Shirkhan at Yas Bakery, and Mrs. Hajian at Vienna Cafe have all given me valuable help.

Special thanks to Elizabeth Garbedian and Hasmig Eskandarian for their helpful suggestions.

For all the typing and research help I wish to give special thanks to Shahrzad and Assim. For editing and proofing, typesetting, and the layout of my thousand and one changes I would like to especially thank Jean Bernard and Christine Schuyler, and Scott Ripley at Mage.

CREDITS

Photographs

Serge, La Colle sur Loup, France: back jacket and flap; pages 1, 4, 8, 14, 34–45, 47, 48, 145, 179, 181, 185, 187, 189, 192–193, 196–197, 200–202, 204, 208, 225, 228–237, 239–240, 308, 309, 310, 312–314, 317–326, 328, 330, 333, 335, 336, 385, 392, 398, 401, 406, 409, 411

Maryam Zandi, Tehran: endpaper; pages 6, 306, 321, 391, 414, 416

Mohammad Batmanglij, Washington, DC: 191, 194, 198, 315, 316

Max Hirshfeld, Washington, DC: page 183

Cover photo: Jon Francis, Washington, DC

Illustrations

Courtesy of the Arthur M. Sackler Gallery, Smithsonian Institution, Washington, DC

S1986.47: Painting from an Iranian manuscript, Habib Al-Siyar, Volume 3. Safavid, 1579–1580 (987 AH). Opaque watercolor, ink, and gold on paper: 27.0 x 15.1 cm, page 238

S1986.221: "A School Scene." Iranian painting attributed to Mir Sayyid-Ali. Safavid, 1530–1550. Opaque watercolor, ink, and gold on paper: 27.00 x 15.1 cm—page 33

S1986.255 "Joseph Enthroned." Painting from an Iranian manuscript, c. 1550. Opaque watercolor and gold on paper: 59.4 x 44.5 cm—page 305

Courtesy of the Freer Gallery of Art, Smithsonian Institution, Washington, DC

46.12: Painting from *Haft Awrang* (Seven Thrones), the 7 *mathnavi* poems of Jami. Persian manuscript, middle of 16th Century (1556–65). Average page: 34.2 x 23.2 cm. Pages 227, 315, 327

53.29: "Two Horsemen Hunting with Falcon." Persian painting by Riza Abbasi. Safavid period, school of Isfahan, 17th century. Drawing in black and red inks on cream-colored paper: 16.0 x 8.7 cm.—page 140

53.29: "Cup Bearer with Big Turban." Persian painting by Riza Abbasi. Safavid period, school of Isfahan, mid-17th century. Drawing in red ink on bluish-green paper: 16.0 x 8.7 cm.—Page 382

08.282: Leaf from a Khamsa of Nizami. Persian painting. Safavid period, mid-16th century. Opaque color and gold on paper: page 31.1 x 19.6 cm painting-17.8 x 14.4 cm.—page 402

53.56: "Scene in the Bathhouse." Persian painting. 16th century. 16.4 x 12.2 cm—page 412

Courtesy of the Arthur M. Sackler Museum, Harvard University, Cambridge, MA

Gift of John Goelet, formerly Collection of Louise J. Cartier

1958.76, miniature, Iran, Safavid, 16th century. Mir sayyid 'Ali, attributed to "Night-time in a Palace," from Shah Tahmasp's Quintet of Nizami, 1539–43 opaque watercolor and gold on paper 283 x 200 mm (image)—page 2, details, pages 76, 281

Gift of John Goelet, formerly Collection of Louise J. Cartier

CREDITS

1960.117.9 painting , Indian, Mughal, 16th c. Nanha, attributed to "Firing up the Poet's Kettle," from a Divan of Anvari, fol. 246b opaque watercolor and gold on paper ca. 13.8 x 8 cm (page)—Page 205
Courtesy of the British Library, London
From the *Ni'matnameh* of Nasir al-Din, circa 1500, pages 195, 199, 250, 264, 320
From a copy of the *Shahnameh,* circa 1560, pages 311, 401
"Majnun brought in chains to Leyla's tent," from the *Khamsa of Nizami*, circa 1530, page 46
Milton S. Eisenhower Library, John Work Garrett Collection, The Johns Hopkins University, Baltimore, MD
Safarnama of Sharafuddin Ali Yazdi, 1467–68, attributed to Bihzad, page 386
Negarestan Museum of 18th- and 19th-Century Persian Art, Tehran, page 360
S'adabad Collection, Tehran, pages 164, 307

Line Art

Perrot, G., and C. Chipiez. *A History of Art in Persia*. London: Chapman and Hall, Limited, 1892. Holle-Verlag, Baden Baden

Persian Calligraphy

Amir Hossein Tabnak, Washington, D.C., and Bijan Bijani, Tehran

Translations

A. J. Arberry, 362
Mohammad Batmanglij, 88, 252, 384, 430
Michael Boylan, 399
Edward Bowen, 110, 393
Amin Neshati, 16, 149, 280, 338, 360, 382, 413, 415

Library of Congress Cataloging-in-Publication Data

Batmanglij, Najmieh,
The New Food of Life: A Book of Ancient Persian and Modern Iranian Cooking and Ceremonies/
Najmieh Khalili Batmanglij.
p. cm.
Includes bibliographical references and index.
ISBN 0-934211-34-5:
1. Cookery, Iranian. 2. Iran—Social life and customs.
TX725.17B373 1992
641.5955—dc20

Second printing

PRINTED IN KOREA

1032 29TH STREET, NW WASHINGTON, D.C. 20007
To receive our current catalog call 800 962 0922, 202 342 1642, fax 202 342 9269

ISBN: 0-934211-34-5